IP VALUATION *for* THE FUTURE

IP VALUATION *for* THE FUTURE

Trends, Techniques, and Case Studies

Weston Anson

ABA Section of Intellectual Property Law
AMERICAN BAR ASSOCIATION

Cover design by Jill Tedhams/ABA Publishing.

Printed in the United States of America.

22 21 20 19 18 5 4 3 2 1

ISBN: 978-1-64105-227-6
e-ISBN 978-1-64105-228-3

Library of Congress Cataloging-in-Publication Data

Names: Anson, Weston, 1942- author.
Title: IP valuation for the Future : Trends, Techniques, and Case Studies / Weston Anson.
Other titles: Twenty-first century intellectual property valuation.
Description: Chicago : American Bar Association, 2018. | Includes index.
Identifiers: LCCN 2018023865 (print) | LCCN 2018025905 (ebook) | ISBN 9781641052283 (ebook) | ISBN 9781641052276 (soft cover : alk. paper)
Subjects: LCSH: Intellectual property—Valuation—United States.
Classification: LCC KF2979 (ebook) | LCC KF2979 .A843 2018 (print) | DDC 346.7304/8—dc23
LC record available at https://lccn.loc.gov/2018023865

Dedication

This has been a three-year process that has involved the support and tolerance of everyone with whom I work. And therefore, I dedicate this book to the entire team at CONSOR.

Contents

Genesis: Birth of a Book

What drives a person to write a book like this? Why? What need are we trying to fill?

In 2005, the American Bar Association (ABA) approached me with a project—they needed a basic book on intellectual property (IP) valuation. The ABA had never published one. Even though I'm not a lawyer, I was a longtime member of the ABA, a speaker, continuing legal education provider, and recognized writer and contributor on topics including IP valuation and the licensing and extension of IP assets. I also had served as cochair of the Trademark Licensing Subcommittee.

The result of that overture was a book titled, *The Fundamentals of Intellectual Property Valuation: A Primer for Identifying and Determining Value*. This was the first "primer" on IP value for the ABA. It became the basic resource for the following:

- A primer on valuing IP for lawyers and financial practitioners alike. Since then, I've written seven books based on specialty aspects of IP including the following:
    - o A guide to bundling and valuing IP and intangible assets, *The Intangible Assets Handbook*, which also includes background on valuation in bankruptcy and reorganization scenarios.
    - o A valuation book unique to the Chinese market, *Fundamentals of Intellectual Property Valuation in China*, reflecting the new awareness and importance of IP in China.
    - o A book on ethics among experts in IP valuation and the use of experts in litigation titled, *Expert Witness, Valuation and Damages*.
        - – Five years after the basic primer came out, we wrote a well-received book titled, *IP Valuation and Management*. This is a more sophisticated look on how and when to value IP and the impact of the law and business on the valuation process.
        - – Most recently, the ABA published, *Right of Publicity: Analysis, Valuation and the Law*.

This brings us to review and restate the principle methods and issues of IP valuation—the legal, financial, and societal issues that are shaping the world of IP and valuation in the future. It's only been a dozen years since the original primer was first published, yet we now find ourselves restating these principles of IP valuation to meet the new market and societal conditions in which we operate.

Who Made This Book Possible?

On the writing and creative side, David Noble, as stalwart as always, donated a key chapter and edited others. Also, three new young writers have contributed to this book; Evan Loker, Sam Ghafir, and Pierce Urban made significant contributions to chapters 9, 10, and 11.

I had substantial support on the administrative and technical side. Our head of legal research, Jamie Majerus, made this book possible with her in-depth research and thorough review of citations. She was referred by Professor Kevin J. Greene of Thomas Jefferson School of Law, a nationally recognized expert in the field of IP. His input during the course of this book was invaluable.

Initial research by Jemma Samala brought order and a framework to the early phases of the book, which I much appreciate. Later in the game, assistance came from Amber Valentine.

Finally, I and everyone at CONSOR acknowledge the key role performed by Rosemary Delaney. She is the master of ceremonies standing in the middle of a three-ring circus and making sure that I got this book published on time, while simultaneously managing the projects, processes, and clients that constantly occupy myself and the other professionals here in the firm.

And, in the end, I can never forget the support throughout the process that I received from my partner, Jeff Anderson.

On a personal note, Wendy Nash gave me great personal counsel during some of those times when writing was difficult – and I thank her forever for her caring.

Introduction

We wrote *Fundamentals of Intellectual Property Valuation: A Primer for Identifying and Determining Value* in 2005; since then, the world of intellectual property (IP) has grown more complex, and the world of IP valuation has grown more sophisticated. Standards of valuation have changed, methodologies have changed, the context in which valuation takes place has changed, and the range of contexts has expanded. Also, the types of IP are growing, morphing and melding together.

There are underlying trends and issues that didn't even exist a decade ago. At the same time that we see new forms of IP, there's also a trend that brings together different types of IP: the merging of technology and trademarks into so-called branded technologies.

There's greater awareness of IP and its value at all levels today—less naiveté, more skepticism. Today, when one thinks about IP portfolios and the management thereof, one thinks "professionalism," which wasn't necessarily true a decade ago. There's greater scrutiny in the boardrooms of America. Corporate directors and officers are increasingly providing tighter oversight of corporate IP portfolios. Ten years ago many boards were not even aware of the potential financial impact of a company's IP holdings on a balance sheet. Today those same corporate directors are not only aware of value but aware of potential liability from shareholder lawsuits and disgruntled investors if they should mismanage that IP portfolio. In general, there's also increased scrutiny by shareholders, both large and small.

Valuation techniques and methodologies have changed. Standards for valuation are certainly tighter today than they were a decade ago, and simple methods of valuation have been dismissed in favor of more sophisticated thinking and analysis. For example, valuation professionals no longer use the 25% rule (calculating an appropriate royalty as 25% of gross profits). Instead, we deal with the smallest saleable patent practicing unit (SSPPU), a concept that was born out of litigation but which is now increasingly being used as a basis for establishing royalty rates and value both within and outside of litigation.

This is the background against which this book is being presented: millennial changes in IP and its valuation. The issues and case studies included in this book present this new world as clearly as possible to the reader. Other factors are increasingly playing a much larger role in the IP world. One is the expanding world of digital assets and social media, another is our legislative and court systems.

In the first case, social media has blossomed over the last decade to generate new and different ways to use IP, both in its primary form as a medium for concepts and ideas as well as a delivery vehicle, e.g., Amazon Prime and YouTube. Over the last decade, the world of litigation and an increasingly active court have brought a new awareness of IP to corporate boardrooms, financial houses, and private citizens alike.

Context: Who Is The Audience for This Book?

This book is intended as a valuation overview for attorneys who need a basic grounding in the principles and financial standards of IP valuation and who can also benefit from a basic review of the core attributes, categories, and permutations of various IP. In addition, it is also intended for bankers, financial professionals, venture capitalists, and other Wall Street professionals. It is also useful for litigation funders who want a better understanding of the basic legal framework and current trends that affect IP, not just valuation trends but trends in terms of litigation, legislation, and categorization of new forms of IP and related intangible assets.

In addition, this book is meant to serve as a resource and quick reference guide for terms and terminology on valuation issues as well as an in-depth analysis and resource on royalty rates, discount rates, and the calculation of actual valuations in transactions and cases. This piece of work is also aimed at a community of IP professionals who engage in licensing, valuation, and evaluation analyses in IP litigation. Hopefully, all of these professionals will be served by having a single volume they can turn to as a quick reference on all matters related to IP value, whether the value is in a transaction, litigation, or other context.

For the last 30 years, my focus has been as a professional IP consultant in licensing and monetization of all IP assets, as well as the evaluation and valuation of the same assets. For many years, I served as a partner and president of a licensing agency, acting as a marketing and sales agent for a number of large corporations. Beginning in the 1980s and into the 1990s, I represented the portfolios of trademarks and brands to extend the reach of those trademarks and brands into new product categories and new geographies both here and abroad. For the last 25 years, my personal focus and the focus of CONSOR, the firm of which I am chair, has been heavily in the area of valuation. During that period, we have written a number of monographs and books on the topics of value and valuation, both in the construct of transactional values as well as value when used in litigation as an expression of damages. As a firm, we lead the way in establishing many of the definitions and refinements in determining today's construct for the standard methodologies used in IP valuation, including what are now some of the more accepted methodologies, such the relief-from-royalty and price premium approaches. In addition, during that time, we developed several proprietary valuation techniques and methodologies, including the VALMATRIX approach and the Brand Value Equation, and we were early adopters and developers of the Technology Matrix approach and others.

With a decades-long background in both monetization and valuation of IP, it must be remembered, however, that we are not speaking from the viewpoint of attorneys. I am not a lawyer by training, nor does our firm practice law. On the other hand, the vast majority of our clients are attorneys in a transactional environment and for litigation. Thus, we have more than a passing familiarity with the legal issues involved in IP, both here and in overseas markets.

Therefore, I must be clear in the following disclaimer: this book is not intended to offer legal advice on any aspect of IP. Instead, it offers very strong and well-reasoned opinions and advice on those aspects of IP that involve monetization, or valuation, regardless of how tangential it may be. The reader will note that wherever possible, we have cited legal cases and legal precedents. The legal discussion is presented as background for the overall topic of valuation. The cites, citing, and footnotes are referrals to more specific discussions of the law, legal precedent, case citing, and more authoritative legal resources. However, chapters 2 and 3 recognize the increasing role of the courts, landmark litigation events, legislation on the valuation process, standards of valuation, methodologies, and new valuation definitions established by the court such as the SSPPU. We recognize the role of the courts and understand how our valuation work must fit within the confines of legal precedent and constraints.

Organization

This book is organized into three sections. The first section, chapters 1 through 3, tracks the IP environment, not just valuation. Although we do have a particular emphasis on the changing world of valuation, we look at the methodologies and the standards of value both inside the courtroom and in transactions. These three chapters focus on the external forces that exact pressure on the world of IP and all forms of IP valuation. Chapters 2 and 3 recognize the increasing role of the courts, the increasing amount of IP litigation, and the fact that legislation at the federal level has been exerting pressure on IP valuation issues and standards in all of it's newly expanding forms as well as both the process and product of IP valuation.

The second part of the book, chapters 4 through 6, is quite practical and specific and is a descriptive knowledge-transfer section. It provides the most updated commentary on valuation methodologies to be found anywhere in the market today. For example, chapters 4 and 5 are the most complete current summary of the primary methodologies being used, not only in the United States but in most overseas markets. Chapter 5 discusses alternative valuation methodologies and provides a brief description of 15 of the most important and interesting alternative valuation methodologies. These range from various option pricing models to the competitive advantage technique. These new and alternative methodologies provide approaches to enable the valuation of both new and expanded characterizations of IP classes, trademarks, copyrights, technology, and digital-based ventures. Chapter 6 is one of the most thorough analyses of royalty rates to be found in one condensed format anywhere. We view licensing royalty rates as the ultimate objective valuation context. We not only provide an historical overview going back more than 100 years but, more importantly, we dig into the analysis of royalty rate trends going back 30 years or more for each of the primary IP classes: patents, trade secrets, copyrights, trademarks, and right of publicity. This analysis is perhaps the best summary of royalty rate statistics to be found in one source anywhere today.

The third part, which is the heart of the book, consists of seven chapters. These chapters cover valuation and the trends, techniques, issues, and market forces specific to IP types and valuation environments that are most critical today on:

- Patents,
- Trade secrets,
- Copyrights,
- Trademarks,
- Rights of publicity,
- Application-based ventures/digital platforms, and
- Assets in international arbitration.

Each chapter is devoted to analyzing the uniqueness of the IP as well as to focusing on unique situations that apply to the evaluation and valuation of each class of assets.

Perhaps one of the most important benefits is that each chapter, as well as throughout the book, includes case studies. The case study method, which formed a good part of my professional training at the Harvard Business School, is obviously still embedded in my psyche (I use it for this reason, and because I truly believe that it is the most effective way to learn). We have included two or three case studies in each of the core chapters. Each case study is a *real* case, not something made up from whole cloth. Instead, the case studies feature transactions, litigation, initial public offerings, or consultations that we have been asked to consult on or to analyze on behalf of the courts, clients, or their financial advisors. Real firsthand knowledge of each case was a requirement for inclusion in the book.

We conclude the book with a look at the future of IP developments. This task could be and should be a book in and of itself. Instead, we only have room to treat it briefly given the constraints of space. Nonetheless, we believe much of what will happen in the next decade is going to be influenced by today's Internet-based/application-based giants. This model is being built by Apple, Microsoft, Alphabet, and Facebook, Netflix and others, and is going to dominate much of the future horizon—and dialogue about—IP formation and valuation.

Chapter 1

Intellectual Property Value and Valuation in a Changing World

The groundswell of forces for change in intellectual property (IP) value and valuation comes from three areas:

- The legal landscape, from Congress to the Supreme Court to bankruptcy courts, Internal Revenue Service hearings, and state courts;
- The emergence of new forms of IP, both organically and as a result of legal changes that interpret what are patents, trademarks, copyrights, and rights of publicity; and
- Greater precision, transparency, and professionalism in the process and standards of valuation, as well as closer scrutiny of the process.

A brief overview of these three areas is useful as we get into the details of IP value and valuation in this new millennium, including subject matter, legal constraints, and valuation standards and approaches. Let's begin with an overview of the last 10 years in the courts to see where we've come from and where we're headed.

Intellectual Property Law from the Supreme Court to the State Courts to Congress—The Changing Landscape

Going back just 35 years, the U.S. Supreme Court heard about 150 cases a year, and rarely did any of those cases involve IP. Today, the workload of the U.S. Supreme Court has gotten considerably smaller. In recent years, the U.S. Supreme Court has heard roughly 75 cases in a typical year. What's telling, however, is the increase in IP cases.

In the term that began October 2013, the court heard 67 cases. Of those, 10, or exactly 15% of its total workload, were cases that dealt with IP. Six dealt with patent issues, two had implications for copyrights, and two were Lanham Act cases in the world of trademarks and related issues.

All of the cases can reshape the world of IP and have had an impact on the value and valuation of these assets. Since 2013, there have been additional landmark cases. In 2014, there was the *VirnetX v. Cisco* case, which dealt with the entire market value rule, as well as a case in 2015 involving *CSIRO v. Cisco* where the calculation of value using Reasonable and Non-Discriminatory based damage analysis for all standard essential patents was dealt with.

Recently, one result has been that an entirely new concept has come into play. When calculating royalty rates and value for part of a multicomponent end product such as a telecommunications product (e.g., a handheld phone or a body fit device), one is now being compelled to use the concept of the smallest saleable practicing patent unit (SSPPU). Not only in litigation, this valuation concept is supplanting that of the entire-market-value rule of calculating value. Also in 2014, the U.S. Supreme Court stepped onto center stage of the IP world, reshaping the landscape and impacting not only the types of IP but in some ways affecting valuation of IP.

This activity in the courts can be summarized in two major points. First, one must be cautious in the area of patent valuations to ensure that the scope of a patent and a patent family is fully understood—and not overstated. This is particularly true when dealing with software and business method patents, particularly in view of the *Alice* and *Bilski* decisions. Second, one must be cautious in applying the entire market value approach to the valuation of patents and technology in general, again to avoid overvaluation of any single patent. Also, new methodologies and new techniques for valuation have been introduced.

There's another aspect to the activity of the law and the courts in terms of value and valuation of IP: the passage of new, stronger, and different laws to support IP. First and foremost among these is the Leahy-Smith America Invents Act,[1] which was signed into law in 2013.

On another front, the Uniform Trade Secrets Act[2] provides reinforcement to the value of trade secrets at the federal level. This act gives new muscle, strength, value, and uniformity to trade secrets. It's a step that's long been needed.

Finally, on the legislative front, the reinvigoration of the Patent Trial and Appeal Board in 2013 has also created something called the inter partes review (IPR), which to some extent potentially weakens patents and shortens their longevity. The IPR essentially allows challenges to almost any new patent that comes to issuance. While it aids greatly in the ability of corporations as well as inventors and creators to challenge the claims of a new patent, it does have one chilling side effect: it can end the life span of a promising new patent. Thus, one has to be cautious in the valuation of these assets.

The Emergence of New Forms of Intellectual Property

As a result, not just of law, legislation and the courts but also of technological activity, social media, and necessity, new forms of IP have appeared, while others have become more circumscribed, such as business method patents. But it isn't just the courts, of course, that have created or circumscribed new forms of IP. It is also the IP community itself, which is constantly pushing to develop new forms of IP along multiple fronts including:

1-1 Leahy-Smith America Invents Act, 112 P.L. 29, 125 Stat. 284.
1-2 UNIF. TRADE SECRETS ACT (UNIF. LAW COMM'N 1985).

- Patents and technology;
- Copyrighted materials, ideas, and concepts;
- Trademarks; and
- Social media.

Each of these have added to the family of IP.

On the patent and technology front, we see new approaches to packaging technologies, encapsulating trade secrets with patents. There is increasing use of trademarks and brands to wrap around a patent or patent family in order to offer a complete bundle of IP for sale or for licensing. In addition, software implemented inventions continue to grow in spite of recent court decisions. At first glance, the *Alice* and *Bilski* decisions seem to limit all software implemented inventions, but in fact they limit simply those that patent an abstract idea, or a "law of nature."[3]

In the world of trademarks, change has been consistent and constant over the last decade. From holographic trademarks, to 3-D trademarks, to the increasing use of colors, smells, sounds, and other sensory perceptions in trademarks, that world continues to expand. The changing world of trademarks means that multiple trademark elements are often to be included in a valuation, and value must often be allocated to individual trademark elements.

Nowhere has change been more evident than in the world of copyrights and social media. Facebook, YouTube, Twitter, Instagram, and Snapchat continue to offer up a never-ending landscape of copyrighted materials and usages as well as trademark uses. Social media is also the new battleground for use and misuse of rights of publicity.

Rights of publicity is an area of growth and change. Many states have added new specific right of publicity statutes in the last 10 years; others have added postmortem rights of publicity statutes. Still others have expanded the scope of right of publicity coverage beyond just a name and likeness. They have expanded into signature, voice, and other unique personal characteristics. In addition to the battle over postmortem, the length of postmortem rights range from state to state from as little as two years up to 100 years. In the middle of 2016, a media frenzy fed a copyright, branding right of publicity case that was watched on TV every night for two weeks: the *Hulk Hogan v. Gawker.com* case. This was the classic battle between an established social media presence and a long-time personality. The confrontation centered first on the right of a personality to protect his or her rights of publicity and, second, on the right of a website to post embarrassing personal material in the name of the First Amendment right of free speech. We will cover that case in Chapter 11, Rights of Publicity Analysis and Valuation.

Finally, the importance of trade secrets has grown from a stepchild form of IP. It was not often valued a decade ago but now has moved firmly into the forefront of the IP discussion—and moved to center stage in terms of valuation and valuation methodologies.

1-3 Laws of nature, natural phenomena, and abstract ideas have been held by the U.S. Supreme Court to be implicit exceptions to patent-eligible subject matter under 35 U.S.C. § 101, with the exceptions rationalized as a means to prevent the monopolization of the basic scientific and technological tools required for future innovation.

Greater Need For Precision, Professionalism, and Transparency in the Valuation Process

Another major trend in the value and valuation process as we move into the new millennium is the greater need for professionalism. While IP valuation professionals have not yet come together to ensure greater financial professionalism in their work, there has been some broader agreement on what are acceptable methodologies for the valuation of IP and intangible assets. The profession has begun to stamp out those firms that, quite frankly, simply created their valuation methodologies out of whole cloth—without any basis in fact or logic. This is not to say we don't still see a number of questionable practices. For example, recently we rebutted a trademark valuation report that based the value of a trademark on a straight-line relationship to the percentage of aided brand awareness. In other words, for each 1% in increased brand awareness, the value of a trademark/brand went up by an equivalent 1% in dollar value. This approach has no intellectual, professional, financial, or logical basis. In fact, it had never been seen by our firm before. Nonetheless, there we were in court rebutting (quite easily as it turns out) a foolish nonstandard approach to "valuation."

Credentials and credentialing of IP valuation professionals is still not standardized and is spotty at best. Consider this: there are at least 25 organizations that hand out valuation credentials. Below is a listing of some credentialing groups. When checking on the credentials of a valuation professional, make sure to examine not only the credentials but also those of the credentialing institution.

Credentialing Groups

- American Bankruptcy Institute (ABI)
- American Institute of Certified Public Accountants (AICPA)
- Association of Insolvency and Restructuring Advisors (AIRA)
- American Society of Appraisers (ASA)
- Certified Financial Analysts Society (CFA)
- Certified Financial Planner Board (CFP)
- Canadian Institute of Chartered Business Valuators (CICBV)
- Chartered Institute of Management Accountants (CIMA)
- Forensic Expert Witness Association (FEWA)
- International Association of Assessing Officers (IAAO)
- International Association of Consultants, Valuators and Analysts (IACVA)
- International Asset Finance Society (IAFS)
- Institute of Business Appraisers (IBA)
- International Business Brokers Association (IBBA)
- Institute of Chartered Accountants in England and Wales (ICAEW)
- International Financial Reporting Standards Foundation (IFRS)
- International Right of Way Association (IRWA)
- Licensing Executives Society (LESI)
- Licensing Industry Merchants Association (LIMA)
- National Auctioneers Association (NAA)
- National Association of Certified Valuation Analysts (NACVA)
- National Association of Independent Fee Appraisers (NAIFA)
- National Investor Relations Institute (NIRI)
- National Society of Real Estate Appraisers (NSREA)
- Turnaround Management Association (TMA)

There is still much work to be done among valuation practitioners to agree on both the more accepted methodologies and new, emerging, and alternative methodologies. Some observations on valuation methodologies are appropriate here:

- Older, simplistic methodologies are leaving us.
- Accepted methodologies such as the income approach, the market approach, and the cost approach continue to blossom but are becoming more sophisticated.
- Variations on these three are being used with more frequency (e.g., the cost savings income approach).
- Comparable transactions and benchmarking analyses are scrutinized much more carefully.
- The use of royalty rate comparables continues to dominate the world of valuation, particularly in litigation-based damages cases. However, a finer touch and a much more in-depth understanding of royalty rates and the other issues in royalty agreements are necessary.
- Comparable from outside "the footprint of the patent" can now be used in damages cases (see *StoneEagle* case, Chapter 7).
- Old rules of thumb are finally past history, including the 25% rule of thumb and the 5% rule of thumb.
- The Georgia-Pacific factors, after 50 years, have finally been buried in recent landmark cases such as *StoneEagle* and others; they are no longer required. Eulogies are being said even as we write these words, but nothing will bring them back to their former robust place in the world of valuation analyses.

The America Invents Acts and the Patent Reform Act of 2013 brought a major overhaul of our patent laws; harmonizing U.S. patent law with that of Europe and most of the rest of the world. One major change was a shift from a first-to-invent system to a first-to-file system that went into effect in March 2013. The system is based on a few of key principles:

- The first person who files a letter application is the one who generally has the prime position in receiving the patent, unless it can be proven that the subject matter disclosed in the application was derived from a venture that files a later application.
- Inventors still have a one-year grace period where their own disclosures or other derivation disclosures may not be used as prior art if they occurred in the prior 12 months.
- Foreign public use and offers for sales will now be considered prior art, which was not the case under our former law.

As part of the changeover, inter partes reexaminations were replaced by a new type of proceeding called an inter partes review, which went into effect in September 2013. This new IPR process is examined more fully in Chapter 7, but suffice to say it provides a new way for a recently granted patent to be challenged under the terms of the new law. In addition, there's a parallel post grant review process that applies to business method patents. In general, the effect of the law has been to allow others who are aware of an inventor's progress to step in and file a first application. Many claim that this new act has worked contrary to the best interest of independent inventors and creators. Another side effect has been that trade secrets becoming increasingly used as a protection for new and creative ideas as a primary form of protection, rather than going with the more traditional patenting process.

Greater Scrutiny, More Stakeholders

Another important change affecting IP, in general, and its value, in particular, is the greater realization by private corporations and by public corporations, in particular, of the value and importance of their IP portfolios. As a result, there are an increasing number of constituencies or stakeholders who have an interest in their portfolios and their value. Ten years ago, when we wrote the original primer on IP value, two things had not occurred (among others of course). First, the great recession of 2008 had not taken place and, as a corollary, the Dodd-Frank Act of 2010 was not yet in place. That market crash and ensuing depression across our economy resulted in recognition by corporate officers, chief financial officers, and Congress that additional financial regulation was needed. Going back to the Sarbane-Oxley Act of 2002, which began to focus on high technology and the fraud that can take place, as exemplified by Enron, one clear conclusion was that the consultants, valuators, and analysts could not deal with the complex financial issues, audits, or IP assets on their own, including valuation or evaluation of IP. Thus, the Sarbanes-Oxley Act set up the Public Company Accounting Oversight Board, a nonprofit private oversight corporation to review the audit of public companies. For the first time, there was also oversight of technologies, thus beginning to put IP in the spotlight. Over time, the general result of SOX has been better-quality reporting and audits, as well as better board and audit committee *oversight*.

However, it took the crash of 2008 and the passage of the Dodd-Frank Bill of 2010 to really put boards of directors of public companies on the line in terms of being responsible for the oversight of their corporations' IP portfolios. Dodd-Frank was aimed primarily at the regulation, control, and oversight of banks, investment banks, financial institutions, and financial advisors. It hasn't worked particularly well, although it has served to destroy most of America's network of small banks. It has, however, had one major effect on corporations' IP and IP value. Boards of directors and individual directors now have a greater responsibility to see that IP portfolios are managed well and that value extraction is maximized. In the current corporate climate, because IP assets tend to comprise a high percentage of most companies' value, the management of these assets will generally fall within the scope of a director's fiduciary duties.

All of this has had positive consequences on IP and its value:

- Greater oversight and scrutiny by multiple parties;
- Greater awareness of IP value and the need to maximize value extraction; and
- Transactions, securitizations, and financings of IP now have a higher priority.

Today, corporate boards and other stakeholders are looking for value extraction alternatives. This has led to companies asking for valuations of their portfolios. In today's world, small patent portfolios are relatively much less valuable than large portfolios on a relative basis, because value extraction costs are not linear. Also, it is harder to get value from small portfolios. Key patents need to be surrounded by an increasing number of flanking patents in order to extract value. Companies today are constantly reexamining their licensing strategies, licensing evaluations, and licensing budgets. Internal licensing teams are being set up to explore sales alternatives as well as licensing alternatives. In fact, entire portfolios have been sold recently.

The same issues arise with large brand and copyright portfolios. The pressure is now on: extend, license, or sell. Single product brands are virtually nonexistent. Extend, extend, extend is the mantra of today's trademark-based brands. Copyright-based companies such as Disney or any of the other entertainment or sports-related conglomerates are all practicing the same strategy. They build on their IP by extending or licensing on a consistent and ever wider family of licensed products and services.

Chapter 2

Here we look at other forces working on IP and its valuation: From the expansion of IP itself to the increase in the amount and type of litigation. In turn, this has led to the rise in litigation-based IP valuations, and a parallel rise in *Daubert* challenges. This chapter also reviews Federal Court activity over the last decade as well as the impact of two key new Federal laws. We conclude with a look at one of the classic IP litigation battles of the 21st century—Apple vs. Samsung.

Intellectual Property Valuation in the Changing World of Legislation and Litigation

Intellectual Property Types Expand

Types of intellectual property (IP) litigation have increased because the range of assets considered IP has increased. Traditionally, IP consisted of patents, trade secrets, trademarks, copyrights, and rights of publicity. But the definition of what is considered IP has expanded at a rapid rate. The reason for that exponential rate of expansion can be directly credited to the use of technology.

Technology has helped create or expand IP categories such as the following:

- trade secrets
- customer data bases
- Internet assets
- proprietary systems
- sensory trademarks
- technical knowledge
- social media platforms
- licensing assets
- international web assets
- right of publicity definition

If you are an IP asset owner, you need to be paranoid in some sense, ever diligent of who is infringing your rights. Not only do you worry about counterfeiters making copies of your songs on electronic servers, but you worry about their unauthorized use on streaming radio or YouTube videos. When a celebrity dies, the estate needs to worry about whether that celebrity's images are being used in postmortem, newly invented products such as hologram concerts or sports gaming apps. The invention of the 3-D printer will soon open up more IP litigation.

Businesses need to be aware of other opportunities to monetize their IP assets and hence more reasons why they need to protect those same assets. For instance, IP assets can be licensed out, which can be a significant source of income for companies that own proprietary technology. Those IP owners need to keep track of avenues where those same assets can be pirated.

There's piracy not only in the music industry but in many technology and medical industries, too—and in high-end consumer goods. In the fashion industry, for instance, when you think of the shortened channels of distribution and shorter product life cycles, there is constant pressure to come up with the "it" product of the day for the ever-demanding consumer. Again, there are more reasons for IP asset holders to be vigilant and ready to pursue infringers if necessary.

The Range and Type of Litigation Cases

Lex Machina (a LexisNexis Company) reported in early 2017[1] that patent litigation filings have been showing a pattern of decline since 2011, when terms of the Leahy-Smith America Invents Act (AIA) went into effect. In 2016, 4,520 patent infringement cases were filed, while there were 5,823 filed in 2015. However, some areas show volatility primarily due to high-volume plaintiffs, which may file 20 to 50 cases within a few days of each other, making the trends look spiky.

Trademark litigation has shown a steady, slight decline going back to 2010. There were 3,458 trademark infringement filings in 2016, while there were 4,239 in 2010. The one spike in trademark infringement trends was when 461 cases were filed in 2014 against the National Football League (NFL) by former NFL players suing for use of their likeness in NFL films and other content. One type of IP case that is seeing an increase is in the area of copyright infringement. In 2016, there were 3,822 copyright infringement cases, while in 2011 there were 2,631 filings. This trend dates back to 2005 when copyright infringement cases nearly doubled from 2004 and stayed above historical levels through 2006. The recent increases are attributable to file sharing cases, which are typically filed against John Doe defendants accused of illegally downloading content. The largest filing party has been Malibu Media, a developer of adult films; in 2015, they filed 589 copyright infringement cases.

2-1 Brian Howard, *2017 First Quarter Litigation Update*, LEX MACHINA (Apr. 12, 2017), https://lexmachina.com/2017-first-quarter-litigation-update/.

Litigation-Based Valuations on the Rise

In general, as IP-related litigation plays a prominent role in the legal universe, in parallel so do litigation-based valuations. While domestic litigation valuations are important, we need to also pay attention to IP valuation on the international scale as well. As the world increasingly functions under a global economy, the need for litigation and arbitrations in front of international tribunals also increases. Most of those disputes require some sort of valuation to validate or invalidate what the disgruntled party is requesting in damages. Since the cost of litigation proceedings are also rising at a rate of roughly 10%–20%[2] per year, getting the valuation done early or prior to the start of litigation is important because you want to know where you stand early in the game.

The use of IP itself has become more complicated, which means a valuation is ever more necessary, simply so that the judge and/or jury can become educated on the value of IP and can make an informed decision as to possible damages that might arise from the infringing use. Factors such as multiple jurisdictions, multiple defendants, multiple types of IP assets in one product, stacked royalties, and the dispersed nature of too much information make valuation necessary. As litigation-based valuations continue to be an important factor, so does the frequency of *Daubert* challenges, resulting in higher standards for experts.

The valuation report is the most important document in determining the amount of damages to be awarded in any IP matter. Because of the reliance on an expert's valuation report, which often includes an explanation of complex IP issues and financial and economic factors, it's only prudent for the litigators to put those valuation experts under a magnifying glass. Therefore, *Daubert* challenges have become much more common. Price Waterhouse Coopers' "*Daubert* Challenges to Financial Experts" report in May 2016 provided a number of interesting statistics from 2000 to 2015 to support this trend. Some of the report highlights include the following:

- In 2015, there were 230 reported challenges to financial experts, an increase of 10% from 2014; 102 of those challenges, or 44%, resulted in partial or full exclusion of the expert. Interestingly, the average over the 2000–2015 period was the same—44% of experts subject to *Daubert* challenges were excluded in whole or in part.
- In 2015, financial experts were most commonly excluded because their testimony was not considered reliable. Courts noted that the experts were unreliable due to lack of sufficient data or use of methodologies not generally accepted. The second most common reason why testimony was excluded was that the expert's testimony was not relevant to the case, usually when the expert went beyond the scope of the expert's role, such as providing legal testimony.
- In 2015, IP cases had the most *Daubert* challenges. During the period 2000–2015, a whopping 49% of IP cases had testimony excluded in full or in part.

2-2 Lawyers for Civil Justice Civil Justice Reform Group, *Litigation Cost Survey of Major Companies* (May 10, 2010), http://www.uscourts.gov/sites/default/files/litigation_cost_survey_of_major_companies_0.pdf.

- For the 2000–2015 period, the highest exclusion rates were in the Tenth Circuit and the Eleventh Circuit, with an exclusion rate of greater than 50%. The Second Circuit had the largest number of challenges in the study period, with 280 *Daubert* challenges.
- In 2015, 63% of *Daubert* challenges were to the plaintiff's experts. For the 2000–2015 period, it was even a little higher, with 68% of *Daubert* challenges going to the plaintiff's side.

In much of the research, there are common themes that we can identify by studying *Daubert* challenges. IP professionals can learn from this when involved in future litigation. Those lessons include the following:

- Gatekeeping—judges have become more active gatekeepers in IP matters. Instead of excluding testimony, they have become more likely to have flaws in valuation become exposed through voir dire.
- Data support—the major reason for testimony being excluded is that data are not supported and often are misused. Examples include not providing sufficient support for calculations and not spending enough time on due diligence to verify client-provided information.
- Qualifications—whether or not an expert is qualified can depend on factors such as skill, years of experience, knowledge, degrees, or industry certifications.
- Goodbye rules of thumb—in the *Uniloc*[3] decision, the court deemed that royalty-rate rules of thumb in IP matters are "fundamentally flawed" valuation methods. Therefore, experts need to become much more specific about methodologies in estimating royalty rates or other income approach standards.
- New methodologies—use of the Nash bargaining solution, the Coase theorem, and the Edgeworth box (see analysis below).
- Second chances—today, courts are more likely to let experts submit revised reports to address any possible challengeable issues.
- Respect boundaries—valuation testimony will most likely be challenged if it goes beyond the scope of the assignment, particularly when trying to provide legal conclusions.

Federal Courts Are More Active on Intellectual Property Issues

With the increase in activity of IP-related matters in federal courts, you would expect a handful of cases to eventually end up on the U.S. Supreme Court docket. A number of U.S. Supreme Court decisions have reshaped how companies need to pursue and protect their IP assets. Let's look at a few significant decisions over the past few years.

- *Alice Corp. CLS Bank Intl.*, 134 S. Ct. 2347 (2014). The Court narrowed the scope of the Federal Circuit's patentable subject matter, such as abstract processes or ideas.

2-3 Uniloc USA, Inc. v. Microsoft Corp., 632 F.3d 1292 (Fed. Cir. 2011).

Claims must have an additional inventive concept that transforms the abstract idea or fundamental principle into something more. Merely stating such a principle and "applying it" using a computer is not transformative of an abstract process or idea. Claims must bring forth an inventive concept or meaningful application of abstract concepts in order to be patent eligible.

- *Octane Fitness v. Icon Health & Fitness,* 134 S. Ct. 1749 (2014). The U.S. Supreme Court made it easier to obtain attorney's fees if a party prevails in patent litigation cases that "stand out from others," regarding strength or frivolity of claims, or unreasonableness in litigation proceedings. Moreover, the Court lowered the standard of proof from clear and convincing evidence to preponderance of the evidence.
- *Highmark v. Allcare*, 134 S. Ct. 1744 (2014). This case further discussed "exceptional cases" and the meaning of such a case in regard to fee shifting statutes, essentially making it easier for a prevailing party to obtain attorney's fees. Again, the U.S. Supreme Court emphasized the importance of the strength of a case when determining whether such a case was "exceptional," as also used in *Octane*. To be successful, a defendant must show they lost a case that lacked merit under a totality of the circumstances analysis.
- *Nautilus v. Biosig Instruments*, 134 S. Ct. 2120 (2014). The U.S. Supreme Court made it easier to find a patent claim indefinite, thus rendering the patent claim invalid. A patent is invalid when its claims, prosecution history, and specification do not reasonably inform an ordinary skilled artisan of the invention's scope. The precision required is to be taken from the point of view of such a skilled artisan at the time of application rather than the time of trial. The Court articulated the indefiniteness standard, stating that claims must "inform those skilled in the art about the scope of the invention with reasonable certainty," ultimately lowering the definiteness threshold.
- *Medtronic v. Mirowski Family Ventures LLC*, 134 S. Ct. 843 (2014). The U.S. Supreme Court clarified that the patent owner has the burden to prove infringement, including a patent owner defendant in a suit of declaratory judgment. When seeking declaratory judgment against a patent holder, the licensee does not bear the burden to establish non-infringement; rather, the burden is on the patentee to show infringement.
- *POM Wonderful v. Coca-Cola, 134 S. Ct. 2228 (2014).* The U.S. Supreme Court addressed the interplay between U.S. Food and Drug Administration (FDA) labeling requirements and Lanham Act claims of unfair competition. Even though the FDA regulates and enforces labeling requirements, according to the Court, a competitor can bring a claim for false or misleading product descriptions under the Lanham Act. Moreover, the Court reasoned that brand competitors often have a deeper understanding of sales, marketing, and consumer activity. POM Wonderful had standing to sue Coca-Cola over misleading labeling.
- *American Broadcasting Companies v. Aereo*, 134 S. Ct. 896 (2014). The Court held that Aereo's streaming TV service publicly performed copyrighted works owned by the petitioners, which mainly consisted of American Broadcasting Company (ABC) programs. Although the Court aimed to encourage the development of new technology, Aereo was more than "an equipment provider" in committing copyright infringement by allowing live and time-shifted programming to be viewed over the Internet.

Patents: All About *Alice*

When you are talking to someone who specializes in legal IP issues and you say "Alice," that person will understand that you are referring to the 2014 U.S. Supreme Court decision in the matter of *Alice Corp. v. CLS Bank International*, briefly described above. The unanimous decision, in simple terms, opined that abstract processes or ideas are not patentable subject matter. Claims need to have an additional inventive concept that transforms the abstract idea or fundamental principle. Merely stating such a principle and applying it by using a computer does not make the abstract process or idea transformative. The claims must bring forth an inventive concept that is eligible for patent protection under 35 U.S.C. § 101. This is significant because under § 101, abstract ideas are not patent eligible.

The *Alice* decision greatly impacted how the courts viewed patent law. It narrowed the scope of the Federal Circuit's view of patentable subject matter. Reigning in previous decisions brought precedent law more in line with Congressional intent. Although not specifically mentioning computer software, the U.S. Supreme Court decision significantly narrowed the eligibility of all *Alice*-type patents, particularly those of software and business method patents.

Prior to the *Alice* decision, there were fewer rejections under § 101, and patents were often drafted in an "apply it" manner. Post *Alice*, the frightening thought to many patent holders was that many patents drafted in the last two decades may now be invalidated. Claims shown to have an inventive concept have survived *Alice* but claims that merely state a fundamental principle and a description to apply it using a computer or software do not qualify as patentable subject matter.

And its progeny? One example is the magnetic resonance imaging (MRI) machine. In late 2016, the Patent Trial and Appeal Board (PTAB) rejected most claims of an application for an MRI machine and classification patent, ruling that the claimed invention was not eligible for patent protection because it was directed toward an abstract idea. The PTAB looked to the *Alice* decision for the two-step test for patent eligibility: (1) whether the claims are directed to a patent-ineligible abstract idea and (2) whether the claims have an "inventive concept" beyond the abstract idea. The PTAB decided the machine was typical of other multistation MRIs and that classification system is an abstract idea.

Additionally, for those in the business of IP valuation, such as CONSOR, the *Alice* decision affects risk assessment assumptions. Valuation professionals will be placed under scrutiny for their revenue projections, underlying assumptions, and data. For instance, if patent bundles are being valued, they may have greater invalidity risk due to potential patent-ineligible subject matter that will result in reduced value. In turn, these reduced values could impact other related transactions, such as software licensing agreements, and research and development (R&D) budgets. More complete due diligence will be a key factor.

Trademarks: Wonderful Labeling and Clever Design

Labeling. In *POM Wonderful v Coca-Cola*, the Court addressed the interplay between FDA labeling requirements and Lanham Act claims of unfair competition. Even though the FDA regulates and enforces labeling requirements, the Court felt that a competitor can bring a claim for false or misleading product descriptions under the Lanham Act. Additionally, the Court reasoned that brand competitors often have a deeper understanding of sales, marketing, and consumer activity. In this case, POM Wonderful was shown to have standing to sue Coca-Cola over misleading labeling.

Although POM had standing to sue, after eight years of litigation, POM eventually lost its case against Coca-Cola. The jury trial lasted six days, and the jury decided that Coca-Cola's labeling of Minute Maid juices did not mislead or deceive consumers into believing the juices had a higher content of pomegranate and blueberry juice and that POM had not suffered any damages. Ironically, POM is still under scrutiny for their own labeling statements of the benefits of drinking pomegranate products.

Design. One interesting trademark case involved a distinct use of color in design, and that case was *Christian Louboutin v. Yves Saint Laurent*—the famous "red sole" case. Fashion designer Christian Louboutin is known for having a signature red sole feature in his shoe designs that is described as sexy, flirtatious, energetic, and passionate, with a towering 5-inch stiletto. For those who can afford it, a pair of Louboutins can fetch upward of $5,000, depending on the style and material.

The fight over red shoes started in the district court for the Southern District of New York when Louboutin sued fashion giant Yves Saint Laurent (YSL), now known as Saint Laurent.

After designing women's shoes for many well-known fashion brands, including YSL, Louboutin started his business in the early 1990s. Using his assistant's nail polish, he first painted the bottom of a shoe red in 1992 to make it stand out. The red lacquered outsole has since become a fashion staple that is instantly recognizable among elite fashionistas such as Christian Louboutin. But in 2011, YSL released an all-red shoe as part of its monochromatic collection, which dated back to the 1970s and included monochromatic designs in green, yellow, and purple.

The district court framed the issue as whether Louboutin's Red Sole Mark should have been issued by the US Patent and Trademark Office (USPTO). If not, the mark would be cancelled and YSL could not have committed trademark infringement. The court opined, "[w]hen Hollywood starlets cross red carpets and high fashion models strut down runways, and heads turn, and eyes drop to the celebrities' feet, lacquered red outsoles on high-heeled, black shoes flaunt a glamorous statement that pops out at once." The district court noted "cognitive bulbs flash" when a person sees a red lacquered bottom, instantly denoting the shoe as Louboutin.

In August 2011, the district court ruled against Louboutin and determined his mark was not worthy of trademark protection because the color red is a functional color reserved for all designers to use. Functionality is the death knell of any trademark. Even worse, the district court found that Louboutin's use of the color red on the bottom of a shoe was not distinctly attributable to Louboutin. Louboutin lost and was at risk of losing his trademark registration on his Red Shoe Mark.

Fortunately for Louboutin, the district court used an improper legal analysis to make that determination, which became exceedingly clear on appeal. On appeal, the Second Circuit enunciated why the district court was wrong in its legal analysis, referring to its reasoning and decisions as "per se" law. The district court erroneously applied the Lanham Act in its decision, and the Second Circuit sought to align the final ruling with the law mandated by the U.S. Supreme Court. The Second Circuit decided that the Red Sole Mark was not functional and distinctly Louboutin. Using the district court's own words against it, the Second Circuit concluded that Louboutin is distinguishable as the shoe's creator because of the fact that the outsole is separately colored red from the rest of the shoe. Ruling the trademark is worthy of protection, the Second Circuit carved out a caveat that allowed both parties a legal win. If the red sole does not contrast with the upper portion of the shoe, as YSL's monochromatic red shoe does not, then it does not infringe Louboutin's trademark. Louboutin did not win his claim of trademark infringement against YSL, and YSL was not able to render the Red Sole Mark trademark ineligible.

On September 27, 2012, the Second Circuit ordered the USPTO to amend the Red Sole Mark registration language to cover "a red lacquered outsole on footwear that contrasts with the color of the adjoining ('upper') portion of the shoe." The result is that YSL, or any designer for that matter, can make monochromatic shoes in red without worrying about infringing Louboutin's trademark.

The practical outcome for trademark users is that brands should be as specific as possible, using carefully selected, precise language when registering their mark.

Internationally, Louboutin continues to fight for their red sole trademark. In February 2017, the Swiss Supreme Court confirmed the invalidity of the trademark in Switzerland. Additionally, Louboutin has ongoing litigation in the Netherlands in a trademark infringement case against Dutch shoemaker Van Haren.

Copyrights: Its Streaming Violations

Technology has brought about a new ease of sharing copyrighted works. In *American Broadcasting Companies v. Aereo*,[4] the Court held that Aereo's TV service violated the Transmit Clause of the Copyright Act. Agreeing with ABC companies, the Court held that Aereo's streaming TV service publicly performed copyrighted works owned by the petitioners, mainly consisting of ABC companies. Although the Court aimed to encourage the development of new technology, Aereo was more than "an equipment provider" in committing copyright infringement; Aereo allowed live and time-shifted programming to be viewed over the Internet at about the same time as the programs were broadcast over the air. ABC also argued that Aereo's services undermined revenue received from cable retransmission fees and the size of their viewership, with cable fees comprising up to 10% of revenue.

2-4 *American Broadcasting Companies v. Aereo*, 134 S. Ct. 896 (2014).

Legislative Impacts: Two Landmark Laws

Leahy-Smith America Invents Act

The AIA is a federal statute that was passed and signed into law in September 2011. It was implemented in three stages, becoming fully functional in 2013. The passing of the AIA brought about the biggest changes to the U.S. patent system since the 1952 Patent Act, changing the U.S. patent system from a "first-to-invent" to a "first-to-file" system, expanding the definition of prior art, eliminating interference proceedings, and developing post-grant opposition.

One purpose for these changes was to align the United States with the international community's first-to-file system. However, the U.S. definition of first to file is different from international standards, including a grace period to disclose any use of the patent application within 12 months of the filing. If it is found that questions are raised about the applicability of prior art during the grace period, then the application could be found unpatentable. For best practices, it is always prudent to file first.

What has been the impact of the AIA? The act has had a dramatic impact on the value of U.S. patents in that it depressed the value of patents. With a first-to-file system, those who invest in patent portfolios have become wary of the risk of investing in assets that may be owned by another party. The uncertainty is what depresses the value of patents and the future benefits of investing in patent R&D.

With regard to the creation of the new proceedings to challenge patents—the inter partes review (IPR) and the covered business review (CBM)—the goal was that the new proceedings would provide a more efficient and inexpensive way to test the validity of a patent and do away with extremely expensive patent litigation trials. On that note, the AIA has done its job since the PTAB now decides on whether to move forward with proceedings based on IPR and CBM petitions with six months. The proceedings are completed within a year, which is much faster than most district court litigation. The cost of PTAB proceedings are on average \$300,000 to \$500,000, while typical patent trial litigation costs a minimum of \$1 million to \$4 million.

But have the time-efficient and less-costly procedures resulted in greater quality of USPTO decisions? That is debatable. Since implementation through 2015, the PTAB found in proceedings that were advanced to a written final decision that 60% were deemed unpatentable claims. This is much higher than the 18% average invalidity rate for district court litigation. In some cases, patent owners are also proceeding in both PTAB proceedings and litigation, therefore adding to costs rather than helping to cut back on costs.

The AIA itself has faced legal challenges. Recently, in *Cuozzo*,[5] the Court upheld the AIA provision barring challenges to IPR institution decisions and approved the use of broadest reasonable interpretation. The door was left open to certain constitutional and statutory

2-5 *Cuozzo Speed Technologies, LLC v. Lee*, 136 S. Ct. 2131 (2016). A unanimous 8-0 decision in favor of Cuozzo essentially created a reexamination procedure called inter partes review, wherein any third party can request the PTO to scrutinize the claims of a patent in order to determine whether the patent should have been issued in the first place in light of prior art. IPR decisions are "final and unappealable."

challenges. Since the *Cuozzo* decision seems to invite patent holders to file administrative procedure litigation, it again creates an atmosphere for parallel district court litigation along with both PTAB proceedings and the underlying patent suit.

As we noted that the value of patents has been depressed due to the uncertainty caused by the AIA, the cost of patent monetization has gone up. Patent owners can usually recover expensive R&D costs by licensing the patents once granted. But in the atmosphere created by the AIA, patent licensing is increasingly resulting in more litigation to prove actual ownership.

While the regulation was created with good intentions, the AIA may have resulted in partially undermining the system it was meant to improve. Those patent holders with large amounts of capital may survive; others will be permanently harmed. Also, innovators will look toward trade secret protection instead, resulting in elimination of some of the benefits of the patent system: inventors receive limited-time monopolies on their inventions in exchange for fully disclosing their innovative work. Rather than encouraging innovation, the result is the opposite.

Defend Trade Secrets Act

The Defend Trade Secrets Act (DTSA) was passed and signed into law in 2016 and allows an owner of a trade secret to sue in federal court when their trade secrets have been stolen. Congress had wanted the DTSA to align with the Uniform Trade Secrets Act, which every state had adopted in some form. In practical terms, the DTSA extended the Economic Espionage Act of 1996, which criminalizes certain trade secret misappropriations. It also grants legal immunity to corporate whistle-blowers.

What has been the impact of the DTSA? One goal of the DTSA is to unify trade secret laws. Although states used the Uniform Trade Secrets Act as a framework, application of trade secrets law varied from state to state. However, the DTSA in practicality supplements state laws rather than replaces them. Therefore, the DTSA works in parallel with state trade secret laws. However, the DTSA has provided easier access to federal courts; in a global and cross-state business atmosphere, as well as in the ever-changing IP industry, this access is needed.

A controversial portion of the DTSA allows courts to issue ex parte seizure orders to prevent the dissemination of a trade secret in extraordinary circumstances under such an order. The trade secret owner may legally seize property of a competitor without providing notice. The court actually holds custody of the property until a court decision. Since this provision can be abused easily, parties are allowed to seek damages if they are harmed by a wrongful or excessive seizure. The seizure provision is the big difference between the DTSA and state remedies, as there is nothing comparable in current state statutes.

In our own practice, we have seen the effect of the DTSA's implementation. For one, there has been a greater demand for valuation of trade secrets. By making trade secrets a protectable asset, companies want to ensure they are able to both monetize those assets as well as pursue damages when their rights have been infringed upon. With the growing importance of trade secrets, we have seen clients internally shift R&D emphasis from patent applications toward more trade secret protection. Over the long term, we expect to continue seeing a reduction in the growth of patent applications in this country in favor of an increase in trade secret programs.

On the other hand, it may be too early to determine how the value of trade secrets will change, if at all. The focus for companies should be on increased diligence in protecting trade secrets before being misappropriated, rather than on using the DTSA to recover stolen trade secrets. Preventative measures are key in keeping the value of trade secret assets.

Battle of the New Millennium

Apple v. Samsung and Its Impact on Valuation

The battle between these two mega tech companies started in the spring of 2011 when Apple began patent infringement litigation proceedings against Samsung. Apple was also involved in separate patent wars with Motorola, Nokia, and Qualcomm. Apple's reputation to pursue a strong multinational patent litigation strategy became known as the "smartphone patent wars." At one point in late 2011, Apple and Samsung were litigating 19 ongoing cases in 10 countries. By 2012, they were involved in more than 50 lawsuits around the world, with billions of dollars in damages claimed between them. We will focus on the bigger of the two U.S. battles.[6]

In this larger of the patent battles, Apple did win a ruling in its favor in the United States when a Northern District of California jury awarded more than $1 billion in damages for patent infringement from Samsung for willfully infringing Apple's design and utility patents and also diluting trade dress relating to the iPhone. Later in 2013, a retrial on damages reduced the award to $930 million. In the meantime, internationally Samsung won rulings in South Korea, Japan, and the United Kingdom. In 2015, the Federal Circuit found that Samsung's entire phone infringed Apple's patents for the face of a smartphone, the nonfunctional ornamental design, ruling that Samsung must pay all of its profits from those phones. However, the courts threw out part of that award, leaving approximately $400 million in damages to Apple. Samsung later appealed to the U.S. Supreme Court.

In December 2016, the U.S. Supreme Court decided not to review damages and instead agreed 8-0 to reverse the decision from the first trial that awarded $400 million to Apple and returned the case to the Federal Circuit court. The reasoning was that the Federal Circuit did not use the correct legal standard to define "article of manufacture" because it is not the smartphone itself that the patents relate to but the individual components, such as the case and the screen. The Court had held that in the case of a multicomponent product, the relevant article of manufacture for arriving at a damages award need not be the end product sold to the consumer but may only be a component of that product. The Smallest Saleable Patent Protected Unit concept, which dates back to the 1880s U.S. Supreme Court case *Garretson*,[7] dealt with mop heads for wet brooms.

2-6 *Apple Inc. v. Samsung Elecs. Co.*, No. 11-CV-01846-LHK, 2017 U.S. Dist. LEXIS 177199 (N.D. Cal. Oct. 22, 2017).

2-7 *Garretson v. Clark*, 111 U.S. 120, 4 S. Ct. 291 (1884).

Further, in February 2017, the Federal Circuit remanded the dispute back to the Northern District of California, stating that since U.S. District Judge Lucy Koh oversaw the original trial, she should preside over the subsequent trial. In October 2017, the court found that "the jury instructions given at trial did not accurately reflect the law and that the instructions prejudiced Samsung by precluding the jury from considering whether the relevant article of manufacture for the purpose of § 289 was something other than the entire phone."[8] The court proceeded to issue a new trial to determine damages and also created a new test to determine the article of manufacture for the purpose of § 289. The test lists the following four factors: the scope of the design claimed in the plaintiff's patent, including the drawing and written description; the relative prominence of the design within the product as a whole; whether the design is conceptually distinct from the product as a whole; and the physical relationship between the patented design and the rest of the product, including whether the design pertains to a component that a user or seller can physically separate from the product as a whole and whether the design is embodied in a component that is manufactured separately from the rest of the product or if the component can be sold separately. At the time of this writing, we are still waiting for Judge Koh to make a final decision on damages.

How does the *Apple vs. Samsung* war affect IP valuation? While we are still awaiting Judge Koh to end the war, we can refer to her order of February 2014 (Public Redacted Version[9]) to gain some sense of how important valuation is in this case. That order granted in part and denied in part certain expert testimony with regard to valuation. Judge Koh's order included the following conclusions:

- The expert "may still rely on her Income and Cost Approaches, as well as her analysis of the *Georgia-Pacific* factors, insofar as that analysis does not rely on the HTC Agreement, the 2010 Apple Proposal, or the remaining licensing agreements [filed exhibits in the record]. As to the form of the reasonable royalty (lump-sum versus running royalty), [the expert] may continue to rely on her overall review of the license agreements in the record. Apple has not shown that [the expert's] choice of a lump-sum form based on [redacted] is improper or otherwise unfairly prejudicial." (Order, page 21)
- Additionally, another's expert testimony using a method to calculate reasonable royalties, where lost profits are not warranted to calculate damages, was allowed. The expert used an Edgeworth Box analysis, and explained the analysis as:

> The likely price at which an agreement can be struck between two parties to exchange a good or asset is bounded by the expected valuations that each party anticipates if the transaction does not take place. These valuations are commonly referred to in economics as forming the boundaries of an "Edgeworth Box," a bargaining range that governs economic interactions between the parties. As the licensor, the patentee takes into consideration that it would generally not be in

2-8 *Apple Inc. v. Samsung Elecs. Co.*, No. 11-CV-01846-LHK, 2017 U.S. Dist. LEXIS 177199 (N.D. Cal. Oct. 22, 2017).

2-9 *Apple Inc. v. Samsung Elecs. Co., Ltd.*, No. 12-CV-00630-LHK, 2014 U.S. Dist. LEXIS 24506 (N.D. Cal. Feb. 25, 2014).

> its economic interest to accept less in royalty fees than the expected financial cost of granting such a license. Correspondingly, as the licensee, the infringer would consider the license fee relative to the expected additional value it would have anticipated realizing as a direct result of having access to the technology taught by the asserted patent. (Order, page 38)

- Therefore, the bottom of the Edgeworth Box is the amount Apple is willing to accept to license its patents, and the top of the box is Samsung's amount they would be willing to pay to obtain those licenses. In extending that analysis, the reasonable royalty is based on Apple's expected loss in profits from licensing to Samsung.

Today, it is more common to see the acceptance of nontraditional alternative methodologies, such as the use of the Edgeworth Box method. As used above, it basically laid the decision on the amount of damages incurred by the plaintiff on the plaintiffs themselves, since the royalties are based on the amount the licensor/plaintiff would accept to license out their patents. While you also need the amount to be agreed to by the licensee as the royalty rate, it was noted by the expert that in a situation like the one Samsung found themselves in, they would be able to build the royalty into their price. The method therefore is much like a residential real estate transaction when there is a low inventory of homes on the market compared to the number of buyers. The buyers are willing to bid above the asking price so that they can have a home. Here, the assumption is that the licensee will pay whatever royalty rate the licensor asks for so that they can have use of the patent. The acceptance of this analysis gives the patent holder a type of monopoly power over any potential licensees.

However, we still note that by allowing certain expert testimony to be included, Judge Koh and the courts, while open to nontraditional methodologies, continue to rely on traditional types of valuation methodologies such as the income and cost methods.

What are our key takeaways with regards to *Apple v. Samsung*?

- Incremental value. There is a trend toward determining incremental values. Apportionment is key. Courts are requiring parties to identify the incremental value of the infringing technology and apportion the royalty base. Identifying the SSPPU is a step toward meeting the requirement of apportionment.
- Goodbye EMVR. The use of the entire market value rule (EMVR) will come under greater attack and be subject to *Daubert* challenges if not proven that its application supports reasonable royalty damages in any given matter. With some high-tech products that use a large number of patented components, the EMVR is simply not logical.
- Design patents can be apportioned. In *Apple v. Samsung*, the Court described a two-step process for calculating damages from the infringement of design patents: identify the article of manufacture to which the infringed design applies and calculate the infringer's total profit made on the article of manufacture. Parties have the ability to show that the infringing feature is a necessary condition for the sale and what motivates consumers to buy the products in the first place.

- Corporate egos create wars. The size of corporate egos running some technology giants cannot be overestimated.
- More important than these first four points, however, has been the impact on the valuation profession and the process. Both have benefitted over the last decade from the greater scrutiny and higher valuation standards that high-profile litigation and legislative changes have brought. The result? These battles in the telecom and high-tech world will likely continue. In response, the future will not only see an increase in technology-related litigation, but IP professionals will use more creative valuation and damages solutions and methodologies.

Impact of the Changes Wrought by the Courts, Legislation, and Litigation

The long-term impact of this decade's legislation and court decisions have yet to be determined since legislation is relatively new and pending rulings, such as *Apple vs. Samsung*, have yet to be finalized. However, it is clear, in our eyes, that the nature of IP itself is always evolving and changing and the related IP community is also changing. That is what makes the IP valuation profession an exciting place to be. To watch the value of IP, and the methodologies and the influences on those values, is much like watching ocean waves upon a beach . . . a constant ebb and flow.

Chapter 3

Changing Valuation Standards and Methodologies

In the most basic terms, the era of valuation simplicity is being left behind, and the simplistic rules of value are being replaced by more complex techniques that push the analytic envelope for the valuation expert, both in transactions and in the courts. As we see below, new concepts such as the smallest salable patent-practicing unit (SSPPU) replaces the old entire market value rule (EMVR). Fair, reasonable, and nondiscriminatory (FRAND)–based royalties are replacing individually negotiated royalties in certain devices. In other words, reasonable and nondiscriminatory bulk royalties are predetermined and then apportioned out for a whole group of patents contained within that particular device to the individual patent holders (see *Commonwealth Sci. & Indus. Research Organisation v. Cisco Sys.*, 809 F.3d 1295 Fed. Cir. 2015).

In Chapter 2, we looked at the activity of the courts over the last decade. We reviewed a number of key cases that have changed the face of valuation and damage calculations, particularly how they affect patents and technology. It is important to note that litigation decisions that affect valuation and valuation standards also affect valuation in a transactional environment. As the world of valuation and its interplay with litigation changes, so too do the methodologies that were developed become adapted to the world of transactions. Why? New asset configurations. New mega licensing concepts, ala FRAND. New complex litigation issues. New and bigger litigation stakeholders. Increased litigation activity. All of these are resulting in increased emphasis on accurate and more precise valuation.

Under federal law, it's clear that reasonable royalties are covered as damages that result from a patent infringement. Damages can be based on the following: "Upon finding for a claimant, the court shall award the claimant damages adequate to compensate for an infringement but in no event less than a reasonable royalty for the use made of the invention by the infringer . . . the court may receive expert testimony and aids in determination of damages what royalty may be reasonable under the circumstances."[1] The Lanham Act addresses trademark damages in a similar manner by saying the following: "[P]laintiff shall

3-1 35 U.S.C. § 284.

be entitled . . . to recover (1) defendant's profits, (2) any damages sustained by the plaintiff."[2] It is interesting to note that in both patent cases and trademark cases, reasonable royalty rates can be established. Of more interest here, however, is that in recent years, district courts and the Federal Circuit have been increasingly cautious and have directed increased levels of examination and skepticism on experts and the techniques and methods that they use in establishing royalty rates. These same courts have been particularly skeptical about traditional methods and rules of thumb used by experts to arrive at their damages calculations.

The 25% Rule of Thumb Is Gone in Litigation—And for Good Reasons

While the 25% rule can still be used in transaction analyses as a final sanity check, it is just that: a quick analysis to help an expert determine if their overall calculations make sense from a broad point of view. It should never be used as the primary or secondary methodology in calculating a royalty rate in any damages case, whether patent, trademark, or copyright. The death of the 25% rule came in January 2011 in the case known as *Uniloc v. Microsoft*, when the court ruled that "as a matter of Federal Circuit law, the 25% rule of thumb is a fundamentally flawed tool for determining a baseline royalty rate in a hypothetical negotiation."[3] From that moment on, the Court of Appeals for the Federal Circuit had finally struck down what had been one of the worst rules of thumb ever developed. This rule of thumb had been used since the 1960s as the foundation for any number of "reasonable royalty analyses."

Hardly reasonable, these were analyses that were done from the simplest point of view and with the least amount of effort. Those so-called experts are now left to try to figure out how they will evaluate royalty damages going forward. As a sidebar, the decision in *Uniloc* did also provide insight from the Federal Circuit concerning the EMVR in its application in royalty rate cases. [*Author's Note: We have been writing about, and railing against, the 25% rule in books, articles, and speeches since the late 1980s, referring to it as the "lazy man's analysis and the easy way out." It's refreshing to be vindicated after all this time.*]

The rule was often used to determine royalty rates, not only in litigation damages but in transaction cases, by a large group of analysts. It was claimed to have been based on the "realities of licensing." However, there was never any real data to support its use, only some anecdotal evidence of success back in the 1960s. The genesis of the 25% rule was actually based on licensing done by a now defunct radio and television corporation, Philco, which licensed and packaged intellectual property (IP) including patents, trademarks, and technical know-how.[4] Because it was a "bundle of intellectual property" being licensed on a nonexclusive basis, the 25% rule was supposedly applicable to all IP, not just patents. No empirical evidence was ever put forward that the 25% rule actually worked. Time moved forward from its original propagation in the 1960s, as much of the recent royalty rate valuation cases, both

3-2 15 U.S.C. § 1117(a).

3-3 *Uniloc USA, Inc. v. Microsoft Corp.*, 632 F.3d 1292 (Fed. Cir. 2011).

3-4 Robert Goldscheider et al., *Use of the 25 Per Cent Rule in Valuing IP*, 37 LES NOUVELLES 123 (2002).

in litigation and transactions, became more complex, the use of the 25% rule became less and less applicable. However, the use of it spread quite far from where it first originated.

A fundamental flaw was that it could never function in the real world where multiple patents were involved. If one thinks about it, the use of a single patent would result in royalties equaling 25% of the profits of a licensee. Therefore, for any product that had more than four patents under license, there would be no profits left for the manufacturer, perhaps the most illogical part of the concept of the 25% rule of thumb. Another significant and obviously illogical part of the 25% rule of thumb was the following question: 25% of what? 25% of gross profit? Operating profit? Pretax profit? Earnings Before Internet Depreciation Taxes and Amortization profit? As anyone familiar with operating businesses is aware, pretax profit is a movable feast and can mean many things to many people in many different tax jurisdictions. However, use of 25% of gross profit would unfairly burden the licensee. Yet, if one uses pretax profit and does a comparative analysis on a company-by-company basis, 25% is such a manipulatable number as to essentially be meaningless. And so, the entire logic of the 25% rule breaks down on these last two points, if on no other.

The 5% Rule of Thumb

An even simpler outgrowth of the 25% rule, also known as the lazy man's analysis, is the so-called 5% rule of thumb. This sprang up in the same time period as the 25% rule of thumb. This simply states that 5% of a licensee's gross revenues is an appropriate rule of thumb for a royalty rate. This smacks of being illogical and bordering on the point of stupidity. Thinking through this on the most basic level, it tells you that a royalty of 5% for a licensee who makes iron ingots would be just as appropriate as for a manufacturer of high profit margin perfumes or other consumer goods. On the surface, one instantly knows that that premise is unworkable. Clearly, 5% of gross revenue royalty would wipe out all profits for the iron ingot manufacturer, while 5% of gross revenues for the perfume manufacturer is hardly a burdensome royalty.

Nonetheless, this 5% rule of thumb has prospered in some quarters for a long time. Thankfully, it was dying a natural death before the *Uniloc* decision was handed down in 2011. Today, it has disappeared entirely from view, at least in the United States. May it rest in peace.

The Georgia-Pacific Factors: Obsolescence After 50 Years

In the 1970s, the 12-inch vinyl LP was partially replaced by the 8-track player, which in turn was supplanted by the cassette.[5] By early 2000 the cassette gave way to the compact disc (CD). Today, the MP3 player has all but replaced the CD. An item, product, or service becomes obsolete when a replacement becomes available that is more advantageous than

3-5 HANS-JOACHIM BRAUN, *MUSIC AND TECHNOLOGY IN THE TWENTIETH CENTURY* 161 (2002).

repurchasing or replacing the original item or service. While 8 track players became obsolete due to the cassette, the cassette in turn became obsolete due to the CD, which in turn became obsolete due to the MP3 player, and finally by direct music downloads.

The Georgia-Pacific factors were first outlined in 1958 in a case that involved royalties to be paid on plywood products. The demise of the Georgia-Pacific factors has come about as a result of time, changing market conditions, and the increased complexity of all IP, particularly technology but also trademarks and other IP as well. We need to take a step back and look at what the Georgia-Pacific factors attempt to do. They were originally outlined as an aide in developing a framework for hypothetical royalty rates in a damages case that involved patents 50 years ago. Over time they became partially codified in our legal system. Unfortunately, these factors were being manipulated in just about every piece of IP damages litigation that one reads about. In fact, they have become so convoluted as to be unrecognizable in recent litigation, most notably, in the *Microsoft Corp. v. Motorola, Inc.* case.[6] In trying to determine appropriate royalties, Judge Robart reworded them to such a degree that some of the factors were, quite frankly, unrecognizable. As a consequence, increasingly, they are no longer recognized by the courts, and some of our most learned judicial minds have spoken out against them.

In July 2012, then chief judge of the U.S. Court of Appeals of the Federal Circuit, Randall R. Rader, discussed the application of the Georgia-Pacific factors and said the following: "whenever I hear *Georgia-Pacific* I bristle a little bit, because the Georgia-Pacific factors are really just a laundry list of various things to be considered. The Georgia-Pacific factors were never meant to be a test or formula resolving damages, and somehow it gets blown out of content. . . . Many of those 15 factors may be overlapping or irrelevant to a particular case. Yet many litigation 'experts' will try to make their case seem more reasonable by stacking up so many Georgia-Pacific factors in their favor, and the rest are stacked for their opponent or neutral. That's not what Georgia-Pacific was ever about. It's a flawed methodology. Those factors are not meant to be counted up the way you count up balls and strikes during a baseball game."

In 1958, the court used the following 15 factors to determine the type of monetary payments that would compensate for a patent infringement in *Georgia-Pacific*:[7]

1. The royalties received by Georgia-Pacific for licensing the patent, proving or tending to prove an established royalty;
2. The rates paid by the licensee for the use of other similar patents;
3. The nature and scope of the license, such as whether it is exclusive or nonexclusive, restricted or nonrestricted in terms of territory or customers;
4. Georgia-Pacific's policy of maintaining its patent monopoly by licensing the use of the invention only under special conditions designed to preserve the monopoly;
5. The commercial relationship between Georgia-Pacific and licensees, such as whether they are competitors in the same territory in the same line of business or whether they are inventor and promoter;

3-6 *Microsoft Corp. v. Motorola, Inc.*, 696 F.3d 872 (9th Cir. 2012).
3-7 *Georgia-Pacific Corp. v. United States Plywood Corp.*, 258 F.2d 124 (2d Cir. 1958).

6. The effect of selling the patented specialty in promoting sales of other Georgia-Pacific products; the existing value of the invention to Georgia-Pacific as a generator of sales of nonpatented items; and the extent of such derivative or "convoyed" sales;
7. The duration of the patent and the term of the license;
8. The established profitability of the patented product, its commercial success, and its current popularity;
9. The utility and advantages of the patent property over any old modes or devices that had been used;
10. The nature of the patented invention, its character in the commercial embodiment owned and produced by the licensor, and the benefits to those who used it;
11. The extent to which the infringer used the invention and any evidence probative of the value of that use;
12. The portion of the profit or selling price that is customary in the particular business or in comparable businesses;
13. The portion of the realizable profit that should be credited to the invention as distinguished from any nonpatented elements, manufacturing process, business risks, or significant features or improvements added by the infringer;
14. The opinion testimony of qualified experts; and
15. The amount that Georgia-Pacific and a licensee would have agreed on at the time the infringement began if they had reasonably and voluntarily tried to reach an agreement.

Finally, in 2015, in *StoneEagle Services, Inc. v. Pay-Plus Solutions, Inc.*,[8] the *Georgia-Pacific* untouchable rules began to collapse after Middle District of Florida Judge Hernandez Covington allowed me, the plaintiff's damages expert, to offer royalty rate analysis without reference to any of the Georgia-Pacific factors. The judge agreed with plaintiff's counsel that the Federal Circuit does not require experts to use any or all of the Georgia-Pacific factors when using a methodology for computing damages. That ruling has changed the way courts weigh the Georgia-Pacific factors when determining whether an expert is subject to a *Daubert* challenge.

I testified in court that the Georgia-Pacific factors were "outmoded," which I have consistently questioned. Subsequently, testimony was allowed based on "market approach" valuation theories, helping the plaintiffs receive a favorable outcome. The jury awarded StoneEagle $2.2 million in royalties for three infringing systems.

This is not the first time that the Georgia-Pacific factors have been questioned as to being the supreme guide to determine if an expert's testimony should be subject to a *Daubert* challenge. In 2011, the *Uniloc* court noted that the Georgia-Pacific factors are not to be thrown out altogether. However, their use is not required and, as in any matter, the use of any theory is best addressed by cross-examination and testimony of the expert witness. After the *StoneEagle* ruling, we can safely say that the Georgia-Pacific factors are no longer the ultimate standard in determining royalty-based damages awards.

3-8 *StoneEagle Servs., Inc. v. Pay-Plus Sols., Inc.*, No. 8:13-cv-2240-T-33MAP, 2015 U.S. Dist. LEXIS 79971 (M.D. Fla. June 19, 2015).

New Valuation Concerns and Methodologies: Who Are Nash and Coase? What Is the Edgeworth Box?

We just read that the courts, market forces, changing technology, and valuation conditions have brought about substantial changes in how IP is measured and valued, particularly in litigation, but equally so in transactional valuations. For example, what used to be a universally used approach called the entire market value rule is giving way to the growing use of the SSPPU. With more co-branding and the use of multiple copyrights and layering of trademarks and copyrights in the same message and on the same product, alternative approaches and methodologies are springing up to better address and more accurately value multiple pieces of IP in a single product or a single usage.

The rise of the SSPPU as a basis for calculating a royalty rate or other damages in a patent infringement case is logical—it is a logical outgrowth of the demise of the EMVR. What do we mean by this? When a product such as a smartphone or other telecommunications device consists of multiple patents, yet only one or two patents are infringed, it would be both unfair and illogical to calculate a royalty to establish damages on the entire selling price of the mobile phone, when, in fact, the patents being infringed represent only a small fraction of the 100 or more patents contained in the phone. Thus, the concept of apportionment of value comes into play, i.e., apportionment of an appropriate amount of value of the entire device to a specific part of the whole device against which a royalty can be calculated and thus, from there, a damages amount can be established.

It springs originally from *Garretson*,[9] a case that dates back to the 1880s and dealt with new technology of floor mop heads.

> This then is the basis from which the SSPPU has sprung. This concept, SSPPU, will eventually spread out to all forms of IP valuation in our opinion. For example, as branded and copyrighted products become more complex and are in turn infringed, I believe that one will see apportionment of royalty rates in damages cases (and in transactional valuations) as one attempts to establish value of only one piece of IP in an overall product. For example, let's imagine a co-branded health and beauty aid product that features a corporate brand name as well as copyrighted elements of either a celebrity's rights of publicity and/or elements of a special promotional packaging provided by an entertainment company. Imagine now that an infringer misuses one of those elements in an outright infringement by selling counterfeit goods in the form of cologne. The damages might be calculated only on the misused trademark and not on the other IP elements, such as the rights of publicity and copyright elements. In this brief example, one would thus be talking in general terms about the SSPPU concept being applied to marketing intangibles—the trademark, the copyright, and the rights of publicity rights contained therein. While I rarely see this specific situation arise, I predict that in the coming few years it will indeed become a more important issue.

3-9 *Garretson v. Clark*, 111 U.S. 120, 4 S. Ct. 291 (1884).

The issue of using the EMVR goes back as far as 1997 in a General Electric damages case where the jury awarded approximately $600 million to that company.[10] Since then it has been back and forth to the Federal Circuit. Beginning in 2009, the concept of apportionment began to firmly take hold in a case that involved Lucent and Gateway.[11] Finally, in a case that involved Cornell and Hewlett-Packard Company,[12] the well-known judge Randall Rader imposed the forerunner of the SSPPU, saying that using the old EMVR approach had no "economic function" and did not use reliable economic principles and methods required for an economic damages expert report. From there, we move steadily forward through a series of cases to 2017, where in the ongoing battle of *Apple v. Samsung*, described in Chapter 2, the U.S. Supreme Court stepped in and reversed a damages award against Samsung, returning the case to the lower courts based on the fact that they essentially agreed that an SSPPU approach to damages would be most appropriate.

Defining the SSPPU

A key issue in these cases is how to define what an SSPPU is. Over the years, the difficulty in the process is to identify what is the smallest unit that can be sold; often this is a theoretical product. The term "article of manufacture" is brought up to encompass an actual product as well as a component, and so the pricing of a theoretical component has to be arrived at before a royalty can be calculated. Unfortunately, in establishing these SSPPU prices, the valuation expert often has to turn to regression analysis to estimate the value of the technology being infringed. Typically, what happens is that a regression model tries to explain and quantify consumer demand for a product as a function of the product's price, its various features, the level of advertising, as well as other factors such as competitive pricing and consumer income.

Hopefully, the regression model is designed so that the quantity demanded, which is the dependent variable, and the factors that affect demand, the independent variables, can identify the relative value and therefore price of the SSPPU. It is, however, in our opinion and that of many others, a very problematical exercise. There is an alternative to the regression analysis that can at least help in the process. The alternative is to engage in a consumer survey among actual potential buyers of the product to determine which feature or features drive their purchasing decision to a greater and lesser extent.

Since the courts seem to be asking that the parties in an infringement suit demonstrate how the infringed patented feature drives consumer demand to some extent in order to justify the royalties chosen for it, it does seem that the survey can provide a workable solution by simply asking a sufficient number of consumers what portion of their demand for the end product is driven by which features within the product. Simplistically, this can work, given that the customer or consumer can divine the differences between the various features. This is not always an easy task, particularly when even simple products like mobile phones get

3-10 *Fonar Corp. v. GE*, 107 F.3d 1543 (Fed. Cir. 1997).
3-11 *Lucent Techs., Inc. v. Gateway, Inc.*, 580 F.3d 1301 (Fed. Cir. 2009).
3-12 *Cornell Univ. v. Hewlett-Packard Co.*, 609 F. Supp. 2d 279 (N.D.N.Y. 2009).

increasingly complex and features gets so multilayered and multifunctional as to be difficult for even the most sophisticated consumer to tell one from the other.

There's one final complicating factor with the SSPPU concept, and here I paraphrase the Federal Circuit:[13]

In determining a royalty base, you should not use the value of the entire apparatus or product unless either, (1) the patented feature creates the basis for the customer's demand for the entire product or the patented feature essentially creates the value of the other component parts of the product or (2) the product in question constitutes the smallest saleable unit containing the patented feature.

Where the smallest saleable unit is in fact the multicomponent product that contains several noninfringing features with no relation to the patented feature, the patentee must do more to estimate what portion of the value of that product is attributable to the patented technology. To hold otherwise would permit the EMVR exception and swallow the rule of apportionment. In other words, the patents may not directly connect to the entire consumer product. In that case, what do you do?

In short, the concept of SSPPU has frankly muddied the water as much as clarified it. However, it is the rule we live with. As a result, two or three new "methods" have arisen to try to help the court address the issue of value in these situations. The two most common are the "Nash bargaining solution" and the "Coase theorem." Also used from time to time is the Edgeworth box, which is simply a fancy phrase to describe an indifference curve. We discuss those briefly below.

New Methodologies

So what are some of these "new methodologies"? Some of them are not new, and I question whether some of them are really methodologies at all, as opposed to economic theorems that users are trying to adapt as valuation methodologies. Below is an overview of these three methodologies, which are experiencing current popularity as valuation analysts and professionals wrestle with SSPPU and the issue of apportionment.

First, as to Mr. John Nash, he was the Nobel prize–winning mathematician whose life formed the basis for the lovely movie starring Russell Crowe, *A Beautiful Mind*. Among other things, he introduced game theory shortly after World War II. Mr. Nash introduced the Nash bargaining solution (NBS), which claims to define the most mutually beneficial outcome in a two-party bargaining situation. Unfortunately, it is one of the most artificial bargaining solutions that you can possibly imagine because it assumes an essentially perfect world.

In the IP valuation world, some damages experts have been using this theoretical bargaining scenario to argue that the starting point of any licensing negotiation (therefore, valuation calculation) is a 50–50 split of the IP's contribution to the licensee or infringers' product. There are a number of problems with using this NBS approach to calculate valuation/damages. Basically, it is such an idealized scenario that it ignores any outside considerations, beyond a simple single negotiation between the two parties in the litigation or transaction. Also, the scenario would ask one to assume that in any licensing negotiation, you have to

3-13 *Uniloc USA, Inc. v. Microsoft Corp.*, 632 F.3d 1292 (Fed. Cir. 2011).

Figure 3.1 Nash Bargaining Solution

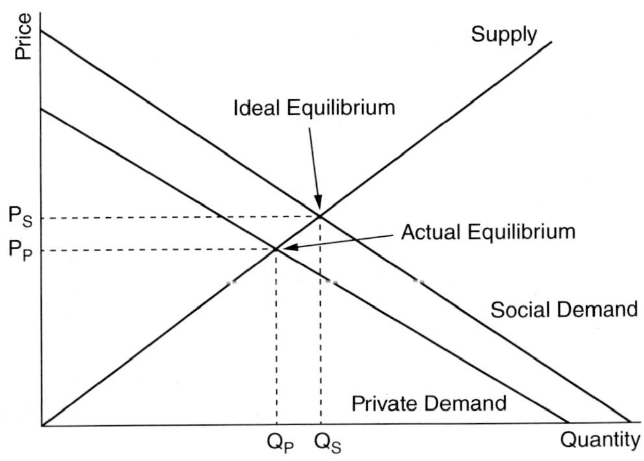

ignore such basic factors as royalties that the licensor may have gotten in other negotiations for the same patent, as well as royalties paid for other comparable technologies in other license agreements. These are facts that would be in evidence and that are basic and important to any negotiation.

The NBS has been allowed in some cases, but other courts reject it because they find it confusing and view it as a complex version of an arbitrary allocation, ala the disgraced 25% rule of thumb. For example, in the case of *Oracle vs. Google*[14] the trier of fact excluded the damages expert's testimony, concluding that it was simply a profit split method that doubled the old 25% rule and then used double talk and complex mathematical equations and that the Nash approach simply invites a "miscarriage of justice." Second, when used in court, the NBS framework is often then combined with the *Georgia-Pacific* factors. What results is a combination of two really bad methodologies, in the author's opinion as well as the opinion of several courts.

Compounding the problem, in order to validate the NBS, you have to have data about the specific contribution of the technology to a product's profitability (rarely available) and the net economic surplus of the parties that adopt the technology (an economist's dream). The utility function of the parties for the particular licensing transaction (a guess at best) needs to be known. Also, knowledge of the bargaining skills of the respective parties is required (again a subjective guess). We have not found a case where experts have been able to modify the NBS to incorporate any new assumptions into the process; in fact, new assumptions are not allowed. (See Figure 3.1 for a visualization of Mr. Nash's Solution.) Most important, we have not been able to identify any licensing professionals who actually use the NBS in real-world deal-making licensing events.

As to Mr. Coase, another obscure but respected economist, his Coase theorem dates back to the 1960s. Dr. Ronald Coase is a Nobel Prize Laureate who had a long tenure at the University of Chicago and based his theorem on his paper titled, "The Problem of Social Cost."

3-14 *Oracle Am., Inc. v. Google Inc.*, 798 F. Supp. 2d 1111 (N.D. Cal. 2011).

Since publication of his original paper in 1960, multiple other economists have added to the Coase theorem. In simplest terms, as shown in the diagram, the Coase theorem deals with predicting outcomes in a negotiating environment that has an absence of transaction costs. In other words, there is perfect knowledge about both the marginal benefits and the marginal costs. His reasoning was that in order to get to the perfect solution for any bargaining situation, one had to assume that no transaction costs could be incurred.

Dr. Coase was applying much of his theorem to costs and fees designed around and for government-regulated fee setting where, in fact, there often is an absence of transaction costs and high knowledge of true marginal costs. However, the obvious problem is that in the real world of transactions, patent litigations, and disputes, real-world transactions costs are high. More importantly, true marginal costs of the two parties involved are rarely known with absolute certainty to the other party. A key criticism therefore is that the Coase theorem is rarely applicable in the realities of a business negotiation or litigation damages analysis. More importantly, the parties to the negotiation obviously choose to distort or disguise the outcome by not providing complete information to the other side about the true costs incurred in their production processes. In other words, both sides in a negotiation, whether it is a transaction or litigation, lack the private information and knowledge of the other side's true costs with absolute certainty; using the Coase theorem to aid them and being able to use this as a meaningful valuation approach are not effective.

In the last few years, his work on the cost of externalities as they affect licensing and licensing agreements has been applied by economists to the question of SSPPUs, in particular, to SSPPUs within FRAND and standard essential patent (SEP) licensing, i.e., those patents included within a SEP grouping and royalties that are set by a standard-setting organization (SSO).

Most notably, in a paper written in 2016, European Professor Nicolas Petit called for the elimination of the concept of SSPPU, claiming that pricing of licensing fees in FRAND transactions is totally inefficient and will inevitably lead to either a patent holder being unfairly compensated and/or the overall royalties being charged in a SEP under an SSO's FRAND rules being grossly overinflated. Neither outcome is desired. Petit also claims that in the long run, SSPPU pricing within SEPs is essentially illegal, unethical, and immoral. His argument that any SSO that is permitted to fix prices is violating antitrust, as well as being anticompetitive, violates laws of any technology based or democratically elected governments of laws appears to have great merit.

This is not the time or place to discuss these moral, ethical, and legal issues. It is enough, however, to say that the Coase theorem, illustrated in the diagram below, seems to support the argument that using the SSPPU approach for FRAND royalty rates under an SSO is not the most efficient way to set royalty rates or to value disputed pieces of IP. The recent litigation over FRAND royalties and the issue of SEPs were reflected in the *Microsoft Corp. v. Motorola*[15] matter, when Judge Robart's ruling on royalties was affirmed by the 9th Circuit Court of Appeals. In his decision, Judge Robart discussed the need to avoid "royalty stacking" or a situation where SEP owners charge high rates and the combined royalty rate is more than the profit on the product.

Mr. Francis Edgeworth is the earliest entrant in our trio of relatively new IP damages theorists. His book on mathematical physics was published originally in 1881. It was

3-15 *Microsoft Corp. v. Motorola, Inc.*, 696 F.3d 872 (9th Cir. 2012).

Figure 3.2 The Coase Theorem demonstrates the equilibrium between marginal cost and marginal benet (MC = MB). If the marginal costs outweigh marginal benets (MC > MB), the enterprise should compensate the other side for producing an extra unit of output.

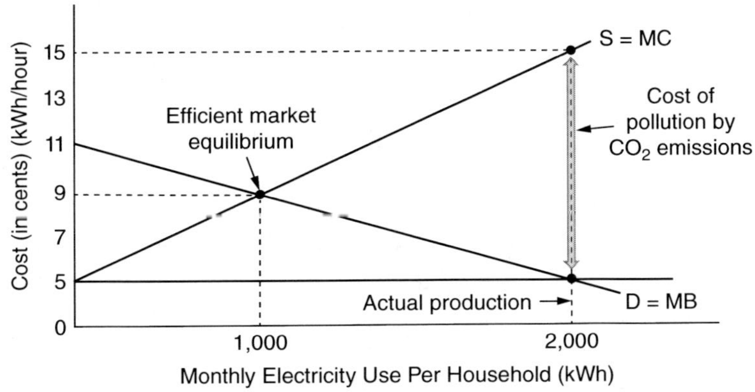

substantially expanded on by Vilfredeo Pareto in 1906 in the *Manual of Political Economy* published by Societe Editrice, 1906, when he added the so-called Pareto curves. In Chapter 2, the Edgeworth box is explained in some detail in connection with the *Apple v. Samsung* case and is shown in the diagram below. Here, we provide some basic background.

Figure 3.3 The Edgeworth Box

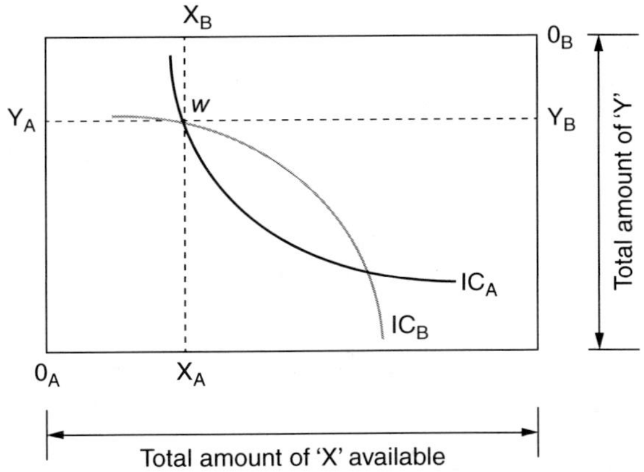

In simplest terms, one can imagine a simple *X–Y* axis graph with a demand curve for a licensor, and separate *X–Y* graph with a demand curve for a potential licensee, each being expressed as a percentage royalty rate. Now, take one graph and invert it on top of the other. You form a box with two curves or straight lines inside of it, and those two curves or lines will cross at some point. You have just constructed an Edgeworth box. The solution within the Edgeworth box is the point at which the two curves or lines cross. Clearly, the process is a bit more complex, but for ease of understanding, this brief explanation should suffice. Again, as with the Nash and Coase approaches, the Edgeworth box makes many simplistic assumptions, including perfect knowledge, lack of substantial external forces, no alternatives, and no other prior royalty agreements. It is an artificial construct. Nonetheless, it has been accepted, at least in the *Apple v. Samsung* case. Will it be used in other cases? Perhaps. Should it be used? When all else fails, new methods need to be tried.

Chapter 4

Valuation Methodologies: Traditional and Accepted

We move now to a review of current methodologies. When valuing intellectual property (IP) assets, it is essential to consider the unique characteristics of the subject asset and the context of the valuation assignment because valuations are needed for many reasons:

- When negotiating a transaction (e.g., endorsement, licensing, merger and acquisition, leveraged buy-out, financing, bankruptcy/liquidation);
- When calculating damages in litigation;
- For financial reporting;
- For tax purposes; and
- For divorce, estate planning, and similar activities.

The methods used to value IP and intangible assets have many elements in common with those used to value tangible assets (e.g., real estate, equipment, or other real property). However, a lack of available information combined with legal and technical intricacies often complicates IP valuations.

Certainty of Valuation

When valuing assets, there is always an inherent level of uncertainty regarding the conclusion of value. This is true even of assets with a seemingly immutable value, such as cash, since inflation and exchange rate fluctuations affect real value. Due to the unique nature of IP assets, the level of uncertainty increases. Unlike real estate or equipment, active markets for the purchase and sale of comparable IP often do not exist, and available information may be skewed toward large deals as smaller transactions are rarely publicized.

Complicating the analysis is the fact that an IP asset, such as right of publicity, can have multiple values at the same time. This seeming paradox is due to the context of the valuation. Unlike a piece of real estate, an IP asset can have vastly different levels of value depending

Figure 4.1 Certainty in Valuation

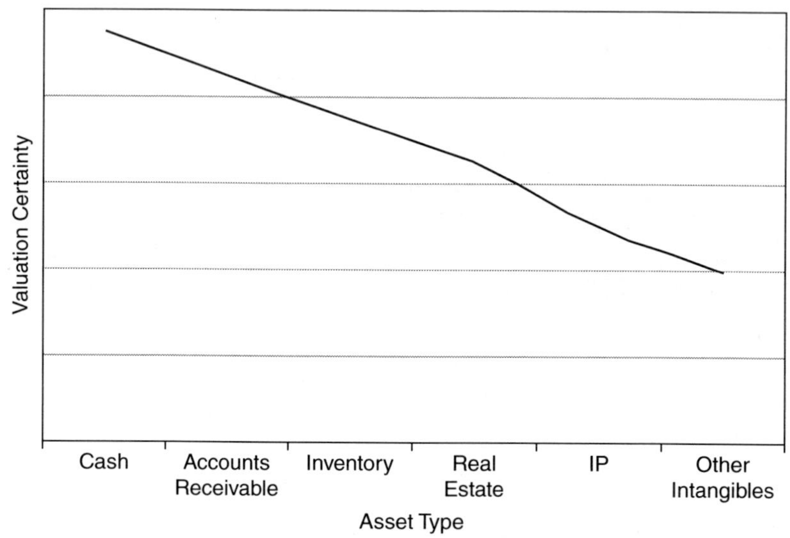

on who owns it and how they intend to use it. As an example, consider a fully commercialized patent held by a pharmaceutical company. There are at least three values for the patent at any given time. The first is the in-place value of the patent as it is currently being used. The second is the value of the patent to a competitor who intends to bring a similar drug to market. Clearly, the value of the patent to the competitor is different than the value to the original owner, as the competitor would be the second or third entrant to the marketplace and unlikely to gain equivalent market share. A third value is the value that a current infringer would pay to avoid litigation. That value, again, will be different than the value to the in-place holder.

Figure 4.1 illustrates this uncertainty concept. The vertical axis is measured in relative certainty of valuation running from 100% to 0%. The horizontal axis identifies six kinds of assets, four being tangible and two being intangible. The slope of the line is a relative slope and simply serves to indicate that there is a range of certainty with any type of valuation.

In this chapter and in Chapter 5, we will review both traditional and alternative valuation methodologies. We begin with a brief introduction regarding the nature of IP, followed by a review of traditional and alternative valuation methodologies. We then conclude with some case studies.

Balance Sheet Treatment of Intangibles

In a 2004 speech, former chair of the Federal Reserve, Allan Greenspan noted, "[t]he economic product of the US has become predominantly conceptual." According to a recent estimate by consulting firm Ocean Tomo, 84% of the market value of companies in the S&P 500 comes from intangible assets.[1] Yet, the vast majority of this value doesn't appear on companies' balance sheets.

From an accounting perspective, intangible assets fall into two categories: those acquired in business combinations and those developed internally. Intangible assets acquired from another party are recorded on the balance sheet at cost, including all acquisition costs and expenditures necessary to prepare the intangible asset for its intended use. However, costs incurred to create intangibles internally are generally expensed. This is an important distinction because costs to develop the asset appear as expenses on the income statement but not assets on the balance sheet.

Numerous explanations have been presented for why this practice makes sense. Costs incurred internally to develop an intangible asset often bear little relation to that asset's value once it is commercialized. The argument states it is often difficult to match internal costs with specific intangibles. However, the end result is that a company's book value (the value of assets on the balance sheet) often bears little relation to the company's true value.

Market Value Defined

There are many definitions of market value. For example, the American Society of Appraisers offers the following:

> The price expressed in terms of cash equivalence at which the property would change hands between a hypothetical willing and able buyer and a hypothetical willing and able seller; acting at arm's-length and in an open and unrestricted market, when neither is under compulsion to buy or sell and when both have reasonable knowledge of the relevant facts. (www.appraisers.org)

Similarly, the International Valuation Standards Council guidelines define market value as "the estimated amount for which a property should exchange on the date of valuation between a willing buyer and a willing seller in an arm's-length transaction, after proper marketing, when the parties act knowledgably and prudently and without compulsion" (www.ivsc.org).

Market value can also be defined as the estimated amount for which a property should exchange on the date of valuation between a willing buyer and a willing seller in an arm's-length transaction after proper marketing, and when the parties have each acted knowledgably, prudently, and without compulsion to do so. Particularly for IP, a fundamental aspect of market valuation is the principle of highest and best use, which can be defined as the most effective use of the IP that is possible given full exploitation that is justified, while still being legally protected, financially feasible, and which results in the highest value of the IP.

4-1 Kristi L. Stathis, *Ocean Tomo Releases 2015 Annual Study of Intangible Asset Market Value,* Insights Blog (Mar. 5, 2015), http://www.oceantomo.com/blog/2015/03-05-ocean-tomo-2015-intangible-asset-market-value/.

Generally Accepted Valuation Methodologies

When valuing IP, we consider each of the different valuation methodologies in light of the information available and the specific circumstances in order to determine the best method for ascertaining value. Traditional methodologies commonly used to determine the value of IP are the cost approach, the market approach, the income approach, and a hybrid methodology known as the relief-from-royalty approach.

Multiple valuation methodologies can be used with IP and other intangible assets; some are well established, some are highly specialized, and some are very technical and situation specific. The multiplicity of methodologies reflects not only the diversity of IP and intangible assets but also the degree of complexity that revolves around valuation of these assets. In general, IP valuation methodologies fall into four broad groups as shown in Figure 4.2.

There is general agreement among valuation analysts and IP professionals on the three broad categories of standard methodologies: the cost method, the income method, and the market-based method. In addition, there are alternatives and subsets to these methodologies that have gained acceptance.

It is both logical and obvious that methods used to value IP and intangible assets must have many elements in common with those used to value tangible assets such as real estate, equipment, and other real property. The unique nature of these assets, however, is combined with an important difference in many IP valuation exercises. That difference is the availability, or lack of availability, of necessary data, such as comparable transactions and/or relevant rates and/or historical costs and other financial information. These data, including benchmarking information and comparable transactions, are needed to establish logical and intellectually sound valuations of the assets. However, they may be difficult to acquire and may take substantial interpretation and interpolation on the part of the valuation analyst, illustrating quite clearly that IP valuation is best left to experts in the field rather than accountants and first-time analysts.

At the beginning of the valuation process, the analyst should have the good sense to consider all of the different methodologies available. It is imperative that the analyst valuing the particular bundle of IP or intangibles consider all methods, both traditional and alternative. This is particularly so because the information available often is neither perfect nor adaptable to one particular methodology. Thus, the valuation analyst should look at multiple

Figure 4.2 IP Valuation Methodologies

Market Approach	Income Approach	Cost Approach	Other
• Market prices in active market • Analogous transactions • Market multiples	• Price premium • Relief-from-royalty method • Excess earnings method • Incremental cash flow method	• Reproduction cost method • Replacement cost method • Imputed cost method	• Options • Elements of value • Return on average equity • Monte Carlo

approaches and compare results before concluding as to a value. There are generally accepted IP valuation approaches, but this does not mean that a given approach is used only with a certain type of IP.

The selection of the best valuation approach and methodology for a given IP or intangible asset is going to depend on four broad basics:

- How unique is the asset?
- How much data is available and verifiable?
- What is the context, purpose, and objective of the analysis?
- What is the judgment of the analyst himself/herself? Hopefully, this is based on extensive earlier experience.

When negotiating a transaction, the ability to develop accurate valuation models will lead to more informed decision making. However, the information available is often imperfect and will affect the choice of valuation methodologies. In the context of litigation, damages calculations require the application of valuation methodologies to determine the value of economic benefits lost, because an arm's-length transaction never occurred. Therefore, the reasonableness of each method must be evaluated based on the context of the specific situation.

Cost Approach

The historical cost to develop an asset is one method used to estimate its value. Based on the economic principal of substitution, one approach to the value of IP can be the cost to replace or reproduce the asset. While the differences between reproduction cost and replacement cost may seem simply a question of semantics, these variations in the cost approach can yield very different results when practiced.

Using the cost approach on a valuation assignment, you must establish the particular definition of cost. Whether using historical or future cost, the basic underlying principal for the cost approach is the same—the principal is substitution, which states that worth or value of any object, asset, or piece of IP is no greater than the cost to obtain that asset or reproduce that asset. The cost can be measured by the cost of reproducing the IP as it can be measured by purchasing it today or replacing it with a substitute asset of equal quality, or by an absolute reproduction of the asset, or by imputing future cost.

Reproduction cost is the total cost that would be incurred, in today's prices, to construct an exact duplicate of the IP being valued. Theoretically, this duplicate IP would be created using the same materials, intellectual capital, standards, design, layout, and quality of work used to create the original IP asset. This would include all costs incurred in the development of the original IP, which may now be obsolete and no longer used.

Replacement cost, on the other hand, measures the total cost needed to create, or acquire an asset with equivalent functionality or utility to the original IP. Due to constant technological advancements, the replacement cost will almost always be lower than the reproduction cost because the replacement cost assumes the asset will be developed in the most efficient manner possible. Another way to think of this is the reproduction cost is historical in perspective, and replacement cost is current or prospective in assessing expenditures that would be necessary in the future to acquire or replace the IP being valued.

The issue with replacement cost is current or that of functionality, in other words, how does the IP work and how many hours, years, or months would it take to acquire or replace the patent, trademark, or other IP with one of equal functionality?

There are subtle differences in the variations to the cost approach and each one uses a somewhat different definition of cost.

Regardless of the cost approach used, the calculation should include several important cost categories:

- Direct hard costs, such as materials and design costs;
- Soft costs and other indirect costs, including development time, e.g., software coding development;
- Overhead costs for management and selling, general, and administrative expense;
- Marketing costs, including costs that have been or would need to be expended on advertising and marketing, and other costs to build or rebuild the market for the particular IP asset;
- Legal costs such as trademark patent and copyright application, registration, and other fees;
- Development costs;
- Personnel and personnel overhead costs; and
- Production and engineering costs, as well as a profit percentage for the development of the asset for the owner or developer.

The primary drawback to the cost approach is that it does not recognize any economic benefits associated with marketplace income or value creation. Therefore, the cost approach is less useful for IP and products that have reached the market and generated revenues. Generally, the cost approach is better suited to analysis of IP and products that have not yet been developed commercially or that could be recreated quickly, because it reflects the cost a company or individual could avoid by purchasing or duplicating a similar development effort. The cost approach is also an effective method for establishing the minimum price of an asset in the context of a proposed transaction, especially if there are other assets available for substitution.

Unless a premium is added to these costs, this method does not give a true indication of the economic benefits or value that the IP has provided or could provide to the owner. This can also be thought of as the opportunity cost, which needs to be added to the costs listed above. Otherwise, the cost approach yields a minimal value for the IP or other asset. In principal, the cost approach is based on the underlying economic concept of substitution, on the premise that a damage calculation or valuation should equal, but not be greater than, the value of the IP being assessed.

Without including opportunity cost, an accurate measure of value will not be reached. There are also the considerations of whether the IP is becoming obsolete or whether the costs of development have declined. For example, many cost items relative to the development

Figure 4.3 Cost Analysis

Summary of Historical Cost	
• Hard costs of development	$100,000
• Personnel and development costs	$ 25,000
• Market development costs	$ 15,000
• Advertising costs	$ 50,000
• Overhead costs	$ 50,000
Total Cost	**$240,000**
Multiplier for current costs	160%
Total value, based on cost, expressed in today's dollars	$384,000

of the IP, such as software coding, which can now be outsourced to India or China, have decreased substantially since the development of the IP. In Figure 4.3 we provide a very simple example of a cost-based valuation for a piece of IP.

Opportunity cost consists of the value of the other courses of action and/or other investment opportunities that were not taken in order to pursue the development of the specific IP being valued. Essentially, this opportunity cost measures the impact of either delayed market entry or the foregone development of an alternative piece of technology, trademark, copyright, or similar item. Another way of thinking about this is to ask the question: What could be earned during the period of development if the financed assets were used elsewhere?

The cost approach is most useful in cases where the IP has no economic activity or income to review, such as an early-stage technology that has not yet come to market or a not-yet-commercialized trademark or copyright. This method is also effective at establishing a minimum price for an asset if the context is a proposed transaction, particularly if there are other assets available for substitution. Again, the primary drawback associated with the cost approach is that it does not recognize any economic benefits associated with marketplace income (unless future imputed income is calculated additional to the cost basis). For example, there is no mechanism with this methodology to incorporate revenue or profit data; therefore, one may be forced to ignore important data by which the value of the assets is typically measured.

Market Approach

The market approach values IP by comparing the subject asset to publicly available transactions that involve similar assets with similar uses. This provides a reasonable indication of value if an active market exists that can provide examples of recent arm's-length transactions with adequate information regarding terms and conditions. Due to the ease of data collection, the market approach is also used extensively in the valuation of real property assets. The residential real estate market, e.g., almost exclusively values properties using the market approach.

In contrast to the other widely accepted valuation methodologies, the strength of the market approach is its reliance on actual arm's-length transactions. As a result, when the

Figure 4.4 Trademark Sales Market Comparables Approach

Agreement A – \$8M cash Agreement B – \$9M: \$4M now, \$5M over two years Agreement C – \$10M: \$2M per year over five years Agreement D – \$8.5M cash Agreement E – \$9M cash **Concluded Value = \$9M**
Based on comparable data interpolation.

necessary data can be found, the market approach has increasingly become the preferred approach to the valuation of intangible assets.

Based on a long history of valuation of all types of assets, the market approach is heavily used for tangible assets. It can, however, be just as effective for intangibles when appropriate market conditions exist. In contrast to the other widely accepted methodologies, the strength of the market approach is its reliance on actual market sales, rents, and transactions. A simplified example of a comparable transaction analysis is shown in Figure 4.4.

Comparable transactions are frequently obscure or hard to interpret. Often it is time consuming and/or impossible to get enough detail to be certain that all of the elements of value that would make it a true comparable have been identified and appropriately considered. Hence, careful analysis is required to ensure that similar IP, in similar environments, used in similar contexts, is included in the set of comparable transactions. When done properly, a close correlation among comparable transactions allows for the triangulation of a value likely to be realized in an arm's-length transaction.

When possible, comparable transactions apply to the same type of IP or intangible, and other information is necessary to establish true comparability. These data include the relevant industry in which the comparable IP is being used, any geographic constraints or differences that may exist, exclusivity or nonexclusivity provisions, payment structures and mechanisms, and, of course, the time frame, among others. Importantly, one also needs to know in what context the transaction took place. In other words, was it related to a bankruptcy filing, an estate settlement, litigation or other judgment, or perhaps a forced transaction or divestiture? Any one of these may render a specific comparable transaction unsuitable for the analysis, unless one takes the time to make compensating adjustments to the transaction.

The valuation analyst should always pay close attention to market conditions at the time that a given transaction took place, as those conditions may have influenced the sale or license terms. Along with these possible considerations, the price information contained in the comparable transaction will frequently have to be adjusted for more precise comparability with the IP being valued, using a common reference point such as sales revenue, profit margins, or net income levels.

The great strength of the market approach is, of course, its connection to actual market sales, licenses, rents, and other transactions. When appropriate data are available, the market approach is practical, logical, and applicable to all types of assets, both tangible and intangible. Finally, as with the income and relief-from-royalty approaches discussed below, the valuation conclusions can be reviewed at any time subsequent to the original valuation analysis in order to see if new data or transactions have appeared and if adjustments in the valuation are necessary. When reliable data are available, the market approach is considered the most direct and systematic method for accurately valuing intangible assets.

Market Multiples Approach

The market multiples approach is a variation of the market approach. The use of market multiples allows for the valuation of comparable assets based on a ratio to some common denominator. This is based on the theory that a ratio that compares value to some company-specific variable is the same across firms.

Common measures used in a market multiples approach are EBITDA multiples, revenue multiples, price to earnings, and others. The market multiple approach can also be used to measure the value of website and online assets. As an example, a website can be valued based on the worth of a single monthly unique user or daily active user. If a group of websites comparable to the target website one is looking to value have exchanged hands and there is publicly available information on the value of those transactions, one simply needs to divide the value of the websites by their number of unique users (or daily active users) to extract a market multiple.

Income Approach

The income approach uses forecasted financial results based on factors such as historical financials, industry trends, and the competitive environment. While the income approach is a widely used valuation approach, it can be complex and requires substantial knowledge and judgment on the part of the individual performing the valuation. There are also numerous derivations of the income approach that can be applied to analyze value. These include direct cash flow models, incremental cash flow models, price premium models, excess earnings models, and relief-from-royalty models.

The concept of the income approach is very simple: it is based on the assumption that the value of a piece of IP or intangible asset results from the future financial benefits that will be generated by it in some form of income or cash flow. There are at least as many income approach valuation methods as there are measures of IP income. However, most methods can be grouped into four areas:

- Direct cash flow models,
- Indirect earnings or savings models,
- Price premium and excess earning models, and
- Relief-from-royalty analyses.

The value of the IP can be thought of as the present value of the future cash flows or other measures of income that can be generated into the future for whatever remaining expected useful life the IP may contain. The three central tasks, therefore, within an income valuation are to first establish the future cash flows that are relevant specifically to the IP.

Figure 4.5 Income Approach

Annual Income Generated from IP	$100,000
• Number of years of income generation	8
• Gross value of income streams	$800,000
• Annual discount rate adjustment	15.0%
• Net value of income streams	≈ **$450,000**

Second, to establish the length of time for which the income levels can be measured with a surety, as shown above. Third is to determine the interest rate or discount rate that should be applied to those income streams.

First, how to measure the "income" attributable to the asset? Is income going to be measured as some theoretical royalty or rent to be received? Or is income going to be measured as the premium price commanded by products using the IP? Or is income going to be measured as some portion of the operating income of a company's overall operations, or for a specific technology or specific brand? Any and all of these can be appropriate and can be used in one IP valuation or another, but one must be careful in selecting the most appropriate measure.

For that reason, the income approach can be misleading, sometimes grossly overstating the potential value of an IP and, more importantly, can become an overly mechanistic approach to valuation. Therefore, an accurate forecast of revenue or income attributable to the IP depends on a thorough understanding of the competitive and economic environment that affects the IP during the time frame of the valuation and into the future.

Importantly, the length of the forecast of future cash flows is also variable as is an accurate estimate of remaining useful life. The discount rate is the final crucial element in appropriately using the income-based approach to a valuation. A discount rate is a calculation that establishes what a future dollar of value will be worth today, applying a constant discount to it over time. Naturally, a dollar 10 years from now will be worth much less than a dollar today. The question being: What discount rate should be used? Later in this chapter, we provide exhibits that illustrate how a discount rate is calculated.

Other comments on the income approach are appropriate. First, it is a flexible approach in the sense that one can value assets from different perspectives. For example, one can use a going concern or fair market value for a transaction. On the other hand, it is possible to include subjective components to reach other values. This is particularly relevant in cases in which a valuation is being carried out for tax purposes, for company transfers, or for bookkeeping purposes. When using the income approach, one is establishing the present value of the income being attributed to the IP (however that income may be defined). It also requires an accurate establishment of the remaining life of the asset as well as an appropriate discount rate.

Regardless of the type of income approach applied, there are three central components to the analysis. First, establish the future cash flows that are relevant specifically to the IP. Second, determine the appropriate rate at which to discount future cash flows. Third, determine the remaining useful life of the IP asset and the length of time for which income levels can be measured with accuracy. An accurate forecast of revenue or income attributable to the IP depends on a thorough understanding of the competitive and economic environment affecting the IP during the time frame of the valuation.

Extrapolation of Income

When dealing with the income method, one often has to project into the future. In doing so, the "extrapolation methodology" or extrapolation methods are used. Variations in income projections are usually based on two things:

- Identifying and analyzing historical trends of income and
- Taking those trends and extrapolating them into the future.

Any observations regarding extrapolation methods have some element of speculation, whether these projections are related to IP or other kinds of asset values, such as business enterprise values. The extrapolation of income, whether specifically for IP, for a transaction, for economic damages, or for some other valuation exercise such as transfer pricing, is always judgmental to some extent.

When one is doing extrapolation of historical income trends into the future, ideally there is a linear relationship between past trends and future results. However, it should be noted that there may be other effects on these trends and result in having multiple variables affecting the projections. While the extrapolation method is based on the simple relationship between time and income to provide the greatest certainty in extending or extrapolating the income projection or other economic activity, it should be noted that this extrapolation methodology can also be affected by external costs or other variables.

In many instances, revenue or income derived from the use of a trademark or other IP asset cannot be isolated from the revenue of the overall company. If this is the case, an analyst can use the income approach to calculate the value of the company as a whole, then allocate a percentage of the company value to the IP asset. The contribution of a given IP asset will vary based on a range of factors, including customer recognition, history of usage, business performance, market conditions, and brand extension opportunities.

Regression-Based Income Method

The performance of a regression analysis is a quantitative way to assist in the estimation of the relationship between several quantitative variables that will predict future income. When using this method, the analyst or valuation expert is attempting to calculate the value of an asset based on other specific variables. Often, the value of IP may be more complex than a simple relationship between one variable to another. Therefore, to be accurate in the estimation of value using regression analysis, more than one variable is often needed to more accurately estimate the target asset's value. For example, the value of a patent or trademark in the food products business may depend on the exclusivity of use of the IP, the prices at which the end product can be sold in various competitive markets, the share of market or market penetration that the product achieves, and the relative profitability of the product in two or more markets. Figure 4.6 shows a simple regression analysis that has two variables; this illustrates how value can be projected using a regression analysis.

Figure 4.6 Linear Regression with Two Variables

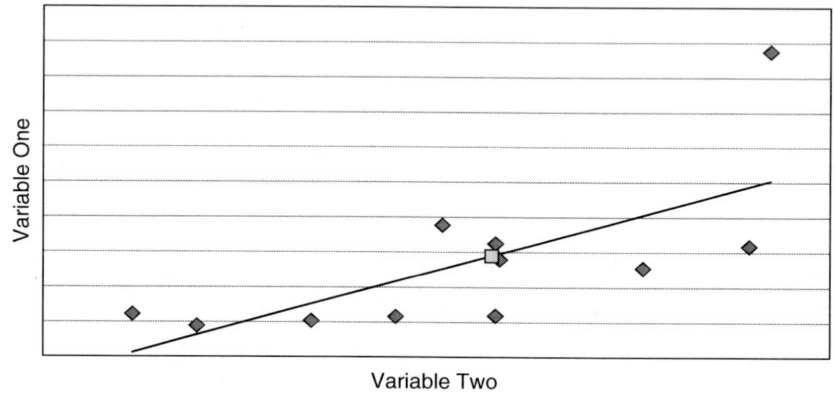

Relief-from-Royalty Approach

The relief-from-royalty approach, one of the most common and most frequently used methodologies, is a hybrid methodology that relies on aspects of the market and income approaches. In this approach, a hypothetical situation is created to estimate what a business would pay to license its own IP assets in an arm's-length transaction. The value is then calculated as the present value of the avoided hypothetical royalty charges.

When used appropriately, the relief-from-royalty approach provides a very accurate indication of value as it isolates the specific income that is or could be generated by an intangible asset. The use of marketplace royalty rates also lends credibility and consistency to value conclusions. In general, more established assets with less risky cash flows will demand higher royalty rates.

When trying to identify appropriate royalty rates, any license agreements that are used as comparables should be reviewed to determine whether they are arm's-length in nature, exclusive, nonexclusive, single product, multiproduct, single-year, multi-year, single-geography, or multi-geography. The comparables should feature attributes similar to the circumstances that surround the IP that is being valued. In common with the market approach described above, the comparable licensing transactions should have parameters that are similar to the type of IP asset, the type of industry, similar payment mechanisms, and appropriate time frames.

The range-of-royalty rates for IP are quite substantial. In our experience, we have seen royalty rates from as little as .25% of a licensee's net revenues to greater than 20%. The differences among these royalty rate ranges are largely due to the relative strength of the properties being licensed, type of IP, industry, geography, uniqueness, and competitive landscape. One major determinant of royalty rates will be the profit margins associated with the products on which they are being used. For example, if a product has an average profit margin of 8%, clearly it is not going to be possible for a licensee to pay a royalty of 10%.

In this methodology, the key to accurate valuation is to use the correct royalty rates in calculating future income streams. An analysis of the relative strength of the assets will help to narrow the range-of-royalty rates. Factors that influence relative strength include growth rates, market share, level of competition, duration of use, registration and legal protection, potential obsolescence, and barriers to entry.

Usually, data from marketplace comparable license agreements are compiled and used as the source for establishing the royalty rate in a relief-from-royalty calculation. It must be noted, however, that there is no such thing as a perfect set of comparable license agreements. By definition, each IP asset is inherently unique. As with other income-based approaches to valuation, the relief-from-royalty method yields results that can be revisited periodically, as royalty rates fluctuate.

Whenever possible, it is advantageous to use multiple valuation methodologies and then reconcile the results to arrive at a reasonable conclusion. Regardless of the valuation methodology used, the assumptions that are relied on will have a huge impact on value. Taking multiple approaches provides the opportunity to check these assumptions and increase the certainty of the concluded value.

Finally, caution is advised when using the relief-from-royalty method. Because it is so simple in concept and easy to calculate, we believe this particular methodology has become overused in the last decade. To some extent, it has been misused and abused in both market valuations and damages calculations for litigation. We believe that far too many theoretical "marketplace royalty rates" are invented out of whole cloth in order to calculate value—rates that, in fact, have no relationship to the particular type of IP under consideration. While it is true that many IP assets, particularly trademarks, brands, and copyrights, have identifiable and comparable market royalty rate data, other IP does not. Nonetheless, when properly used, and when appropriate royalty rates are available, the relief-from-royalty rate method is a highly effective valuation tool.

Discount Rate Analysis

To calculate the present value of forecast future earnings, a discount rate that is indicative of the level of risk involved in an investment in the IP must be applied. The discount rate represents the opportunity cost of funds, or the rate of return required by investors to compensate them for their contribution of capital. No investor will willingly invest in an asset unless the expected return meets or exceeds what they could receive in an investment of comparable risk. As certain IP assets cannot generate a return on investment without the contribution of other assets, an investment in IP may be considered to be of greater risk than an investment in an entire corporation.

The example below shows how an actual discount rate was calculated by our firm. XYZ Company (XYZ) represented a potential buyer of the target IP assets we were valuing. Therefore, we used their operating results as the basis of our Weighted Average Cost of Capital calculation. The equation describing the WACC model is as follows:

$$WACC = \frac{E}{D+E} \times r_e + \frac{D}{D+E} \times r_d$$

where: r_d = the pretax cost of debt
r_e = the cost of equity
D = market value of debt
E = market value of equity

Estimating Cost of Debt (r_d)

In the notes to their financial statements, XYZ disclosed that in 2017 the effective annual interest rate under their credit facilities was 3.28%.

Estimating Cost of Equity (r_e)

The cost of equity (r_e) is the required annual rate of return that a company's equity investors expect to receive. Financial professionals typically use the capital asset pricing model to accomplish the task. This is done with the following equation:

$$Cost\ of\ Equity\ (r_e) = r_f + \beta_L \times (r_m - r_f)$$

where: r_f = risk-free rate
β_L = levered beta
r_m = expected return on the market
$r_m - r_f$ = market risk premium

As a proxy for the risk-free rate, we relied on the normalized 20-year U.S. Treasury yield of 4.00% as reported by Duff & Phelps. The market risk premium ($r_m - r_f$) is the difference between the expected market return over the risk-free rate. It is important to have an appropriate time period for the market return, as it will heavily impact the market risk premium and cost of equity. As an estimate of the market risk premium, we relied on the Duff & Phelps recommended risk premium of 5.5% for 2017.

The beta (β) is the measure of the covariance between the rate of return on a company's stock and the overall market return (systematic risk). Traditionally, the S&P 500 is used for the market data. A beta that is 1.0 will have a return equal to that of the market; a beta less than 1.0 has lower systematic risk than the market; and a beta greater than 1.0 has a higher systematic risk. A higher beta is associated with a higher cost of equity and vice versa. As a measure of beta, we relied on XYZ's actual historical beta of 1.27.

Using the inputs outlined above results in the following cost of equity calculation:

$$Cost\ of\ Equity\ (r_e) = r_f + \beta_L \times (r_m - r_f)$$

$$Cost\ of\ Equity\ (r_e) = 4.00\% + 1.27 \times (5.50\%)$$

$$Cost\ of\ Equity\ (r_e) = 10.99\%$$

Using the cost of equity calculation and XYZ's 3.28% cost of debt in 2017, we calculated XYZ's WACC. As of June 30, 2017, financial net debt comprised 26.33% of XYZ's capital structure.

Using the inputs outlined above results in the following WACC calculation:

$$WACC = \frac{E}{D+E} \times r_e + \frac{D}{D+E} \times r_d$$

$$WACC = (73.67\% \times 10.99\%) + (26.33\% \times 3.28\%)$$

$$WACC = 8.96\%$$

Remaining Useful Life

The remaining useful life for IP can vary substantially from situation to situation, and there can be several definitions for remaining useful life. For example, in the case of a patent or copyright, there are statutory lives attached to these assets. In the case of patents, 20 years for utility patents and 14 years for design patents. In the case of copyrights, based on the latest revisions to the Copyright Act, the statutory life for works created after January 1, 1978, is a term lasting for the author's life plus an additional 70 years beyond death. For works for hire and anonymous and pseudonymous works, the copyright duration is 95 years from first publication or 120 years from creation, whichever is shorter (if the author's identity is later revealed, the term then becomes the author's life plus 70 years). Trademarks, of course, can be renewed indefinitely.

However, there can also be a contract life attached to a piece of IP. For example, one may be valuing a trademark, patent, or copyright in an environment where the life is determined by how long a license has been granted in regard to that piece of IP. For example, if there's a trademark license with only 7 years left on the contract with no possibility of renewal, then the remaining useful life is clearly 7 years. Also, in some litigation settings, there's a judicial life that determines the period for which damages are to be calculated, in which case, one uses that period of time as the remaining useful life. Most often, however, the remaining useful life is really a function of the remaining economic life, which in turn can be a function of remaining technological life for patents, trade secrets, and other technologies. Remaining economic life in the case of technologies can be affected by changes in the environment, the economy, and the basic technology itself.

The above commentary on the life span of IP needs to be considered when engaging in valuation, whether one is using an income approach or not, because obviously the remaining useful life affects valuation in a market approach, an income approach, or a relief-from-royalty analysis. Therefore, the so-called analytical life span of the IP is ultimately the measure of the asset's remaining useful life. Analytical life is the qualitative and quantitative analysis of the IP as performed by the people in charge of the valuation. This analytical life takes into account any issues of statutory life, contract life, judicial life (if this issue exists), technologies, technological and economic issues, along with other effects on remaining useful life, such as those that can affect trade secrets that may have a declining or wasting remaining useful life.

The point is that unlike tangible assets such as buildings and equipment, remaining useful life is a topic that has to be carefully thought about in the valuation process and when choosing a valuation methodology.

Selection of Valuation Methodology

The decision of which approach to use is generally based on four factors: how unique is the asset; how much verifiable data are available; what is the context, purpose, or objective of the analysis; and the judgment of the valuation professional, which (one would hope) is based on extensive prior experience. Numerous alternative valuation methodologies exist that may be applied based on the issues and context of the valuation. We introduce some of the other available methodologies in the next chapter.

Chapter 5

New, Developing, Proprietary, and Alternative Valuation Methodologies

When valuing intellectual property (IP), reliance solely on traditional cost, income, and market-based valuation approaches may not provide reasonable indications of value. Accurate analysis requires detailed research, use of multiple methodologies whenever possible, and a thorough understanding of each party's economic alternatives. In the context of litigation, valuation experts are placed in a position of advocacy, creating the potential temptation to seek extreme valuations. However, especially in light of the increasing scrutiny placed on valuations by the courts, it is essential to conduct unbiased analysis.

In addition to the traditional methods used to value IP, numerous alternative methods are available. Many are derivations of the traditional approaches. In addition, there are proprietary techniques that have been developed by valuation professionals. A detailed explanation of each methodology could fill a book. This chapter serves as an introduction to these alternative valuation methods.

A number of alternative valuation methodologies are listed in Figure 5.1. This is not an exhaustive list but merely a sampling of some techniques used by valuation professionals. Whenever possible, it is advantageous to use at least two valuation approaches; this provides the valuation professional with the opportunity to check the inputs and assumptions relied on in their analysis. If the two approaches yield drastically different conclusions of value, it is a good indication that the data and assumptions need to be re-evaluated.

Figure 5.1 Alternative Valuation Methodologies and Techniques

Brand Value Equation Methodology	Monte Carlo Analysis
Competitive Advantage Technique	Premium Pricing Analysis
Decremental Cost Savings	Profit Split Methodology
Income Differential Analysis	Subtraction Method
Income Capitalization	Technology Factor Analysis
Liquidation Values	VALMATRIX Analysis

The Brand Value Equation Methodology

The brand value equation methodology (BVE_Q®) is based on the premise that when valuing a brand, more than one asset element may be involved. This proprietary technique recognizes the principle that brand value is often comprised of a bundle of assets. There can be multiple intangibles and IP elements, including trademarks, logos, corporate colors, trade dress, slogans, and similar items. In this methodology, a value for the core trademark is calculated (CBV), and then each of the other individual assets attached to the core trademark have their values calculated (IVE). Therefore, the sum of the core trademark value plus the incremental assets becomes the total brand value, as shown below. The methodology can be expressed in an equation as follows:

$BVE_Q = CBV + IVE_1 + IVE_2 \ldots IVE_n$

1.	Core brand value (Coke trademarks)	CBV	\$10.0B
2.	Incremental value elements	IVE_1	0.2 (e.g., corporate colors)
		IVE_2	0.5 (e.g., umbrella Ads)
		IVE_3	0.3 (e.g., foreign trademarks)
		IVE_N	1.8 (e.g, diet Coke trademarks)
	Total brand value		**\$12.8B**

The Competitive Advantage Technique

The competitive advantage technique is best used when the subject company has a complex portfolio of IP. The technique works on the supposition that the IP is giving its owner an advantage over its competitors because of proprietary patents, technology, trademarks, software, or other intangibles. This method attempts to measure that advantage in a number of ways. The competitive advantage can sometimes be quantified based on market share, market growth, higher competitive pricing, or other benchmarks. While individual pieces of IP within a company's overall portfolio may be difficult to measure, this approach allows one to estimate the value of the entire portfolio as used in one or more business units of a corporation.

Decremental Cost Savings Valuation

Decremental cost savings valuation quantifies a decrease in the level of costs being experienced by the IP owner/operator. If, in fact, the IP owner can quantify lower levels of capital or operating costs connected directly with the ownership of the IP, then those lower costs can be a direct measurement of the value of the specific IP. For example, company A may have a trade secret that consists of a superior blending process that enables it to reduce the number of people and the amount of raw materials needed to produce a specific product. These lower costs calculated as a net present value of future savings would express the value of the IP.

Income Capitalization or Direct Capitalization Methodology

Income capitalization is sometimes used to estimate the value for IP that has no predetermined statutory expiration (such as trademarks) and for which net income (royalties or profit) is not expected to vary greatly over time (e.g., due to contractually defined license fees). This involves taking an estimate of the expected annual royalty stream (or profit) and multiplying this amount by a factor known as the capitalization rate.

The suitable capitalization rate will, in principle, reflect the interest rate environment and trends, the state of investor return expectations, prevailing attitudes and incentives to take on financial and management risk, and how closely royalty payments track inflation. In practice, capitalization rates are typically derived from observations of comparable ratios of revenue to sales price in actual transactions.

One notable use of this method is found in the pharmaceutical industry, where a leading company is credited with applying a quick method when valuing marketed product lines for acquisitions. The direct capitalization formula in this case is, on average, equivalent to multiplying annual sales times a capitalization rate of 2.7, conceived as 2 plus 2/3 of the remaining economic life of the product line (or its patent).

Income Differential Analysis

Income differential analysis is a variation of the income method that applies the phrase "income differential" literally. It simply means that a company that manufactures and sells a product with a particularly strong trademark or unique technology will receive more income than a competitive company that produces the same product but without the addition of the specific IP, such as the trademark or patent. A simple example is the income differential between what Land O'Lakes receives for a pound of its butter versus the income received by a second-tier local producer. That income differential capitalized over a number of years then becomes the value of the IP (see also premium pricing).

Liquidation Value

Liquidation value is used in a distressed environment and its value curve is shown. Liquidation value is the lowest price at which an asset will be pegged to ensure that there will be an acquisition. Found most often in bankruptcy situations, as the name implies, liquidation value for any piece of IP is the lowest price that the asset is virtually guaranteed to be sold at in a distressed situation. Litigation value scenarios arise most often in a Chapter 7 bankruptcy cases.

These liquidation values are much affected by other assets that may be available. For example, in selling off the Heilig-Meyers brand and trademarks in the time period, we established liquidation value partially based on selling prices for similar retail trademarks and

Figure 5.2 Context Continuum™

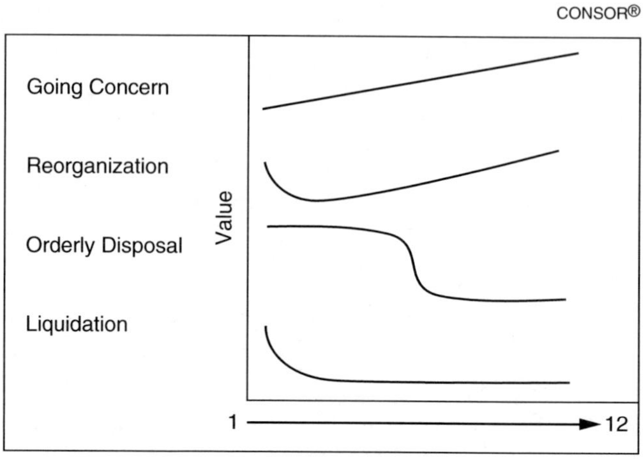

brands such as Montgomery Ward and Service Merchandise. In its simplest form, liquidation value is that price below which we can, with some certainty, guarantee the price will not fall (Figure 5.2). Although it is important to note that with each passing month in a liquidation scenario, the value of the IP can decrease rapidly, sometimes by 5 or 10% per month or more.

Monte Carlo Analysis of Value

The Monte Carlo analysis is based on techniques that have long been used in engineering and aerospace applications to test various physical operating models. It is used to evaluate how possible future outcomes can affect the decision of whether or not to use a new piece of IP based on possible value. Remember that this methodology is most useful in valuing early-stage, noncommercialized technology. It is particularly useful where there are many unknowns and numerous scenarios related to the future development of the technology. It is also useful when a single discounted cash flow analysis is problematical at best, given the uncertainty. In using this approach, one runs simulated operating and cash flow analyses for all of the scenarios, taking values from the outcomes of each scenario and then incorporating those into a probability analysis (often as many as 1,000 scenarios). The result of the analysis is a distribution of present values of the many possible future outcomes. Therefore, one can predict first, second, third, and fourth quartile values based on the possible future outcomes.

Options Pricing Techniques

Monte Carlo analysis is a variation of the options pricing theory. Patent licensing shares at least one attribute with all other relevant business decisions: it involves risk. Where decisions that involve financial risk are concerned, sound management principles suggest considering ways and vehicles to hedge that risk. A central vehicle for hedging risk in modern finance is an "option." A financial option on a stock, for instance, is simply the right to buy the stock for a predetermined price before the option expires, but it does not entail any obligation to buy. Similarly, a patent can be seen as the right to invest in or to license (or enforce through litigation) an underlying technology or product line during the term of the patent. Therefore, an uncommercialized patent can be valued from this options perspective.

Other Modeling Techniques and Permutations

Other modeling techniques include the Black Scholes formula and the binomial options pricing model, which provides sophisticated analysts a general method for valuation of options or decisions based on optional actions, such as when to delay an investment. It has been widely used for the last 40 years in developing answers to valuation issues where other models can't easily be applied. However, it is based on a description of an underlying action or financial instrument over a period of time. It is most often used to value marketplace options that are exercisable to acquire stock or other financial instruments. However, it can be used as a substitute for a Monte Carlo analysis. The binomial options pricing model often uses what is known as the binomial lattice method and can be used very effectively for modeling the outcome of Chapter 7 or Chapter 11 bankruptcy proceedings, in particular, as intangible assets or other assets enter into the liquidation value phase.

More interesting here, however, is the real options methodology, which can be used effectively in connection with more traditional income approaches to establish the net present value of an asset. At the end of this chapter is a brief discussion on linking a net present value analysis using an income approach with a real options valuation analysis. The application of option valuation analysis to patent valuation requires, nevertheless, careful consideration of similarities and differences to achieve significant results.

Premium Pricing Analysis

Of all the variations to the income approach, premium pricing analysis is perhaps the most easily understood because the value of an asset is established by looking at the difference in the price that it can command in the market, typically at wholesale, and the average price in the market. The difference between these two prices is the price premium. This, then, is projected out on an annual basis, and a net present value is established. A price premium approach can be used with consumer goods such as soft drinks, with Internet search engine pricing, and with mobile telephone handsets, where the price premium can be directly attributable to software and features. However, it is important to note that the method may overstate the value of a particular technical asset because of market perceptions as opposed to actual utility.

Profit Split Methodology

A form of the income approach, profit split methodology can be tricky to apply accurately because the method attributes a share or portion of a company's profitability to a particular intangible asset. This method requires that the valuation analyst understands the IP to such an extent that he or she can isolate and expressly separate the intangible asset's profit generation potential from all the other business assets and then allocate that portion of profit split to the company's IP and capitalize that value over a number of years.

The method is recognized by several authorities, most notably the Internal Revenue Service, and is often used in valuation environments that are driven by tax allocation and intercompany transfer pricing issues.

This method is more technically complex because it is similar to an accounting calculation for purchase price allocation. The value of the IP or intangible assets is essentially determined by first calculating the value of all of the various asset classes. Every company has several classes of assets, ranging from real estate and equipment to inventory and intangible assets, and each can expect to have a different return on investment. For example, a company's real estate might expect to have an annual return of 5% on its value. Therefore, that amount of income as a return on the value of the real estate would be calculated and isolated from the remainder of the company's total income. This process is then repeated for each tangible asset group such as inventory, plant equipment, and working capital. After proper returns are calculated for these other assets and deducted from the company's income, what is left represents the return to be allocated to the intangible assets as a whole. This amount can then be capitalized and expressed in today's dollars. Note, however, that while technically inspired, this method is best used when one is attempting to establish a single value for all of the intangible assets within a company's portfolio as a group. It is far more difficult to use this method if one is attempting to establish a value for a single piece of IP.

Subtraction Method of Value or Benchmark Method of Value

Establishing the value of a company against another company by comparing them on a so-called benchmark basis is the premise of this approach. The benchmark value is for a company that owns a particular trademark or patent, and the second value is for a comparable company that does not have that same asset. For example, one might value the cash flows associated with a producer of generic detergent against those of a branded manufacturer such as Proctor & Gamble. If the value of the company without the branded product is $200 million and the value of the company with the branded product is $300 million (on a comparable level of sales), then the subtraction value theory says that the value of the IP is the difference between the two, or $100 million.

The Technology Factor Approach

As the name implies, the technology factor approach is applicable only to technology. This methodology is designed to measure the portion of a business unit's overall market value that is based on the utilization of its underlying patents and technology. The willing buyer–willing seller aspect of a fair market value definition is incorporated by scoring a series of attributes for the technology as to whether they favor a buyer or a seller in a hypothetical negotiation. Accurate use of this technique depends on ascertaining the appropriate technology factor scale and components. The components within the technology factor scale help determine an upper limit for the contribution of value provided by the given technology used in a particular industry. A relative strength analysis of the various utility and competitive attributes is then performed in order to narrow the contribution of the subject technology to a specific percentage within the overall value.

Industries that use products that feature large contributions from technology, such as scientific instruments and pharmaceuticals, have relatively high upper limits on their technology factor analysis, while companies with products that feature few contributions from technology, such as mining and other mineral extraction, have relatively low technology factor attributes. Examples of utility attributes for technology include the current stage of the technology, the level of capital required to commercialize the technology, the size of the potential market, and the potential margins. Competitive attributes for the technology should include the existence of alternative technologies, the potential for obsolescence, and the likely response by competitors to the technology's potential to displace their existing products. Once these attributes are selected, weighed, and scored, a higher or lower value will be assigned. The utility and competitive attributes averages may also be weighed according to the relative contribution to the overall determination of technology value. The mean of these two averages (utility and competitive) is then combined to arrive at the final technology factor. That factor is then multiplied by the net present value of the subject business unit to arrive at the value of the technology, thus, separating the technology value from that of other assets of the business enterprise.

VALMATRIX® Analysis Technique

The VALMATRIX proprietary valuation methodology is a two-part technique that combines marketplace comparable data, both from propriety databases and public sources, with the VALMATRIX scoring system. This proprietary system was developed by CONSOR more than two decades ago. It uses a matrix of the most important predictors of value for a trademark, patent, or piece of software. The technique is an integral part of the analysis of royalty rates and comparable transaction analyses performed in many of our valuation projects.

The predictors for each type of IP are unique. Essentially a relative strength analysis, VALAMTRIX objectively measures 20 attributes associated with the IP being valued and the past, intended, and potential usage of the asset. The attributes cover factors such as financial performance, legal strength, marketing activities, and competition, among others. They are used in a unique manner—to score a given IP asset against its peers on a numerical scale of 1 to 5.

The numerical score, generated by assessing and weighing the 20 factors in the VALMATRIX approach, is used to establish a percentile ranking relative to all similar IP assets, i.e., similar trademarks, similar patents, or similar software. This relative value ranking is applied to the appropriate range of market comparables or streams of income. Over time, the VALMATRIX technique has proven to be especially useful in ascertaining at which point in the spectrum of comparable IP values an asset is positioned.

This methodology is also a useful predictor of future commercialization or future licensing potential. There is indeed a strong correlation between the relative score for a trademark or brand (or patent) and its future success. As the score that a trademark earns in the VALMATRIX scoring process moves into the second and ultimately the first quartile of all comparable scores, the chances of future licensing success grow and its relative value increases.

Testing New Approaches with New IP

When assessing IP (or many asset classes for that matter), valuation techniques and methodologies should most often be complementary. Valuation conclusions reached using two methodologies that vary widely or are widely inconsistent with each other should serve as a strong signal that something is fundamentally wrong, either with one of the methodologies or with the basic analysis. On the other hand, if two or more valuation methods produce consistent results, then client and analyst should take great comfort from the valuation work. How does one value a new patent? A revolutionary, but still unproven technology? Snapchat or Twitter in their pre-revenue days? Any new social media platform? In these cases, there are no cash flows yet, and no real comparables. Cost analysis doesn't necessarily work well in these cases. Valuation analysts can do cash flow projections and hypothetical discounted cash flow, but is there an alternative? Is there a better way? Perhaps. Real options analysis combined with a discounted cash flow analysis may be an answer.

As background, investments or technologies such as those named above are typically analyzed based on their expected cash flows and discount rates (typically quite high) at the time of the analysis. The net present value is then computed on that basis as a measure of the value of the technology or other IP. The result is a simple one—relatively low net present values based on the discounted cash flow analysis—and this typically substantially reduces the value of the high-risk and as yet unproven technology or other revolutionary IP. However, perhaps it's possible to combine a discounted cash flow analysis with a real option analysis and use the two approaches to arrive at a more balanced view of the potential future value of the patent, technology, or other IP.

Because traditional discounted cash flow analysis of highly speculative technologies and other new IP yield such relatively low values, the challenge is to find a way to capture or express some of the upside value for these assets through an alternative valuation technique. This is done in order to not only identify what the upside value might be but also to paint a more balanced picture of what the IP assets value might be in the long term.

A valuation that uses the real options approach may provide this second, alternative valuation approach to balance the discounted cash flow analysis. The real options approach to value is essentially an analysis that looks at the possibility of the technology achieving its full potential. The value of an options analysis therefore increases as the uncertainty of the new technology (or other underlying IP asset) increases. If the valuation professional thinks about it in this way, then the discounted cash flow analysis and the real option analysis are complementary. As a result, an unproven technology's or other new IP asset's total value becomes the sum or a weighted value of the two approaches, with the discounted cash flow or income approach valuation providing a lower or base estimate of value and the real option valuation providing the input to the more positive potential upside value. If one can accept the thought that both the discounted cash flow analysis and a real option analysis can be done in a given situation, then it also must be obvious that the proportion of the total valuation contributed by each methodology will vary according to the amount of uncertainty associated with the new technology or other IP.

In sum, we are suggesting three things:

- First, on the more tactical or granular level, the valuation analysis can have two distinct approaches that accept two different premises: a traditional discounted cash flow analysis and a more untraditional options analysis brought together in a weighted average to arrive at a concluded value.
- Second, on the broader, more philosophical level, this leads inevitably to the conclusion that two approaches to value—whether or not real options is one of the approaches—should be pursued whenever possible in any valuation situation.
- Third, the more complex the valuation scenario, the more compelling is the argument that two or more valuation approaches should be taken.

IP valuation is a complex issue, and assuming that a single methodology can always address that complexity is an assumption fraught with danger.

Chapter 6

Royalty Rates: The Ultimate Value Context

Royalty rates are as old as the licenses that were given to the Nuncios in various papal states, which allowed the pope's emissary to collect taxes in the pope's name. The term "royalties" is connected to royal warrants or licenses given to purveyors of goods and services using the warrant or shield of a royal family in the middle ages. Thus, payments came to be known as royalties. A brief history of royalties and licensing is laid out below.

Royalties are an objective, data-driven, measurable value indicator for intellectual property (IP). They not only serve as an indication of value for individual deals. When analyzed collectively as a group of royalties for a specific type of IP, they become a barometer of value, measuring over time the rise or fall in relative value compared to other forms of IP. For example, as we shall see, royalties for software have declined over time while trade secret royalties have risen.

The Historical Beginnings of Licensing

The earliest examples of licensing date back to the Middle Ages when the popes granted *warrants*, or licenses, to local entrepreneurs to collect taxes and forward a royalty percentage to Rome. We then move forward to the early 1700s when two ladies of the British nobility lent their names to a line of facial cosmetics in return for a royalty on sales. Based on our own research, subsequent milestones in licensing's history have included the following:[1]

1913: Teddy Roosevelt lends his name to the "Teddy" bear in return for a royalty that supported his efforts to establish a network of national parks.

1918: Raggedy Ann rears her stuffed head, followed two years later by Raggedy Andy.

6-1 Weston Anson, Fundamentals of Intellectual Property Valuation: A Primer for Identifying and Determining Value (2005).

1928: Walt Disney introduces Mickey Mouse to America.
1929: Buck Rogers appears and becomes an early licensing success. The first morning that Buck's licensed rocket pistol goes on sale at Macy's in the early 1930s, all 20,000 pistols were sold out before noon.
1930: The Lone Ranger hi-ho's into America's consciousness.
1932: Herman Kamen establishes Disney's licensing program and Disney's acknowledged leadership in the industry begins.
1930s: Six million licensed Shirley Temple dolls are sold.
1940s: Hopalong Cassidy and Tom Mix gallop into our lives on the backs of palominos bought from royalties on toys, premiums, and endorsements.
1950s: Zorro slashes his way into the limelight.
1955: Disney builds the first complete family of licensees around a TV character, Davy Crockett.
1960s: Batman mania takes over.

Not until the 1970s did we witness the emergence of licensing as a major industry. The success scored by entertainment and sport properties such as Star Trek, Snoopy, the Fonz, Star Wars, and NFL team emblems, to name just a few, awoke corporate boardrooms everywhere to licensing's potential.

In the 1980s, licensing took on a new respectability—it became a science. As Greg Battersby was the first to report in the January 1983 issue of *The Merchandising Reporter*, a character named Strawberry Shortcake was literally "born to be licensed." It didn't stop there. Licensees no longer focused on just the property. They wanted to know the licensor's marketing program and the property's expected exposure. It no longer was enough for the licensor simply to have a cute property.

Growth was steady in the 1980s and early 1990s. Since then, sales growth has been steady. Reliable research and industry data exist concerning the size and growth of the licensing industry over the years. Based on the estimates reported regularly in *The Licensing Letter*, North American retail sales of trademark licensed products in 2017 were $109 billion.

Royalty Rates as a Representation of Value

A royalty rate is a representation of value for the underlying IP and will vary based on a range of factors, including prestige, utility, and ubiquity. Typically, what the licensee is paying for is one or more of the following:

- Scarcity
- Uniqueness
- Utility
- Leading edge positioning
- Technology
- Speed

- Compactness
- Fashion
- Entertainment
- Function
- Ease of use
- And the list goes on

The context of the royalty rate that is being paid is a reflection of one or more of the parameters listed above or a reflection of future uses that the licensee identifies. But it is always, after all, a representation of marketplace value as perceived by the licensee rather than the licensor. In a licensing negotiation, it is a willing seller and, more importantly, a willing buyer that consummate a licensing contract. As is always the case, time and marketplace conditions will bring market value into line with market conditions. In other words, in the context of the license, whether for a transaction, onward development process, or other use, the royalty will ultimately express value. For example, as rights of publicity become a more frequently monetized asset and as more A-level celebrities enter the right of publicity endorsement game, royalty rates and celebrity endorsement fees may be held down because the number of A-level celebrities who are available in the marketplace increases. As more individuals begin participating, the incentive to pay higher royalties to any one celebrity will diminish. We can see this by looking at Figure 6.1, which maps out average royalty rates for celebrity licensing over the past decade.[2] Rates have remained relatively flat, with a slight decline over that time period. Again, it is self-evident that while celebrity right of publicity licensing remains very much in the forefront of marketing today, royalty rates are not going up.

Figure 6.1 Celebrity Licensing Royalty Rates

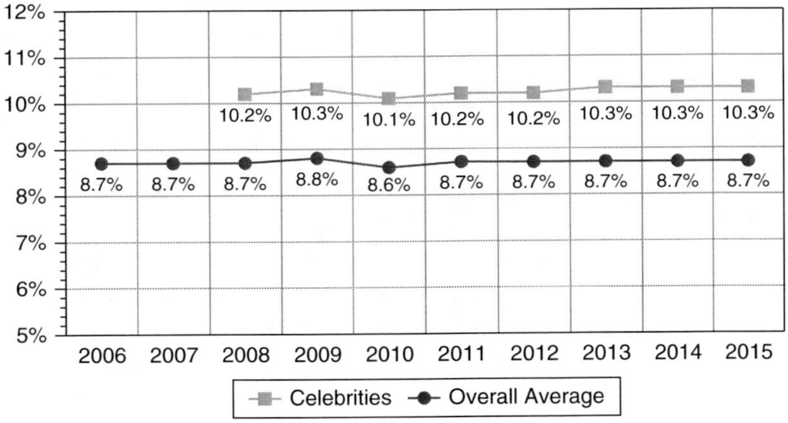

6-2 Royalty Trends Report 2016, The Licensing Letter, Plain Language Media, LLLP 2016.

Figure 6.2 Estate-Based Licensing Royalty Rates

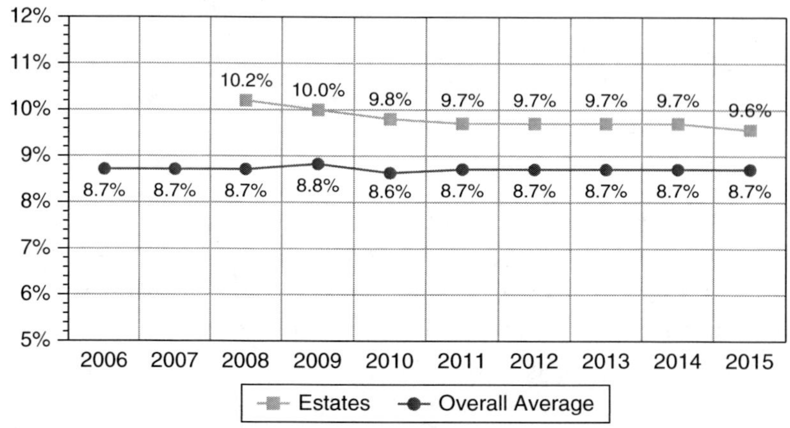

Figure 6.2 maps out royalty rates for estate-based licensing, which is increasing in popularity.[3] The fame of deceased celebrities is being leveraged in an ever more active way. Today, when deceased celebrities are used for licensed consumer products, their estates command a royalty premium above what average royalty rates are for all consumer goods. However, as we point out above, we have seen a declining trend over the last decade in those royalties as more and more celebrity estates make their imagery available to the licensing community.

What Form Can Royalties Take?

There is a misperception in the marketplace that all royalties must be calculated at a fixed percentage of sales on an ongoing basis. We constantly work to dispel this misconception. In general, there are two types of royalty agreements: a running royalty and a fully paid-up license agreement. The latter entails a lump-sum payment, expressed either in a single, upfront payment in the currency of the licensor's choice and/or a structure where two or three fixed fee payments are stretched out over a period of one to three years. In either case, these payments are predetermined at the time of signing and represent the maximum amount the licensee shall pay during the term of the license agreement.

In the alternative, which is observed in the majority of license agreements, a running royalty is paid that consists of periodic payments on a monthly, quarterly, semiannual, or annual basis. In this scenario, a royalty can be calculated based on a variety of formules. These can consist of the "standard" system of paying a percentage on either gross or net sales. Alternatives call for a sliding scale of percentage payments, while still others call for a fixed monthly fee plus a percentage of sales. In other agreements, royalties are calculated based on an amount per unit. There are many other alternatives where royalties can vary with volume, as well as others that are expressed as a percentage of incremental sales. In Table 6.1, we

6-3 Royalty Trends Report 2016, The Licensing Letter, Plain Language Media, LLLP 2016.

present 22 alternative approaches. These are included as examples of what can be negotiated in any given license agreement between two parties committed to finding a way to make a royalty structure work for both of them.

Table 6.1 Alternative Royalty/Fee Arrangements

	Alternative	Group	Rationale
1	Percentage royalty rate on sales	Single component fee	Payment based on one primary component
2	Per unit royalty rate	Single component fee	
3	Fully paid-up license, also known as a single up-front payment	Single component fee	
4	Annual flat fee	Single component fee	
5	Annual fixed fee plus per unit payments	Tiered fee	Payment changes as variable changes
6	Annual cap on percentage or per unit fees	Tiered fee	
7	Fees vary per Stock Keeping Unit	Tiered fee	
8	Cumulative cap on fees for each contract period (i.e., three or five years)	Tiered fee	
9	Fees declining over time	Tiered fee	
10	Royalties based on components of value	Future dependent	Payment changes based on future, nonfinancial events
11	Royalties based on percentage utilization within a product	Future dependent	
12	Fees plus royalties on new markets or new product developments	Future dependent	
13	Fee, plus % for each new upgrade/design	Future dependent	
14	Royalty on any increase in sales when applied to an existing product	Results based	Payment changes based on future financial performance
15	Royalties based on profits or margins	Results based	
16	Royalties (% or $/unit) declining with sales or unit volume	Results based	
17	Royalty on sales less deductions for marketing costs or other allocation of relevant expenses	Results based	
18	Royalty on gross sales less direct manufacturing costs	Results based	
19	Royalties on cost of product	Results based	
20	Royalty with per unit and fixed fee elements	Mixed fee	Total fee includes multiple components
21	Cost-plus fee with contingent royalties	Mixed fee	
22	Trilevel or multilevel fees	Mixed fee	

Royalty Rates Vary by Type of IP

The above heading may seem obvious to some but it bears repeating. Clearly, the royalty for a patent will be different from that of a trade secret, which will be different from a copyright, which will be different from a trademark, which will be different from a right of publicity. This is self-evident, and we will discuss it further below. Before we do that, let's think about what other major influences there are on royalty rates. They include the following:

- Geography
- Product or service
- Profit margins
- Length of time of the license agreement
- Competitive environment
- Currency
- Restrictions on usage
- Size of the market
- Competitive pressures
- Other licensors

It bears saying again, context is key. Changing terms and conditions will affect the value of a license agreement, and determining the appropriate royalty rate is highly dependent on the

Figure 6.3 Key Factors to Considered When Negotiating a License Agreement

Licensing Agreement Key Factors (Non-Technical)

1. Pre-Agreement Considerations
- Category research, market research
- Understand the needs of the consumer
- Understand the needs of the retailer or distributor
- Pre-negotiation due diligence (financial, etc.)
- Availability of trademarks

2. Grant of License: Core Considerations
- Exclusive or nonexclusive
- Limitations to the grant

3. Goods to be Licensed
- Description and definition
- Pricing parameters
- Complimentary goods being licensed

4. Territory
- One country only or multiple territories
- On-line versus off-line
- Geographic options
- Exclusive versus nonexclusive territories

5. Term/Timing
- Length of contract
- On-sale dates
- Timeline
- Geographic rollout
- Retail rollout
- Marketing schedule
- Disposal period

6. Renewals, Options and Extensions
- Renewal options
- Additional product options
- Unilateral versus bilateral options
- Automatic extensions
- Exercise period
- Term of option
- Other geographies

Licensing Agreement Key Factors

7. Fees, Financial Terms and Conditions
- Initial fee
- Royalty rates
- Advertising payments
- Minimum royalties
- Other fees
- Minimum annual sales guarantees
- Payment details
- Currency considerations and remittance issues
- Registration of agreement required to make payment from outside of U.S.
- Tax considerations: country of payment

8. Advertising, Promotions, Marketing
- Contributions to advertising
- Approval of marketing plans
- Joint licensor-licensee advertising pool
- Advertising and promotional commitments
- Media schedules
- Imagery decisions
- PR management

9. Approval Process
- What has to be submitted
- Steps of process
- How are submissions to be made
- When can licensee sell and ship

10. Controls and Monitoring
- Financial
- Products
- Design
- Advertising
- Promotion
- Distribution channels

11. Quality Assurance
- Product standards
- Packaging
- Advertising
- Requirements for testing
- Test results and certifications to establish compliance

Licensing Agreement Key Factors

12. Ownership of Artwork and Designs
- Trademark notices
- New works of license
- Interpretive rights
- Derivative works from artwork and designs of licensor

13. Warranties/Indemnification
- Legal versus marketing warranties
- Licensee's: Product quality
- Licensor's: Trademark ownership

14. Insurance
- Product liability
- Advertising liability
- Coverage
- Additional insured/notice
- Amount

15. Confidentiality
- Requirements
- Publicity
- Public offerings

16. Termination Rights
- Causes
- Cures
- Damage
- Immediate
- Right to cure

17. Dispute Resolution
- Choice of law
- Jurisdiction and venue
- Arbitration
- Litigation

18. Assignability and Sub-Contracting
- Sub-licensing
- Contract manufacturing
- Sale of business or assets
- Change of controlling interest
- Change of management

ability to evaluate both subjectively and objectively the relative importance of the IP to the business, process, or product in which the IP will be used. An entire book can be and should be written about royalty rates and other license agreement terms and conditions. Figure 6.3 outlines the key factors that should be considered when negotiating a license agreement and royalty rates in a typical trademark/copyright license or in hybrid licensing that covers multiple types of IP.

Royalty Rate Trends

Now, we turn to royalty rates for different types of IP and look at general trends over the last 30 years.

Like a barometer that moves slowly across the dial with shifts in atmospheric pressure, so too do royalty rate trends and medians shift over time for each type of IP, be it a trade secret, copyright, patent, trademark, or right of publicity. Shifting conditions can lead to observations of the relative strength and importance of these major groups of IP. However, medians are just that: a middle point or average, not an appropriate rate for any individual piece of IP for any specific deal.

We think it is useful to look at royalty rate trends for the five major groups of IP on a long-term comparative basis. Based on this premise, we plotted out royalty rate trends from 1981 through 2015 on a rolling five-year basis. As a common basis for data selection, we used data from Royalty Stat, which specializes in collecting royalty rate information from publicly available documents globally (with a heavy emphasis on North America). Their services can be procured on a subscription basis or by acquiring royalty agreements on an individual purchase agreement basis. This analysis was done for five major groups of IP:

- Patents;
- Trade secrets, know-how, and propriety information;
- Copyrights;
- Software; and
- Trademarks and tradenames.

The median royalty rates for each group are described below. Some general conclusions include:

- Over the last several decades, royalties for copyrights have experienced a meaningful increase. Over the same time frame, royalty rates for software have had a substantial decline.
- As we noted earlier in this chapter, right-of-publicity royalty rates are high and have remained relatively stable. We were not able to include a 20-year chart here because licensing activity in this area has not been monitored and reported for a sufficient period of time.
- Median trademark and tradename royalties have increased by approximately 50% over the last 30 years. This is not surprising given the increased use of trademarks as a licensing vehicle and the increase in hybrid or bundled licensing.

Patents, Know-How, and Trade Secrets

We can observe the obvious in Figures 6.4 and 6.5 for patents, and know-how and trade secrets. The rise in median royalties from 5% to just over 6% for trade secrets between 1986 and 2015 was not unexpected, particularly given both increased legal protection and use of trade secrets as an alternative to patents. As stated above, the flatness of the median royalty rate for patents is not unexpected; while average royalty rates for patents *appear* to be rising.

However, some equally important data were reported in the journal *les Nouvelles* in March 2017 in the study titled "Royalty Rates in Biopharma Alliances" by Mark G. Edwards of BioScience Advisors. In doing his research, Mr. Edwards looked at the BioSci deal database, which is available for general search and consists of 19,000 file contracts and amendments, according to Mr. Edwards. This serious piece of research looked at deals from 1987 through 2016 to see what patterns emerged in terms of royalties as shown in figure 6.6.

Figure 6.4 Patent Royalty Rates

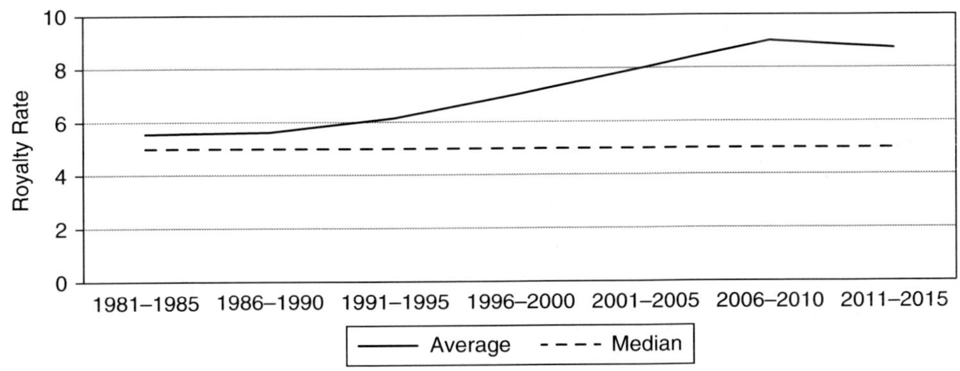

Figure 6.5 Know-How and Trade Secrets Royalty Rates

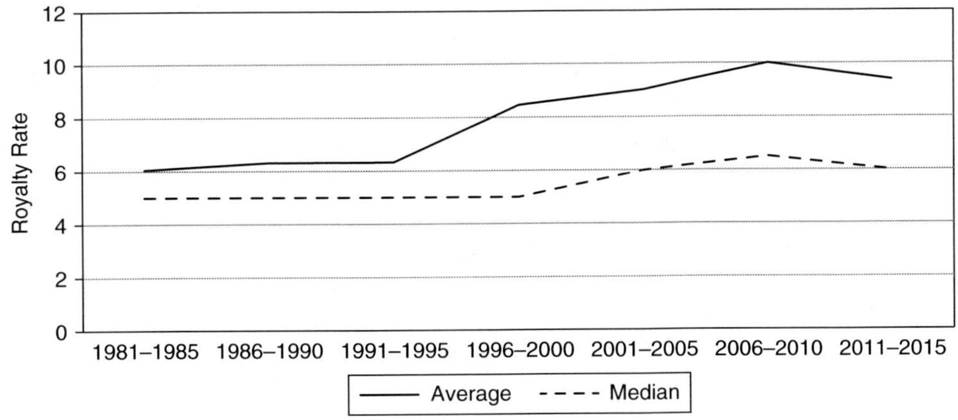

Understanding some caveats, the data proved in general that royalties for patents in the biopharma area have fallen consistently over the last 10 years. In comparing deals from the 1997–2006 period to deals from the 2007–2016 period, Mr. Edwards found a decline of 2–3% in the effective royalty rate (EFR) charged in these deals. This represents a drop of about 25% in the average royalty rate being charged.

Remembering, however, that the royalty rate is only one aspect of the licensing agreement, he did find that there are higher upfront fees today in most deals, but they are not sufficient to offset the lower royalty rates being charged. The most notable conclusions from the *les Nouvelles* article are that the EFR in biopharma deals range from 3% to 17% and are higher if a corporation is the licensor as opposed to a university. Most importantly, the data showed that for biopharma deals since 2007, the average EFR *declined* by 2–3% compared to deals in 1997–2006. These are for deals that focused on worldwide rights. Also, in an important footnote, Mr. Edwards found that in preclinical deals in biopharma today, royalty rates are 4–5% lower than they were prior to 2007, while royalties deals that are ready to go to market are 3% higher. This indicates a clear risk adverse strategy opposed to 10 years ago. However, the most important thing is a summary of the findings that compare 1996–2006 to 2007–2016 as summarized in Figure 6.6 from *les Nouvelles*.[4] The findings speak for themselves. Clearly, patent royalties in this arena are falling.

Figure 6.6 Biopharma Alliances From 2007 Through 2016: Average EFRs Declined 2–3% for All but Discovery and Regional Deals

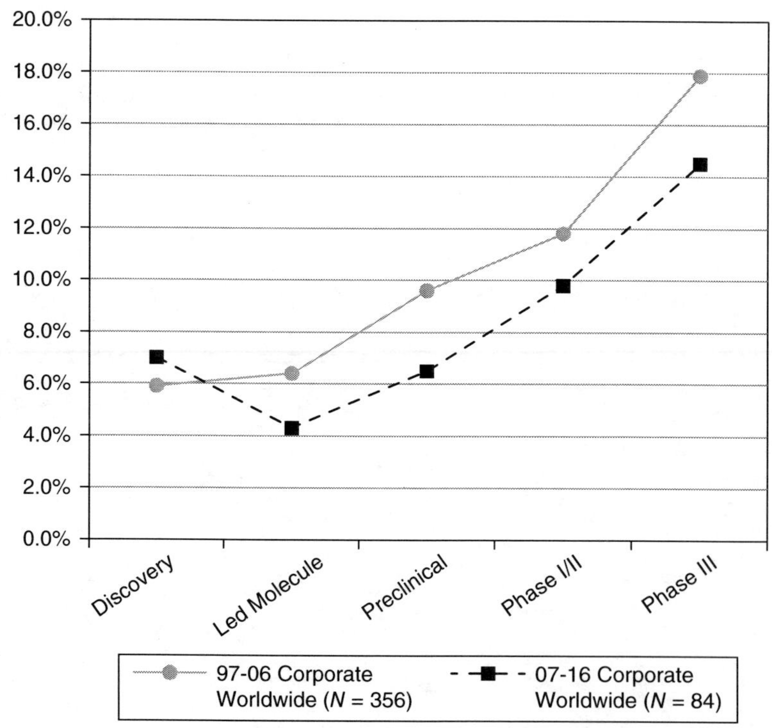

6-4 Royalty Trends Report 2016, The Licensing Letter, Plain Language Media, LLLP 2016.

Copyrights

Of the major groups of IP, the area of copyrights is perhaps the hardest in which to generalize about royalty rates. The reason? Copyrights cover a wide range of properties, including music, art, databases, published works, and even software. The median royalty rate for copyrights has had a generally upward trend since 1986 when the median was at 4.0%. It has since risen to 6.5% but had a jump in the early 2000s to 10% (Figure 6.7). We believe the long-term median rate is between 6.5% and 7.0%. This reflects increased copyright licensing, not just in music but also in art, fashion, and publishing.

Some royalty rates under the copyright umbrella are set by statute or by industry regulation, such as mechanical royalty rates for music, while others are strictly negotiated on a free market basis. Some royalty rates are unique, such as very high fees that are charged for reproductions of high-level limited-edition reproductions, e.g., the Robert Rauschenberg collection and the Robert Mapplethorpe photography library. At the same time, other artists are charging more standard royalties for their mass market licensing programs. These include artists such as Andy Warhol and Thomas Kinkade, the estates of which have substantial licensing programs.

Also, in some copyright situations, a body of work such as music will command two distinct types of royalties. As we just mentioned, much of the music world has a set of royalty rates dictated by industry and statutory bodies, such as mechanical royalties and performance royalties. On the other hand, there is an active business in merchandise based on music, mostly the souvenir variety such as t-shirts, jackets, caps, and pins. Most of this is sold at concerts or general retail distribution with a split at concert venues and at traditional and online retail stores. Even in these situations, the royalties for the sales are split between very high royalties at venues of between 15% and 25% and lower royalties for retail. However, on average over the last six years, the royalty rate being commanded in the industry is 8.2% for licensed music merchandise (according to *The Licensing Letter*).

Finally, databases and proprietary information can have fixed fee royalties that can range from $10 or $20 per issue to thousands of dollars for annual subscriptions. These fees are of course set depending on the scarcity of the data, the size of the audience, and the relevance and currency of the data to the current marketplace.

A final comment on copyright royalty rates—while analyzing the data on median rates is useful to show an overall trend, it certainly does not provide the whole story. Figure 6.7 provides a brief overview of the difficulty in establishing what is "an average royalty" within the IP group called copyrights.

Software

Software has suffered the most precipitous decline of any IP group, going from a 15% median rate in 1986 to a 7% median rate in 2015 (Figure 6.8). This is accounted for by a couple of things, most notably that increased competition combined with open sourcing have depressed royalty rates for software in general. Second, as software becomes secondary in

Figure 6.7 Copyright Royalty Rates

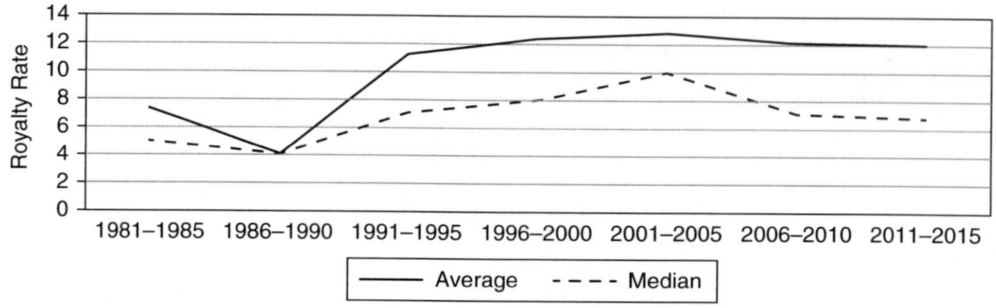

Figure 6.8 Software Royalty Rates

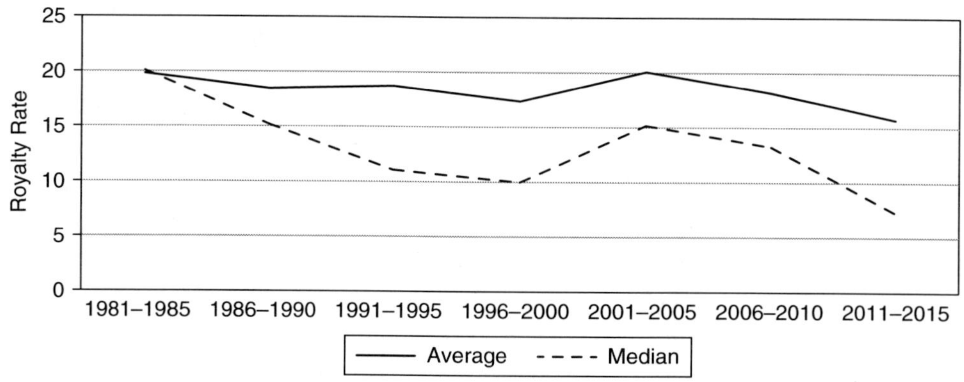

importance to programmable apps and algorithms, there is general downward pressure on software royalty rates.

Trademarks and Tradenames

There has been a slow and steady rise in median royalty rates for trademarks since 1986, with the median rising from 4% to 6% during that period of time—a 50% increase. As we describe in more detail below, while the median has had a 50% rise, average royalty rates, particularly in consumer goods, are substantially higher than the 6.0% median, with rates averaging nearly 9% and rising to the 12% to 15% level.

The median royalty rate for trademarks has had steady upward pressure over the last 20 years. As seen in Figure 6.9, the median royalty has increased 50% in the 20-year period. However, it's useful to look beyond the median to see what the other data can tell us about trademark royalty rates. First, one must remember that the 20-year median data included in the figure tracks licensing of all trademarks on all products, ranging from AT&T license agreements for home communications accessories to Louis Vuitton fashion

Figure 6.9 Tradename and Trademark Royalty Rates

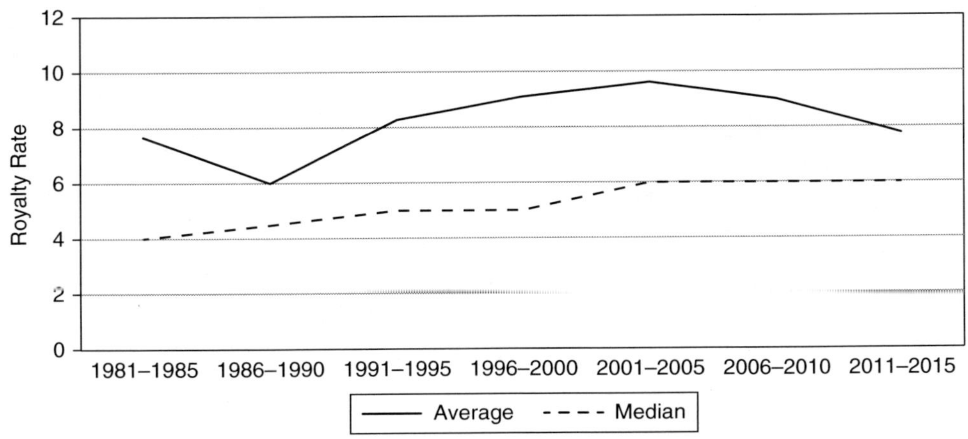

accessories, and everything in between. Trademark licensing, particularly in the consumer goods area, is highly dependent on two factors to determine an appropriate arm's-length royalty rate:

- The type of property: an entertainment or character property, versus a fashion property, versus a nonprofit, versus a celebrity or estate.
- The product category: apparel versus consumer electronics, versus health and beauty aids, versus publishing.

Each factor, if plotted on longitudinal and latitudinal axes, enables one to predict with some degree of accuracy the royalty rate for a given product. For a better understanding of these determinates, refer to Figures 6.10 and 6.11. This is the most recent data available covering 2016 and was published in mid-2017. In Figure 6.10, average royalty rates by property type are presented for 2016; you will note that royalties range from automotive trademarks at 4.1%, up to celebrities, entertainers, and models at 10.4%. On the product side (Figure 6.11), we find consumer electronics commanding the lowest royalty at 5.3% and toys, games, and software commanding the highest royalty at 10.5%. This serves to demonstrate that a median royalty for an overall class of intellectual property may have little or no meaning when negotiating a specific deal.

There is, however, one other point to be made. The average royalty rate for consumer goods licensing has maintained a very steady 8.7% for the last 10 years. From 2008 moving forward, the average royalty rate ranged from 8.65% to the current 8.75% as reported by *The Licensing Letter* for 2017.

Finally, the overall market for trademark licensed consumer merchandise reached $109 billion, based on the annual survey of *The Licensing Letter*. This number is based on reports from their readers and from Licensing, Industry Merchandisers Association members.

Figure 6.10 2016 Average Royalty Rate by Property Type

Category	Overall
Art and	6.2%
Art and Artists	6.2%
Museums	6.1%
Celebrities	10.3%
Entertainers/Models	10.4%
Chefs/Home-Related	9.7%
Collegiate	10.0%
Entertainment/Character	10.0%
Estates	9.6%
Fashion	8.5%
Apparel	8.4%
Footwear	7.1%
Home	7.5%
Music	8.2%
Non-Profit	8.3%
Publishing	8.5%
Books	7.9%
Newspapers/Magazines	8.2%
Comic Books/Strips	9.6%
Sports	10.0%
Trademarks/Brands	7.7%
Automotive/Motor Vehicle	4.1%
Food/Beverage	5.6%
Restaurants	5.9%
Sporting Goods	7.0%
Traditional Toys/Games	8.2%
Videogame/Interactive/Online	9.0%
Overall Average	8.7%

Source: The Licensing Letter, Plain Language Media.

However, given the narrow dataset, there is reason to believe it grossly understates the size of the trademark licensing business by a factor of 2 to 3. It is interesting to look at what types of properties drive consumer goods trademark licensing. The three largest types of licensors are corporate trademarks and brands, which account for nearly 30% of the total market, followed by fashion licensing with 20% of the market and entertainment licensing, with 15% of the market depending on how one categorizes entertainment.

The important takeaways from this brief discussion of trademark licensing and royalty rates is that median royalty rates are rising. Second, average royalty rates for consumer goods are substantially higher than the median, running at a steady 8.7% for the last 10 years. Third, there are two determinates of royalty rates for consumer goods: the type of property being licensed and the type of product upon which the trademark is being licensed.

Figure 6.11 2016 Average Royalty Rate by Product Category

Category	Average Royalty Rate
Accessories	9.1%
Eyewear	8.3%
Handbags, Backpacks, Messenger Bags	8.9%
Headwear	9.9%
Hosiery	8.6%
Jewelry and Watches	7.7%
Luggage and Travel Accessories	10.1%
Scarves and Ties	7.3%
Apparel	9.5%
Consumer Electronics	5.3%
Domestics	8.9%
Food/Beverage	6.0%
Footwear	8.1%
Furniture/Home Furnishings	7.5%
Gift/Novelties	8.6%
Health and Beauty Aids	9.0%
Fragrance	9.3%
Cosmetics, Hair Accessories, Other	8.4%
Housewares	6.3%
Infant Products	8.6%
Publishing	9.6%
Sporting Goods	9.8%
Stationery/Paper	8.9%
Toys/Games	10.5%
Videogames/Software	10.5%
Overall Average	8.7%

Source: The Licensing Letter, Plain Language Media.

Conclusions

We began this chapter by calling royalty rates the objective context of value, and indeed they are. The financial terms of a license agreement, or royalty rate, is a true barometer of IP value and represents the marketplace value of IP. A royalty rate is an objective, data-driven, measurable, and quantifiable value that has been placed on the IP in an agreement. What else do we know about royalty rates?

- There is no such thing as an average or standard royalty rate.
- Royalty rates vary by the type of IP.
- There have been major trends in the last 30 years that are discernable and have been mapped in this chapter.
- While trade secret royalty rates are up, patent royalty rates are no better than stable and in fact are trending down.
- Trademark royalty rates are trending upward, but vary by property type and category of product being licensed.

- Copyright royalty rates have increased over time, but copyright royalty rates are complex and multilayered, and the category itself has multiple components.
- Right-of-publicity royalty rates have been stable over the last decade, but the volume of use is increasing year after year.
- Not all royalty rates are based on a percentage of sales.
- The changing terms and conditions of a license agreement can be more important and more valuable than the stated royalty rate itself.
- Finally, as with much in the world of IP value, context and time are the main drivers in establishing fee structures in license agreements.

We summarized what the current status of royalty rates and fee structures is in the world of IP. Tomorrow's context may change that.

Chapter 7

Patent Valuation: Trends and Cases Contributed by David Noble

As described by the US Patent and Trademark Office, "[a] patent for an invention is the grant of a property right to the inventor, issued by the U.S. Patent and Trademark Office. The right conferred by the patent grant is . . . 'the right to exclude others from making, using, offering for sale, or selling' the invention in the United States or 'importing' the invention into the United States."[1]

While governmental entities grant patent rights, they do not automatically enforce them. In general, it is the responsibility of the patent holder to police the use of the invention in the marketplace and, if necessary, bring legal action. There is also a range of criteria an invention must meet to be patent eligible, including:

- *Patentable subject matter:* There are numerous forms of subject matter that are excluded from patentability including materials or substances that already exist in nature, scientific theories or mathematical methods, biological processes, and methods of treatment for humans or animals.[2]
- *Industrial applicability (utility):* The invention must be of a kind that can be applied for practical purposes and not be purely theoretical.[3]
- *Novelty:* The invention must be new in the sense that it is not anticipated by prior art. "Prior art is, in general, all the knowledge that existed prior to the relevant filing or priority date of a patent application, whether it existed by way of written or oral disclosure."[4]
- *Inventive step (non-obviousness):* An invention cannot be patented if it is obvious. This restriction "is based on the premise that protection should not be given to what is already known as part of the prior art, or to anything that the person with ordinary skill could deduce as an obvious consequence thereof."[5]

7-1 *General Information Concerning Patents,* USPTO, https://www.uspto.gov/patents-getting-started/general-information-concerning-patents#heading-2 (2015).
7-2 World Intellectual Property Organization, Intellectual Property Handbook 18 (2nd ed. 2004).
7-3 *Id.*
7-4 *Id.* at 19.
7-5 *Id.* at 20.

- *Disclosure of the invention:* An additional requirement for patentability is that the application details the invention in a manner sufficiently clear that a person of skill could carry out the concept.[6]

In recent years, rulings in several prominent cases have altered the patent landscape in the United States by providing guidance on what is patent eligible, the appropriate royalty base in damages calculations, and the appropriate venue for patent lawsuits. The rulings in several of these relevant cases are briefly addressed throughout this chapter. In addition, I touch on the somewhat controversial role of nonpracticing entities in patent litigation.

To conclude the chapter, I present two case studies based on recent projects that illustrate the practical (albeit somewhat simplified) application of patent valuation methodologies. The first case study presents a valuation for the purpose of raising capital. The second case study outlines a damages analysis conducted in the context of a patent infringement lawsuit.

Challenges in Patent Valuation

As with other forms of intellectual property (IP), there is a range of contexts in which patent valuations are required: acquisitions, dispositions, transfer pricing, securitization, litigation, and others. However, the nature of patents provides unique valuation challenges not incurred with other forms of IP.

For example, high-tech products that utilize one trademark may incorporate hundreds, or thousands, of patents. To value an individual patent, this presents the challenge of determining the relative contribution of the specific patent. As a result, patents are often valued in bundles.

A similar challenge arises when calculating patent infringement damages in litigation. In recent years, the courts have made it clear that if only a single patent, or subset of a product's patents, is infringing, damages should (often) be calculated on the smallest salable patent-practicing unit (SSPPU), not the cost of the entire product.

This was described in the 2012 *LaserDynamics, Inc. v. Quanta Computer, Inc.* decision:[7]

> Where small elements of multi-component products are accused of infringement, calculating a royalty on the entire product carries a considerable risk that the patentee will be improperly compensated for non-infringing components of that product. Thus, it is generally required that royalties be based not on the entire product, but instead on the "smallest salable patent-practicing unit."
>
> We reaffirm that in any case involving multi-component products, patentees may not calculate damages based on sales of the entire product, as opposed to the smallest salable patent-practicing unit, without showing that the demand for the entire product is attributable to the patented feature.[8]

7-6 *Id.* at 21.

7-7 *LaserDynamics, Inc. v. Quanta Comput., Inc.*, 694 F.3d 51 (Fed. Cir. 2012).

7-8 *Id.* at 67–68.

As discussed in the ruling, calculating damages based on the overall price of a multicomponent product could potentially lead to a patent holder being improperly compensated for non-infringing aspects of the product. This is illustrated in the (highly simplified) example below.

> *SSPPU damages example:* As of the preparation of this chapter, the base model 2017 Lexus IS Turbo had a listed sticker price of $38,820. As with many automotive manufacturers, optional features could be included for an additional cost. If one of these features, the "intuitive parking assist" for example, was determined to infringe on a patent held by a competitor, the appropriate royalty base on which to calculate damages would be the incremental cost of the parking assist feature, not the price of the car. This is illustrated in Figure 7.1.

While SSPPU serves to provide useful guidance when calculating damages, it is not an absolute rule that must be applied in all instances. This was addressed in *Commonwealth Sci. & Indus. Research Organisation v. Cisco Sys.*, a lawsuit originally filed in 2011, alleging patent infringement related to WiFi chips. On appeal to the Federal Circuit, Cisco argued District Court Judge Davis erred in his 2014 ruling by (among other alleged errors) "not beginning its damages analysis with the wireless chip which it found to be the smallest salable patent practicing unit."[9] In December 2015, a three-judge Federal Circuit panel rejected the argument that all patent damages methodologies always must start out using the smallest salable patent-practicing unit[10]:

The rule Cisco advances—which would require all damages models to begin with the smallest salable patent-practicing unit—is untenable. It conflicts with our prior approvals of a methodology that values the asserted patent based on comparable licenses. Such a model begins with rates from comparable licenses and then accounts for differences in the technologies and economic circumstances of the contracting parties. Where the licenses employed are sufficiently comparable, this method is typically reliable because the parties are constrained by

Figure 7.1 Damages Calculations Using SSPPU

	Disregarding SSPPU	SSPPU Damages
2017 Lexus IS Turbo—Base Model Price	$38,820	$38,820
Optional Features		
Backup Camera	$ 350	$ 350
Intuitive Parking Assist	$ 500	$ 500
Power Rear Shade	$ 210	$ 210
Total Price	**$39,880**	**$39,880**
Royalty Base	$39,880	$ 500
Appropriate Royalty Rate	3.5%	3.5%
Damages per Vehicle Sold	$ 1,396	$ 18

7-9 *Commonwealth Sci. & Indus. Research Organisation v. Cisco Sys.*, 809 F.3d 1295, 1301 (Fed. Cir. 2015).
7-10 *Id.*

the market's actual valuation of the patent. Moreover, we held in Ericsson that otherwise comparable licenses are not inadmissible solely because they express the royalty rate as a percentage of total revenues, rather than in terms of the smallest salable unit. Therefore, adopting Cisco's position would necessitate exclusion of comparable license valuations that—at least in some cases—may be the most effective method of estimating the asserted patent's value. Such a holding would often make it impossible for a patentee to resort to license-based evidence.

Accordingly, we conclude that the district court did not violate apportionment principles in employing a damages model that took account of the parties' informal negotiations with respect to the end product.[11]

In the District Court ruling, damages were determined as a fee per unit sold (as opposed to a percentage of revenue). Thus, the royalty base did not factor in the calculation; the per unit royalty could equally be interpreted as a royalty per WiFi chip without impacting the damages calculation.

Useful Life

In addition to challenges related to the high volume of patents contained in many products, determining the remaining useful life of a patent can be challenging. In the United States, patents can be protected for "a term beginning on the date on which the patent issues, and ending 20 years from the date on which the application for the patent was filed."[12]

However, the useful life of a patent can significantly differ from the 20 years of protection set forth in 35 U.S.C. Section 154. When advising clients, we often recommend bundling multiple forms of IP as a means of extending the length of time they can effectively be protected. Unlike patents, trademarks can be perpetually renewed. By closely associating a trademark with the patented product, it may be possible to extend its useful life.

While some would argue it is detrimental to innovation, an alternative preferred by some entities is to rely on trade secrets as opposed to filing a patent application. The preference for trade secrets can be two-fold. First, trade secrets can be maintained indefinitely. In addition, some consider a patent to provide a roadmap by which competitors could attempt to circumvent the innovative elements contained in the invention.

While there are methods for attempting to extend the useful life of a patent, the useful life of most patents is significantly less than the 20 years of protection. As innovation continues, older patents often become obsolete as they are replaced with new inventions. According to law professor Dennis Crouch from the University of Missouri School of Law, the average utility patent in the United States is allowed to expire approximately 11 years after the issue date.[13]

7-11 *Id.* at 1303–04.

7-12 35 U.S.C. § 154.

7-13 Dennis Crouch, *Reduced Average Patent Life*, PATENTLYO (Oct. 26, 2014), https://patentlyo.com/patent/2014/10/reduced-average-patent.html.

Use of Intellectual Property for Securitization

Further convoluting the understanding of the value of IP is the disparity between corporations' true value and the value of their assets reported in their financial statements. As noted 15 years ago by Alan Greenspan, Chair of the Federal Reserve of United States, "[t]he economic product of the U.S. has become predominantly conceptual."[14] According to some estimates, as much as 90% of the value of publicly traded companies in America comes from intangible assets. Yet, the clear majority of this value does not appear on companies' balance sheets.

From an accounting perspective, intangible assets fall into two categories: those acquired in business combinations and those developed internally. Intangible assets acquired from another party are recorded on the balance sheet at cost. This includes all acquisition costs and expenditures necessary to prepare the intangible asset for its intended use. Costs incurred to create intangibles internally, however, are generally expensed. This means that costs to develop the asset appear as expenses on the income statement but not as assets on the balance sheet.

Numerous explanations have been presented for why this practice makes sense. These include the argument that costs incurred internally to develop an intangible asset often bear little relation to that asset's value once commercialized and the argument that it is often difficult to match internal costs with specific intangibles. However, the result is that a company's book value (the value of assets on the balance sheet) often bears little relation to the company's true value.

As the percentage of corporate value derived from IP has increased, the use of IP as collateral in loans has and will likely continue to increase. The use of IP as collateral is not a novel concept; in the late 1800s Thomas Edison used his patent on the incandescent light bulb to secure financing to start the General Electric Company.[15]

However, the use of patents for securitization purposes does come without challenges. Patents are inherently unique, which complicates the valuation process and increases the cost associated with obtaining a valuation. In addition, patents have a finite life, and the risk of invalidation has increased following the *Alice* decision and the increase of inter partes reviews. To help mitigate this risk, lenders will often require borrowers to bundle their patents.

Patentability

As discussed in Chapter 1, the issue of patentability has been an area of focus in recent years. Under 35 U.S.C. Section 101, "Whoever invents or discovers any new and useful process, machine, manufacture, or composition of matter, or any new and useful improvement thereof, may obtain a patent therefor."[16] "Laws of nature, natural phenomena, and abstract ideas have been held by the U.S. Supreme Court to be implicit exceptions to patent-eligible

7-14 Alan Greenspan, The Federal Reserve Board, April 4, 2003.
7-15 See ANDRE MILLARD, EDISON AND THE BUSINESS OF INNOVATION 43–46 (1990).
7-16 35 U.S.C. § 101.

subject matter under §101, with the exceptions rationalized as a means to prevent the monopolization of the basic scientific and technological tools required for future innovation. These judicial exceptions arguably did not play a large role in U.S. prosecution or enforcement of biotechnology and pharmaceutical patents until recent years."[17]

For example, the Supreme Court has established that a naturally occurring DNA segment is a patent-ineligible product of nature and does not become patent eligible based simply on isolation from the genome.[18] By contrast, the Supreme Court unanimously held that complementary DNAs that have been synthetically modified to omit noncoding sequences found in nature are sufficiently different from natural sequences for patent eligibility.[19]

The 2012 implementation of the inter partes review process and the 2014 ruling in *Alice* have led to an increase in scrutiny over the issue of patentability as follows:

- *Inter partes review:* a trial proceeding challenging the validity of a U.S. patent conducted by the Patent Trial and Appeal Board, an administrative body of the U.S. Patent and Trademark Office.[20] The process provides an opportunity to challenge an issued patent under 35 U.S.C. §§ 102 and 103 based on prior art patents or printed publications. A petition for inter partes review is made by any party other than the patent owner and is available for any issued patent (i.e., both first to invent and first inventor to file patents), subject to certain restrictions. Most notably, inter partes review is only available during the first year after a client (or a privy) is served with a patent infringement complaint.[21]
- *Alice:* In the *Alice* decision, the U.S. Supreme Court established a two-part test for determining patent eligibility under 35 U.S.C. § 101. First, determine if the patent claim at issue is direct to a patent ineligible concept such as a natural phenomena or abstract idea. Second, determine if the claim elements individually (or in combination) contain an inventive concept that transforms the claim to ensure the patent amounts to significantly more than an abstract idea.[22]

In the wake of the *Alice* ruling, a large number of patents for computer-related inventions (software patents in particular) were invalidated. The two-part test outlined in *Alice* also left a great deal of uncertainty or confusion regarding what is and is not patentable. Despite providing the framework of the two-part test, the Supreme Court failed to provide a definition of what is considered an "abstract idea." In addition, the court failed to provide clear guidance of the level of transformation necessary to ensure the patent is more than an abstract idea. This lack of clear guidance put the lower courts in the difficult position of attempting to determine how the two-part test should be applied.

Numerous courts have discussed the difficulty in establishing the line between what is and is not patent eligible. For example, the Court of Appeals for the Federal Circuit has said,

7-17 http://www.skgf.com/uploads/1378/doc/LSIPR_Jan15_AfterALice.pdf.
7-18 *Ass'n for Molecular Pathology v. Myriad Genetics, Inc.*, 569 U.S. 576, 133 S. Ct. 2107 (2013).
7-19 *Id.*
7-20 *Inter Partes Review*. USPTO, https://www.uspto.gov/patents-application-process/appealing-patent-decisions/trials/inter-partes-review (2017).
7-21 35 U.S.C. § 315(b).
7-22 *Alice Corp. Pty. Ltd. v. CLS Bank Int'l*, 134 S. Ct. 2347 (2014).

"Distinguishing between claims that recite a patent-eligible invention and claims that add too little to a patent-ineligible abstract concept can be difficult, as the line separating the two is not always clear."[23] Similarly, District Judge Rodney Gilstrap in the Eastern District of Texas, who has more patent cases on his docket than any other judge, has remarked, "[T]he contours are often unclear between those inventions that are directed to an abstract idea and those that are not."[24] Another district judge has likened the analysis to Justice Stewart's famous statement concerning obscenity: "hard to define '[b]ut I know it when I see it.'"[25]

Patent Reviews Following *Alice*

In approximately two years after the *Alice* decision was issued in June 2014, only one Federal Circuit decision (*DDR Holdings LLC v. Hotels.com*) found a patent eligible under the two-part *Alice* test. That trend changed in 2016 when the Appeals Court reversed several Lower Court decisions in which computer-related patents had been deemed ineligible, including *Enfish LLC v. Microsoft Corp.*[26]

- *DDR Holdings:* The *DDR Holdings* case was the first in which a patent was upheld under the two-part *Alice* test. The patent at question was a method for allowing a host website to maintain user web traffic while offering digital advertising. Generally, when an individual clicks on a digital advertisement, they are redirected from the host's website to the website of the advertised company. As a means of keeping traffic on the host's website, the patent "generates a webpage that combines certain visual elements of the host website (i.e., look and feel) with the content provided by the third-party merchant."[27] In applying the two-part *Alice* test, the court determined the patent included an inventive concept as opposed to generic use of the Internet to perform a known business practice. Thus, the patent was upheld.
- *Enfish:* In 2012, Enfish LLC sued Microsoft alleging one of its products infringed on the company's patent for a "self-referential table" in database products. At trial, Judge Mariana R. Pfaelzer of the Central District of California concluded the patent was invalid under the two-part *Alice* test. On appeal in May 2016, the Federal Circuit reversed the District Court's ruling and determined the invention was patent eligible and not related to an abstract idea. In the decision, the court provided the following guidance for interpreting *Alice*: "We do not read Alice to broadly hold that all improvements in computer-related technology are inherently abstract. . . . Software can make non-abstract improvements to computer technology just as hardware improvements can. . . . We thus see no reason to conclude that all claims directed to improvements in computer-related technology, including those directed to software, are abstract. . . .

7-23 *DDR Holdings, LLC v. Hotels.com, L.P.*, 773 F.3d 1245,1255 (Fed. Cir. 2014).
7-24 *Clear with Computs., LLC v. Altec Indus.*, No. 6:14-cv-79, 2015 U.S. Dist. LEXIS 28816 (E.D. Tex. Mar. 3, 2015).
7-25 *Jacobellis v. Ohio*, 378 U.S. 184, 84 S. Ct. 1676 (1964) (Stewart, P., concurring).
7-26 See *Enfish, LLC v. Microsoft Corp.*, 822 F.3d 1327 (Fed. Cir. 2016).
7-27 See *DDR Holdings, LLC v. Hotels.com, L.P.*, 773 F.3d 1245 (Fed. Cir. 2014).

> In this case, however, the plain focus of the claims is on an improvement to computer functionality itself, not on economic or other tasks for which a computer is used in its ordinary capacity."[28]

The *Enfish* ruling, along with subsequent decisions, has given rise to a slight shift in the interpretation of *Alice*, with more software patents being upheld. Richard Hung of Morrison & Foerster LLP states: "Given the scarcity of cases, there was very little supportive authority for district courts finding a patent valid under 101.What we're really seeing now is the Federal Circuit tilting back and saying that many computer and internet patents are patentable."[29] Hung asserts, "Defendants will still frequently seek to invalidate patents under *Alice*, but Enfish and the other decisions give courts more precedent to support arguments by patent owners that the claims are valid, he added, so 'we're going to see a lot more losses on Section 101 motions than we did previously.'"[30]

TC Heartland and the Eastern District of Texas

Historically, the Federal Circuit has allowed patent suits to be filed in any district where the defendant made sales. This has led to the process of "forum shopping" in which parties file a complaint in the jurisdiction in which they believe they are most likely to prevail. This has led to a disproportionate number of cases being filed in the reputedly plaintiff-friendly Eastern District of Texas.

In March 2017, the *New York Times* reported that more than 40 percent all of patent infringement lawsuits in the United States were filed in a federal court in East Texas, with a single judge (based in Marshall, Texas) overseeing approximately a quarter of the patent cases nationwide. This represented more than the number of patent infringement cases handled by all federal judges in California, Florida, and New York combined.[31]

Figure 7.2 shows the percentage of all U.S. patent infringement lawsuits filed in East Texas on a quarterly basis.[32]

Many have speculated that the high volume of filings is attributable to the court's propensity for expediting the trial process as well as the district's reputation for friendliness to plaintiffs. For example, in 2006 the *New York Times* reported that in Marshall, Texas, patent holders were victorious 78 percent of the time compared to an average of 59 percent nationwide and less than 50 percent in New York.[33]

7-28 *Enfish, LLC v. Microsoft Corp.*, 822 F.3d 1327,1335 (Fed. Cir. 2016).

7-29 Ryan Davis, *Patent Litigation Trends to Watch in 2017*, MORRISON FOERSTER, Jan. 2, 2017, https://www.law360.com/articles/876203/patent-litigation-trends-to-watch-in-2017.

7-30 *Id.*

7-31 Adam Liptak, *Supreme Court Considers Why Patent Trolls Love Texas*, N.Y. TIMES, Mar. 27, 2017, https://www.nytimes.com/2017/03/27/business/supreme-court-patent-trolls-tc-heartland-kraft.html?mcubz=0.

7-32 Brian Howard, *2017 First Quarter Litigation Update*, LEX MACHINA, Apr. 12, 2017, https://lexmachina.com/2017-first-quarter-litigation-update/.

7-33 Julie Creswell, *So Small a Town, So Many Patent Suits*, N.Y. TIMES, Sept. 24, 2006, http://www.nytimes.com/2006/09/24/business/24ward.html?mcubz=0.

Figure 7.2 Percentage of Patent Infringement Cases Filed in the Eastern District of Texas

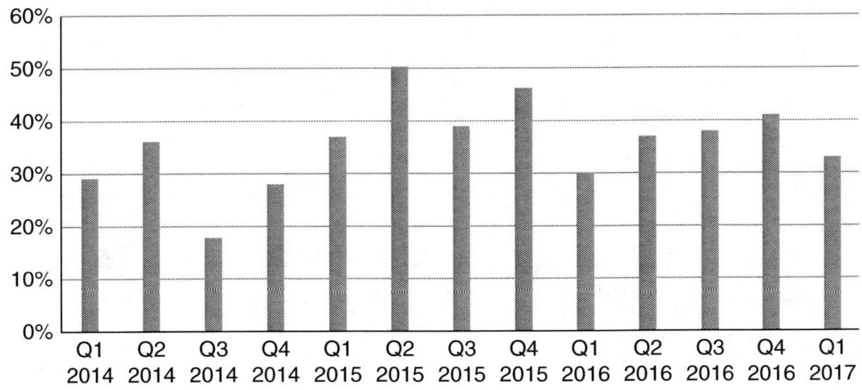

In December 2016, the U.S. Supreme Court agreed to hear a challenge in *TC Hartland LLC v. Kraft Foods Group Brands* regarding venue selection. "TC Heartland sought to move the case to Indiana, but lower courts refused, relying on a 1990 decision of the U.S. Court of Appeals for the Federal Circuit, a specialized court that handles patent appeals. That decision said defendants in patent cases, as in other cases, may be sued essentially anywhere they do business."[34]

In the decision, the court ruled as follows:

> The question presented in this case is where proper venue lies for a patent infringement lawsuit brought against a domestic corporation. . . . In [*Fourco Glass Co. v. Transmirra Products Corp.*, 353 U. S. 222, 226], this Court definitively and unambiguously held that the word "reside[nce]" in §1400(b) has a particular meaning as applied to domestic corporations: It refers only to the State of incorporation . . . Accordingly, we reverse the judgment of the Court of Appeals and remand the case for further proceedings consistent with this opinion.[35]

This decision is likely to create a substantial shift in the way in which patent litigation proceeds in the country. Moving forward, the primary patent litigation venue will likely shift from East Texas to Delaware, where many entities are incorporated.

Non-Practicing Entities

In recent years, there has been a great deal of media coverage regarding the role of non-practicing entities (NPEs) in patent litigation and the possible need for reform. An NPE is an entity that owns a patent for a process or product but does not generate revenue from manufacturing or selling goods. While individual inventors or research organizations could be

7-34 *TC Heartland LLC v. Kraft Foods Grp. Brands LLC*, 137 S. Ct. 1514 (2017).
7-35 *Id.* at 1516.

considered NPEs, the issue has focused on what are commonly referred to as "patent trolls." These are entities that acquire patents (often large portfolios at auction) with the intention of filing patent infringement claims or forcing the alleged infringer to enter a license. Given the high costs of litigation, defendants often find themselves in an unfavorable position regardless of the perceived merits of the claim. Proponents for reform have pointed to examples of what they consider to be patent trolls attempting to "enforce patents of dubious quality or with questionable infringement claims, and then settling for amounts far less than the defendants' litigation costs."[36]

In October 2016, the Federal Trade Commission (FTC) released a study on patent assertion entity (PAE) activity. A PAE is the official term by which the FTC differentiates between patent trolls and other forms of NPEs. In the study, the FTC analyzed information from 22 PAEs and more than 2,500 of their affiliates. In their findings, the FTC divided the PAE activity into two business models: portfolio PAEs, which licensed large portfolios, and litigation PAEs, which largely engaged in what could be considered nuisance litigation:[37]

- "*Portfolio PAEs:* Portfolio PAEs negotiated licenses covering large portfolios, often containing hundreds or thousands of patents, frequently without first suing the alleged infringer. The value of these licenses was typically in the millions of dollars. Although Portfolio PAEs accounted for only 9% of the reported licenses in the study, they generated 80% of the reported revenue, or approximately $3.2 billion. Portfolio PAEs typically funded their initial patent acquisitions through capital raised from investors, including institutional investors or manufacturing firms."[38]
- "*Litigation PAEs:* Litigation PAEs typically sued potential licensees and settled shortly afterward by entering into license agreements with defendants covering small portfolios, often containing fewer than ten patents. The licenses typically yielded total royalties of less than $300,000. According to one estimate, $300,000 approximates the lower bound of early-stage litigation costs of defending a patent infringement suit. Given the relatively low dollar amounts of the licenses, the behavior of Litigation PAEs is consistent with nuisance litigation. For each separate patent portfolio that they acquired, Litigation PAEs characteristically created a new affiliate entity, which often held ten patents or less. They generally operated with little or no working capital and relied on agreements to share future revenue with patent sellers to fund their businesses. Litigation PAEs filed 96% of the cases in the study and accounted for 91% of the reported licenses, but only 20% of the reported revenue, or approximately $800 million."[39]

7-36 Dennis Crouch, *Analyzing the Role of NPEs in the Patent System*, PATENTLYO (Aug. 21, 2012), https://patentlyo.com/patent/2012/08/analyzing-the-role-of-npes-in-the-patent-system.html.

7-37 Federal Trade Commission, *Patent Assertion Entity Activity* (Oct. 2016), https://www.ftc.gov/system/files/documents/reports/patent-assertion-entity-activity-ftc-study/p131203_patent_assertion_entity_activity_an_ftc_study_0.pdf.

7-38 *Id.*

7-39 *Id.*

In presenting their findings and recommendations, the FTC noted that 77% of license agreements entered by litigation PAEs were valued below the estimated cost of defending a patent lawsuit through the end of discovery. In addition, when an agreement was reached, the cases tended to settle early: 34% within 6 months of filing, 66% within a year, and 83% within 18 months.[40]

While the FTC recognized the important role of infringement litigation in the judicial system, it also noted nuisance lawsuits "can tax judicial resources and divert attention away from productive business behavior."[41] As a result the FTC proposed the following reform:

1. "Address discovery burden and cost asymmetries in PAE litigation;
2. Provide the courts and defendants with more information about the plaintiffs that have filed infringement lawsuits;
3. Streamline multiple cases brought against defendants on the same theories of infringement; and
4. Provide sufficient notice of these infringement theories as courts continue to develop heightened pleading requirements for patent cases."[42]

Royalty Rates in Transactions Versus Litigation

Since 1990, more than 70% of patent damage awards by district courts have involved reasonable royalty determinations. More than 50% of awards were calculated exclusively using reasonable royalties and 17% with a combination of reasonable royalties and lost profits. However, there has been a distinct disparity between royalty rates used in litigation versus those negotiated in arm's-length transactions (Figure 7.3).[43]

This disparity can be attributed to the context of the analysis. In arm's-length transactions, valuations are conducted by each party with their own respective interests in mind. However, the parties share the joint interest of reaching an agreement. In the context of litigation, valuations are conducted by adversarial parties with distinctly different goals. This provides incentives for the use of greater levels of speculation. A damages calculation is the valuation of an enforced transaction conducted at a single point in time. As a result, adversaries often conduct all or nothing analyses where extremes, rather than mid-points, are sought. This will likely lead to increased scrutiny from the courts when evaluating the reasonableness of damages analyses presented by opposing experts.

7-40 *Id.*
7-41 *Id.*
7-42 *Id.*
7-43 GREGORY J. BATTERSBY & CHARLES W. GRIMES, LICENSING ROYALTY RATES 294 (2010).

Figure 7.3 Royalty Rates: Litigated Versus Arm's Length (1990–2008)

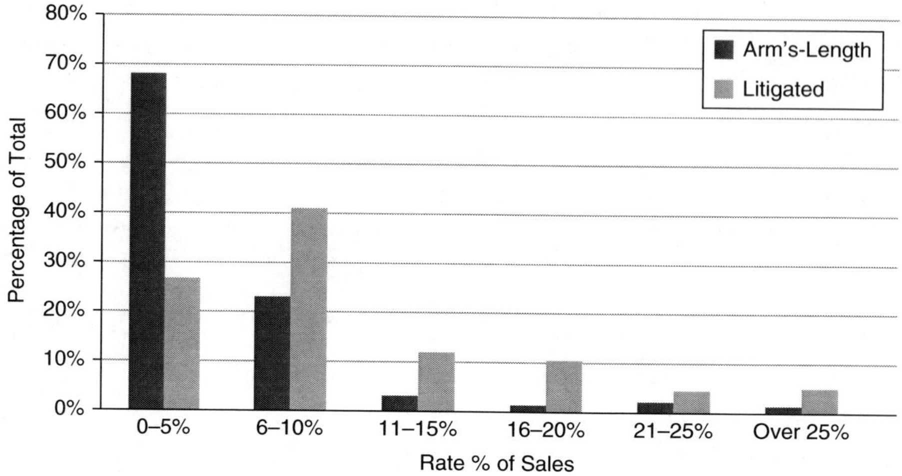

Case Studies

To conclude this chapter, two case studies are provided to illustrate the ways in which valuation methodologies are applied to patents. The first valuation was conducted in the normal course of business with the intention of raising capital. To protect the confidentiality of our client, all names and numbers have been changed. In the second case study, we were retained to analyze damages resulting from patent infringement. Since all information was made publicly available in the course of litigation, the actual names and numbers are presented in the case study.

Case Study 1: Consumer Electronics Co.

We were retained by Consumer Electronics Company to provide an opinion regarding the value of their portfolio of patents (the patent portfolio), broken down into two subcategories: consumer wearable and commercial medical.

Industry overview: Consumer wearable and commercial medical devices are rapidly becoming an integral part of personal fitness regimes and healthcare services. These devices measure a range of vital signs and deliver corrective suggestions, along with storing or transmitting data in communication with smartphones, tablets, PCs, and similar devices. Wearable devices are no longer just focused on one measurement, such as the number of steps taken in a day, but are now focused on a variety of bodily measurements. Devices often include a combination of sensors, actuators, storage, and encryption mechanisms, depending on the user's needs.

In recent years, there has been a growing trend of home-based medical diagnostics to cut down on rising hospital costs. These wearable devices also open doors to patient empowerment and personalized medicine. Based on product segments, this market has been segmented into wearable therapeutic medical device (further subsegmented into hearing aids, insulin pumps, and respiratory therapy devices), wearable monitoring and diagnostic devices (further subsegmented into fetal and obstetric devices, continuous glucose monitoring devices, and cardiac monitoring devices), and health and fitness devices (vital signs monitoring).

Patent strength analysis: To determine the strength of Consumer Electronics Company's consumer wearable and commercial medical patent portfolios, we conducted a comparative analysis of the patents in view of the global landscape. To accomplish this, effective sets of keyword strings were formulated for each of the two major categories. From this, a global patent dataset corresponding to each category was obtained from the Thomson Innovation database.

A total of 1,934 U.S. granted patents in this domain were identified, with many of these patents overlapping into both consumer wearable and commercial medical. There are 1,580 patents applicable to the consumer wearable space and 1,260 applicable to the commercial medical space. Of the 1,934 U.S. granted patents, 54 are held by Consumer Electronics Company, amounting to 3%.

A total of 158 and 126 seminal U.S. patents were identified in consumer wearable and commercial medical, respectively. "Seminal patents represent an invention so important that it creates or shifts a particular technology space. Other inventors cite it as prior art for their own inventions, which can be improvements or enhancements to the original idea."[44] Notably, approximately 18% (28 out of 158) and 21% (27 out of 126) of these seminal patents are owned by Consumer Electronics Company in each of the respective categories. This indicates that Consumer Electronics Company's patent portfolio is of high value compared to other industry players.

To further analyze Consumer Electronics Company's patent portfolio we retained iRunway whose COMPASS^{SM} tool was used for calculating and analyzing patent strength. The tool reduces subjectivity by providing a "patent score" that is used to compare a set of patents. In addition, we reviewed forward citations. Figure 7.4 compares the average count of forward citations of Consumer Electronics Company's U.S. patents to the average count of forward citations of patents held by the other assignees. The large discrepancy highlights the importance of Consumer Electronics Company's patent portfolio.

Valuation methodology: Based on the context of the situation, we chose to use the relief-from-royalty approach as the most reasonable indication of value for the patent portfolio. The relief-from-royalty method is a variation of the income approach that establishes the value of the IP as the capitalized value of the royalties that the company is relieved from paying due to its ownership of the assets. This approach provides a measure of the value by determining the avoided cost.

7-44 Denise Deverelle Crown, *Tips for Identifying Seminal Patents*, INNOGRAPHY (Jul. 7, 2014), https://www.innography.com/blog/post/tips-for-identifying-seminal-patents.

Figure 7.4 Average Count of Forward Citations

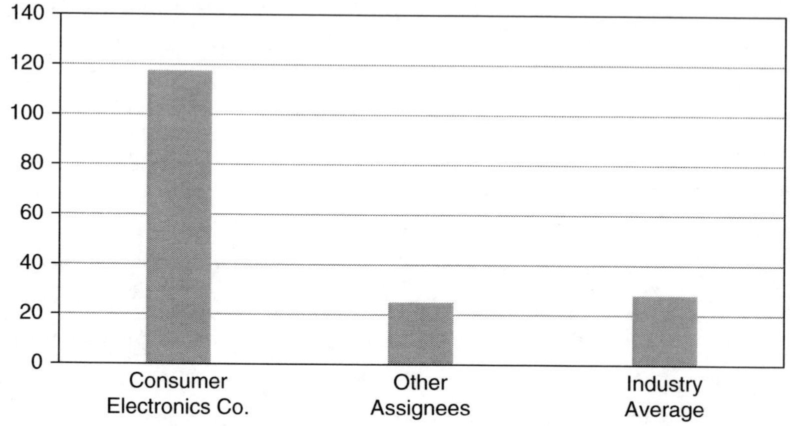

Figure 7.5 Royalty Rate Conclusions

Consumer Wearable Patents	5%
Commercial Medical Patents	6%

This method is appropriate to use when the assets in question have comparable licensing information to use.

Royalty rate research: A key element of the relief-from-royalty approach is to identify appropriate royalty rates for use of the IP. To determine the fair market value of a royalty fee for use of the consumer wearable and commercial medical patent portfolios, we used the market approach to identify comparable license agreements. Royalty rate transaction data were collected from various sources. Specifically, we used annual royalty rate industry surveys, public documentation from corporate 10-Q and 10-K forms, our internal database of license agreements, and third-party databases containing tens of thousands of publicly available licensing transactions.

Based on our research, we identified license agreements for patents comparable to both the consumer wearable and commercial medical portfolios. Our royalty rate conclusions are presented at Figure 7.5.

Revenue projections and valuation: To estimate the market size of the consumer wearable and commercial medical industries, we relied on publicly available industry estimates in combination with our internally developed assumptions. Based on our industry research and technical analysis of the patent portfolios, we estimated that the average remaining useful life of both patent portfolios was 8.5 years. This was in line with the average remaining protectable life of Consumer Electronics Company's U.S. granted patents. Based on our analysis, we arrived at the value conclusions shown in Figure 7.6.

Figure 7.6 Range of Value Conclusions

Consumer Wearable Valuation Matrix ($US in Millions)

		Market Share		
		5%	10%	15%
Discount Rate	40%	$71	$142	$213
	30%	$90	$179	$269
	20%	$122	$243	$365

Commercial Medical Valuation Matrix ($US in Millions)

		Market Share		
		10%	15%	20%
Discount Rate	40%	$170	$255	$340
	30%	$210	$315	$420
	20%	$277	$415	$553

Summary Range ($US in Millions)

Summary Range		
Low	Selected	High
$241	$494	$918

Case Study 2: StoneEagle Services, Inc. v. Pay-Plus Solutions, Inc. & Premier Healthcare Exchange, Inc.

CONSOR® IP Consulting and Valuation (CONSOR) was retained on behalf of StoneEagle Services, Inc. (StoneEagle or plaintiff) to provide consulting services and patent infringement damages analysis in relation to litigation against Pay-Plus Solutions, Inc. (PPS) and Premier Healthcare Exchange, Inc. (PHX) (collectively, the defendants). The litigation referred to was case no. 8:13-cv-02240-VMC-MAP in the U.S. District Court, Middle District of Florida, Tampa Division (the case). Specifically, we were asked to provide an opinion regarding the actual damages sustained by StoneEagle, as a result of the defendants' unauthorized use of StoneEagle's healthcare provider reimbursement system (the StoneEagle patented system).

> *Case background:* Stone Eagle has been a provider of "innovative product administration systems and data driven business solutions since 1967. StoneEagle offers a suite of web-based software solutions that automate, simplify and integrate business processes."[45]

7-45 *StoneEagle Servs., Inc. v. Pay-Plus Sols., Inc.*, No. 8:13-cv-2240-T-33MAP, 2015 U.S. Dist. LEXIS 79971 (M.D. Fla. June 19, 2015).

The defendants marked and sold a system for the electronic payment and documentation of claims for healthcare providers and payors. According to the complaint, the system sold by the defendants infringed on the StoneEagle patented system. We were asked to analyze damages.

Damages analysis: As a measure of damages, we analyzed what StoneEagle would have received in royalty payments for use of the StoneEagle patented system. Since StoneEagle did not authorize the use of the StoneEagle patented system, they did not derive an economic benefit from its use by the defendants. Actual damages were calculated by analyzing what an arm's-length charge would have been to obtain the legal right to use the StoneEagle patented system.

As described by the courts, a reasonable royalty represents the lower bound of appropriate damages: "Upon a showing of infringement, a patentee is entitled to 'damages adequate to compensate for the infringement, but in no event less than a reasonable royalty for the use made of the invention by the infringer.'"[46]

The key element of the assignment was to determine the appropriate arm's-length royalty payment for use of the StoneEagle patented system. After reviewing thousands of license agreements, we identified seven comparable agreements for patents used to facilitate payment processing. These agreements are summarized at Figure 7.7.

Figure 7.7 Royalty Rate Charged in Comparable License Agreements

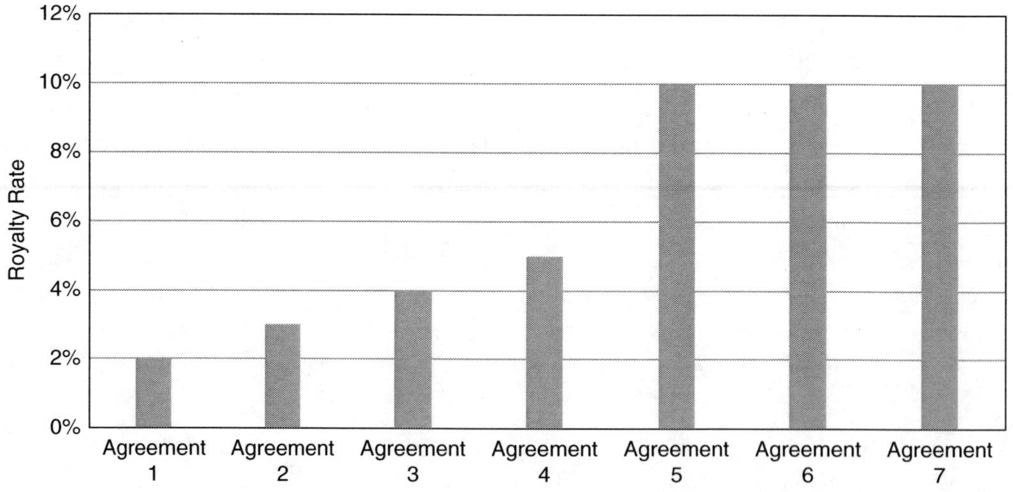

7-46 *ResQNet.com, Inc. v. Lansa, Inc.*, 594 F.3d 860, 868 (Fed. Cir. 2010) (quoting 35 U.S.C. § 284).

Figure 7.8 Actual Damages Calculation

	2012	2013	2014	2015 YTD (Jan–May)
Total Revenue	884,902	9,209,807	35,316,037	16,932,667
Reasonable Royalty Rate	5.0%	5.0%	5.0%	5.0%
Hypothetical Royalty Charge	**44,245**	**460,490**	**1,765,802**	**846,633**
Total Actual Damages	**3,117,171**			

In our analysis, we relied on the median royalty rate of 5%. Applying this royalty to the revenue generated from the defendants' sales of infringing products resulted in the damages conclusion summarized at Figure 7.8.

Defendants' rebuttal: In our report, we explicitly stated that we did not rely on the Georgia-Pacific factors in our analysis. In an attempt to discredit our analysis, the defendants retained a rebuttal expert who opined that our opinions and analysis should be excluded for failure to consider the Georgia-Pacific factors.

- *Georgia-Pacific:* In the landmark 1970 case, *Georgia-Pacific Corp. v. U.S. Plywood Corp.*, Judge Tenney of the Southern District of New York established a list of 15 factors to consider in the determination of appropriate royalty rates for damage calculations. The Federal Circuit has endorsed these 15 factors, which have become known as the Georgia-Pacific factors.

  With the technological advancements of the past 40 years, the application of these factors has become more challenging. In the 1970 *Georgia-Pacific* case, a single patent covered the entire product. "[T]he contribution of the [patented] invention cannot be isolated as a separate physical part. The invention permeated the [Georgia-Pacific] plywood panel to such a degree that it should be considered as covering the article as a whole."[47] Today, it is common for products to be comprised of hundreds or thousands of patentable parts. This creates the difficulty of determining the relative contribution of a specific infringing input.

While the Georgia-Pacific factors can be incorporated in damages analysis, their inclusion is not mandatory. In addition, when the Georgia-Pacific factors are considered by experts, the actual application is often flawed. The limitations of the Georgia-Pacific factors for use in damages analysis have been discussed by former Chief Judge of the U.S. Court of Appeals for the Federal Circuit, Randall R. Rader. In a 2012 interview, Judge Rader described *Georgia-Pacific* as follows:

> *Chief Judge Radar:* Whenever I hear "*Georgia-Pacific*" I bristle a little bit because the Georgia-Pacific factors are really just a laundry list of various things to be

7-47 *Georgia-Pacific Corp. v. U.S. Plywood Corp.*, 318 F. Supp. 1116 (S.D.N.Y. 1970).

> considered. The Georgia-Pacific factors were never meant to be a test or a formula for resolving damages issues. They are merely a list of things to consider. And somehow it gets blown out of context—I see it time after time after time. I can tell you exactly how it gets blown out of context.
>
> The expert—I trust this is not you gentlemen—is sitting on the stand and he or she will testify: "Well, there are 15 Georgia-Pacific factors and six of them favor us and the other nine are neutral." Well, that is an attempt to convert this laundry list into some kind of a methodology. However, many of those 15 factors may be overlapping or irrelevant to a particular case. Yet some will try to make their case seem more reasonable by stacking up so many Georgia-Pacific factors in their favor and the rest are against their opponent or neutral. And that's not what the *Georgia-Pacific* case was ever about and it's a flawed methodology. Those factors were not meant to be counted up the way you count up balls and strikes during a baseball game.

Court ruling and jury verdict: In response to the defendants' motion to exclude the damages presented by CONSOR, the court agreed that it was not mandatory to incorporate the George-Pacific factors in damages analysis. In her order, U.S. District Judge Virginia M. Hernandez Covington ruled as follows:

> "This Court denied Defendants' Motion to Exclude Mr. Anson (Doc. # 144), and determined that Mr. Anson's opinions – which utilized the 'Market Approach' as opposed to the Georgia-Pacific factors in determining a reasonable royalty rate in this action – were based on sound and reliable methodology."[48]

At trial, the jury ruled in favor of StoneEagle and awarded patent infringement damages of $2,220,850.[49] Moving forward, we anticipate the views of Judge Rader will become more widely accepted, and the role of *Georgia-Pacific* in damages analysis will diminish.

Current State of the US Patent System

Finally, some comments from the Licensing Executives Society Inc. (United States and Canada; LES) and the U.S. Chamber of Commerce on the current state of the U.S. patent system:

> [LES] is deeply concerned by recent evidence of further decline in the effectiveness of the U.S. patent system. On February 8th, [2018] the U.S. Chamber of Commerce Global Innovation Policy Center released the 6th edition of its International IP Index. The Index finds that the U.S. patent system has fallen to 12th place in the

7-48 *StoneEagle Servs., Inc. v. Pay-Plus Sols., Inc.*, No. 8:13-cv-2240-T-33MAP, 2015 U.S. Dist. LEXIS 79971 (M.D. Fla. June 19, 2015).

7-49 Jury Verdict Form, filed August 12, 2015.

> world. It's lowest ranking in the six years of the history of the Index. This comes after last year's surprising fall from first to 10th place, tied with Hungary.[50]

The U.S. Chamber attributes the decline to a 'growing level of uncertainty for innovators, particularly in relation to patent protection and technology licensing.' The Index specifically cites uncertainties resulting from inconsistent interpretation of Supreme Court attempts to define patent-eligible subject matter by lower courts and the U.S. Patent and Trademark Office. The Index further cites challenges innovators face in post-grant opposition proceedings, which 'involve a great deal of cost and lack of predictability for patent owners compared with other post-grant opposition systems.[51]

7-50 Licensing Executives Society Concerned by Further Decline in US Patent System (Feb. 15, 2018) http://www.lesusacanada.org/news/387151/Licensing-Executives-Society-Concerned-By-Further-Decline-in-US-Patent-System.htm.

7-51 Licensing Executives Society Concerned by Further Decline in US Patent System. Feb. 15, 2018.

Chapter 8

Trade Secrets Valuation: Trends and Cases Contributed by Evan Loker

For decades, trade secrets have been glossed over in intellectual property (IP) valuation discussion, the Ringo Starr of IP so to speak, and for good reason. Originally lacking the robust federal protection and regulation afforded to its more well-known brethren (copyrights, trademarks, rights of publicity, and patents), trade secret regulation was covered almost exclusively by state law and, at times, even lacked a good definition. Trade secrets have made up a lot of ground in recent decades. As the business landscape continues to evolve rapidly due to increased technology utilization and globalism, one could argue that trade secrets are now the Paul McCartney of the IP world.

Certainly, as valuation professionals, we have seen a rise in both the use and value of trade secrets. In this chapter, we will cover and discuss many aspects of trade secrets and their journey pre- and post-millennium. Additionally, we will review and analyze recent trade secret–related legal cases and conclude with a brief discussion on where trade secrets might be headed in the next decade.

Benefits and Drawbacks

Trade secrets are not a panacea; they are not going to cover the entirety of a company's IP. However, trade secrets do provide certain benefits and protections that the other forms of IP do not. For example, when a company files for a patent, it must disclose some of the subject matter and details to the U.S. Patent and Trademark Office (USPTO), making those elements available to the public. Anyone or any company can view those filings and attempt to circumvent the patented elements.

With the advent and proliferation of the Internet and globalism over the past few decades, the ability to circumvent or reverse-engineer a patent has increased exponentially. Add to that cheap labor from all over the world and you get a business landscape that is increasingly litigious and more reliant than ever on trade secrets. Another advantage of trade secrets is that they can be kept in perpetuity, unlike other forms of IP. From the list below of famous trade secrets, there are a handful that are several decades old, and one that has been around for well over a century. Compare this with the 20-year life span of a utility patent or the 14-year life span of a design patent, and you can see why some companies would choose to never patent their invention and instead simply keep it under lock and key forever.

Famous Trade Secrets

- Research and development information
- Algorithms
- Designs
- Ingredients
- Methods

Specific

- McDonald's secret sauce
- Coca-Cola formula
- Google search algorithm
- KFC recipe
- Lena Blackburn's baseball rubbing mud
- *New York Times* bestseller list
- WD-40
- Listerine formula
- Twinkies preservatives
- Krispy Kreme doughnuts process

There are some disadvantages to trade secrets, of course, most in the form of legal recourse should your trade secret become public. Until recently, if your trade secret became public (legally), you did not have an easy way to regain the secretive nature of your company's advantage, determine the monetary value of the trade secret, or punish the entity that made your secret public through legal means. By definition, if a company's trade secret, e.g., a database, algorithm, proprietary method, or process, becomes public, then it is no longer secretive and it will quickly cease to provide the company with any economic benefit once its competitors implement it. Whereas patents, trademarks, and copyrights cover discrete forms of IP, trade secrets cover things that are much more difficult to assign a monetary value to; therefore, it is much more difficult to determine the monetary damage done to a business. For a long time, the ability to seek legal recourse for trade secret misappropriation had been a relative patchwork of varying state laws. However, trade secret law has made a lot of progress on this front, culminating in the 2016 Defend Trade Secrets Act (DTSA) that sought to provide companies with the ability to file civil lawsuits in federal court under the Economic Espionage Act (EEA), greatly strengthening trade secret protection into the new millennium.

Increasing Use and Strength of Trade Secrets

The use of trade secrets in business has steadily increased over the past few decades. As the protections surrounding trade secrets have become stronger and as IP has evolved in this increasingly globalized and digitized landscape, the traditional stalwarts of IP have lost some of their luster while the value of trade secrets has increased substantially. This is evidenced by the number of litigation cases that involve misappropriation of trades secrets. They doubled between 1988 and 1995, doubled between 1995 and 2004, and are projected to have doubled once again between 2004 and 2017.[1]

Trade secrets are valuable to all companies in all industries. However, the higher up the technology value chain one goes, the more important trade secrets become to a company. As of the time of this writing, Google's parent company, Alphabet, was suing Uber for misappropriation of nine trade secrets related to self-driving vehicles.[2] Alphabet is claiming $2.6 billion in damages for just one of the nine trade secrets that came from a former Google executive downloading 14,000 files and taking them to Uber.[3] This is the highest purported value ever placed on a single trade secret and shows just how valuable today's companies view trade secrets.

A survey of businesses showed that "intellectual property protection was of importance to only 20 percent of firms investing in sales or distribution outlets, but that it mattered to 50-60 percent of firms investing in manufacturing of components or complete products, and to 80 percent of firms investing in R&D facilities."[4] It is not that surprising that 80% of firms that invest heavily in research and development (R&D) consider trade secret protection of great importance as "[e]conomically-powerful innovations originate primarily in advanced economies where commitments to research and development are strong . . . and intellectual property rights are respected."[5] One could argue that spending on R&D is the bellwether of a company's or a country's future economic health and prosperity.

For decades, the United States has spent more than any other country on R&D, and the country subsequently reaped the enormous benefits of all of that spending. In recent years, as China has evolved the nature of its economy, it has aggressively spent more and more money on their own R&D efforts because it has seen how the IP born out of basic R&D has shaped and propelled the U.S. economy. Figure 8.1 shows historical R&D spending for the five countries that currently spend the most on R&D.

8-1 CHAMBER OF COMMERCE OF THE UNITED STATES OF AMERICA, THE CASE FOR ENHANCED PROTECTION OF TRADE SECRETS IN THE TRANS-PACIFIC PARTNERSHIP AGREEMENT 11, https://www.uschamber.com/sites/default/files/legacy/international/files/Final%20TPP%20Trade%20Secrets%208_0.pdf.

8-2 *Waymo LLC v. Uber Techs., Inc.*, 319 F.R.D. 284 (N.D. Cal. 2017).

8-3 Johana Bhuiyan, *Alphabet's Waymo Wants Uber to Pay $2.6 Billion in Damages for a Single Allegedly Stolen Trade Secret*, RECODE (Sept. 20, 2017), https://www.recode.net/2017/9/20/16340046/alphabet-waymo-self-driving-car-uber-stolen-trade-secret-billion-damages-lawsuit-trial-hearing.

8-4 CHAMBER OF COMMERCE OF THE UNITED STATES OF AMERICA, THE CASE FOR ENHANCED PROTECTION OF TRADE SECRETS IN THE TRANS-PACIFIC PARTNERSHIP AGREEMENT 6, https://www.uschamber.com/sites/default/files/legacy/international/files/Final%20TPP%20Trade%20Secrets%208_0.pdf.

8-5 Robert J. Shapiro & Kevin A Hassett, *The Economic Value of Intellectual Property*, 5, http://www.sonecon.com/docs/studies/IntellectualPropertyReport-October2005.pdf.

Figure 8.1 Gross Domestic Spending on R&D, 2000–2015[6]

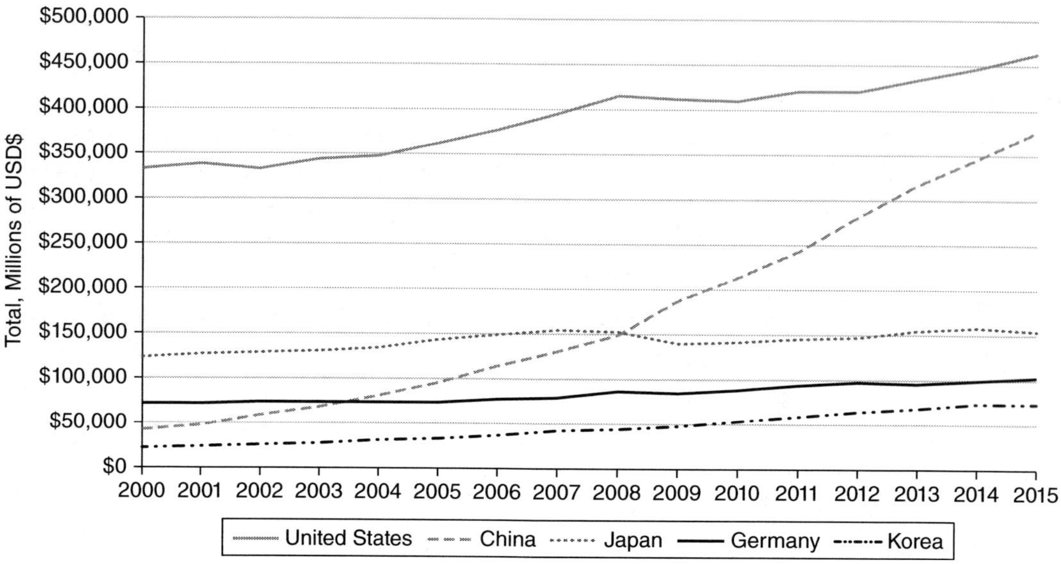

Trade secrets born out of R&D are of great value to businesses and countries. A 2010 study by Forrester Consulting found that trade secrets "comprise an average of two-thirds of the value of firms' information portfolios. In knowledge-intensive industries like manufacturing, information services, and professional, scientific, and technical services, that percentage increases to some 70 to 80%. In the aggregate, this value is immense. Publicly traded U.S. companies own an estimated $5 trillion worth of trade secrets."[7] Additional surveys further bolster the view held by U.S. businesses that trade secret protection is vital to their success. A 2008 survey conducted by the National Science Foundation asked U.S. businesses with significant R&D activity about the importance of various types of IP protection. Figure 8.2 includes a summary of the findings.

Figure 8.2 Importance of Various Forms of IP Protection to U.S. Businesses with R&D Activity[8]

	Very	Somewhat	Not
Trade Secrets	45%	22%	33%
Trademarks	33%	27%	40%
Utility Patents	26%	15%	60%
Design Patents	15%	18%	67%
Copyrights	25%	25%	49%
Mask works	4%	6%	90%

8-6 OECD, Gross domestic spending on R&D (indicator), doi: 10.1787/d8b068b4-en, https://data.oecd.org/rd/gross-domestic-spending-on-r-d.htm (last visited Mar. 11, 2018).

8-7 CHAMBER OF COMMERCE OF THE UNITED STATES OF AMERICA, THE CASE FOR ENHANCED PROTECTION OF TRADE SECRETS IN THE TRANS-PACIFIC PARTNERSHIP AGREEMENT 10, https://www.uschamber.com/sites/default/files/legacy/international/files/Final%20TPP%20Trade%20Secrets%208_0.pdf.

8-8 *Id.*

Trade secret protection is more important now than ever before. As the digital age continues across the globe, countries are revisiting, or even creating for the first time, their legal framework around IP, in particular, trade secrets.

How Do You Keep Trade Secrets a Secret?

As more and more of a company's proprietary formation gets stored on computers, the ability of a single person to steal or leak that information is increasing. Later in this chapter we will discuss a case where misappropriation occurs, along with the subsequent damage that can be dealt to a company as a result.

While legal recourse is the only option once a trade secret is made public, it is not a great deterrent simply because it is reactive instead of proactive. If you are taking legal actions against violators of your trade secrets, then it is already too late. The best defense is to be proactive with your company's rules, procedures, and access regarding your company's trade secrets.

If your trade secret meets the current definition under the DTSA, then the following major steps should be taken to keep your trade secrets secret. We look at these steps when valuating trade secrets.[9]

1. Identify and assess
   - Make sure that your IP falls into the definition of a trade secret.
   - Conduct a risk assessment to understand what your company's trade secrets are, where they are stored, and who within the company has access.
   - Determine the level of importance of your company's various trade secrets.
2. Lock and key
   - Create agreements, internal policies, procedures, and records to bolster information protection and confidentiality.
   - Establish physical and electronic security measures to limit access to trade secrets.
3. Educate and assign
   - Conduct employee and vendor training to educate personnel on what is expected of them when handling this type of information.
   - Determine a hierarchy of ownership for your trade secrets.
   - Assign ownership and responsibility for the different trade secrets or levels of importance.
4. Monitor and measure
   - Institute an information protection and monitoring person or team so that someone takes ownership of the company's trade secret protection.
   - Establish measurement metrics with which to gauge the trade secret protection personnel, as well as regular company and vendor personnel.

8-9 Barbara Weltman, *5 Steps for Protecting Your Trade Secrets*, SMALL BUSINESS ADMINISTRATION (Sept. 10, 2015), https://www.sba.gov/blogs/5-steps-protecting-your-trade-secrets.

5. Continual improvements and corrective actions
   - Revisit your trade secrets list and your company's protocols around ownership and access, and update any policies or procedures as your company grows.
   - Understand the laws that surround trade secrets and the corrective measures that can be taken if trade secrets get misappropriated.
   - Take swift legal action in the case of misappropriation, as courts view a company's prompt response as a strong indication that the trade secrets are of great commercial value to the business.

Trade Secret Legal Protection—Pre-Millennium

Trade secret protection in the United States has made up a lot of ground in the past few decades. While the other forms of IP have had strong legal protection for several decades, if not a century or more, trade secret protection has been relatively slow to catch up. Prior to the millennium, the U.S. relied on common law and two statutes to govern trade secrets and misappropriation across the country. After the millennium, Congress passed new statutes that further bolstered trade secret protection.

Statutory law protecting trade secrets in the United States prior to the millennium was principally based on the Uniform Trade Secrets Act (UTSA) and further strengthened by the EEA. The UTSA, published by the Uniform Law Commission in 1979 and amended in 1985, was a uniform act of the United States, disseminated in an effort to provide a clearer legal framework to better protect the trade secrets of U.S. companies that operated in multiple states. The UTSA was intended to codify and align standards and remedies regarding misappropriation of trade secrets that had evolved under U.S. common law on a state-to-state basis.[10] At present, every U.S. state, except for Massachusetts and New York, has adopted the UTSA in one form or another. The major contributions to trade secret law that the UTSA brought were revisions for:

- The definition of a trade secret,
- The definition of trade secret misappropriation, and
- Legal recourse/remedies/enforcement should trade secret misappropriation be found.

The UTSA's definition of a trade secret notably goes beyond the definition originally provided in the 1939 §757 Restatement of Torts. In particular, a trade secret was originally required to be continuously used in a business's operations.[11] The UTSA "expands protection to a plaintiff who has not yet had an opportunity or acquired the means to put a trade secret to use. The definition includes information that has commercial value from a negative

8-10 UNIF. TRADE SECRETS ACT (UNIF. LAW COMM'N 1985).
8-11 RESTATEMENT OF TORTS § 757 (1939).

viewpoint, for example the results of lengthy and expensive research which proves that a certain process will not work could be of great value to a competitor."[12]

More than a decade after adoption of the UTSA, Congress passed another piece of legislation that went even further in protecting trade secrets and deterring misappropriation. The House Judiciary Committee recognized how important trade secrets were to the United States and how they had become "a prime target for theft precisely because it costs so much to develop independently, because it is so valuable, and because there are virtually no penalties for its theft."[13] In 1996, Congress passed the Economics Espionage Act to signal just how important it viewed trade secrets to be by deeming any trade secret misappropriation a federal crime.[14]

U.S. common law, the UTSA, and the EEA served as the country's trade secret protection for a long time, and served it well. In the decades leading up to the millennium, the country's stance on trade secrets and legal protection expanded steadily in response to the quickly evolving global business landscape.

Trade Secret Legal Protection—Post-Millennium

After the millennium, it would take more than a decade for another piece of trade secret legislation to emerge. In 2011 and 2016, Congress passed the America Invents Act (AIA) and the DTSA, respectively, both of which affected the IP landscape after their passage.

America Invents Act

The AIA was discussed in more detail in Chapter 2. In this section, we will briefly discuss how the passage of this law, while focused on patents, inadvertently affected the importance and value of trade secrets. The major changes to the U.S. patent system ushered into law by the AIA include the following:

- *From first-to-invent to first-to-file:* This change means that an inventor must submit their application to the USPTO even earlier than previously required because they can no longer rely on first-to-invent evidence to prove that they should be the true patent holder. Inventors now must disclose their invention sooner, which shortens the life of the patent and subsequently lowers the perceived value of the patent.
- *From inter parte reexamination to inter parte review:* Inter parte reexamination is closer to ordinary patent examination, while inter parte review is more like ordinary patent litigation. Any third party can request inter parte review, and it greatly increases the amount

8-12 Unif. Trade Secrets Act (Unif. Law Comm'n 1985).

8-13 Chamber of Commerce of the United States of America, The Case for Enhanced Protection of Trade Secrets in the Trans-Pacific Partnership Agreement 23, https://www.uschamber.com/sites/default/files/legacy/international/files/Final%20TPP%20Trade%20Secrets%208_0.pdf.

8-14 18 U.S.C.S. § 1831.

of time that a patent can be litigated, resulting in increased legal fees to the inventor, greater exposure, and less time to practice.

- *Addition of post grant review:* Once a patent is issued, a post grant review must be requested within the first nine months following issuance. The process for post grant reviews and inter parte reviews are quite similar. The only difference is that a post grant review can challenge a broader scope of patentability questions that might have nothing to do with prior art.

These major changes to patent law in the United States, coupled with the increased legal protection and remedies for trade secrets and trade secret misappropriation and with the fundamental differences between patents and trade secrets, have greatly affected the difference in value between patents and trade secrets. These changes to patent law have affected trade secrets because by calling into question the extent of patent protection for business methods and diagnostics, trade secrets now play an especially significant role and may become the primary way for companies to protect innovations in those areas. In fact, a greater focus on trade secrets and interest in offsetting lost patent protection might even result in certain companies treating information that was previously shared with the industry as trade secrets.

Defend Trade Secrets Act

In 2016, Congress overwhelmingly passed the DTSA. While it was modeled after the UTSA in many respects, it also included some noteworthy differences. The goal of the DTSA was to "further harmonize the law through a single federal statute, allowing for the development of more predictable, nationwide case law. It would also give litigants easier access to federal courts, which supporters say are better equipped than state courts to handle cross-state and international cases, as well as complex technological issues."[15]

The DTSA created three significant changes to trade secret law. First, it slightly altered the definition of a trade secret to require it to be used in interstate commerce. Second, the "DTSA provides for ex parte seizures of property when necessary to prevent the dissemination of a misappropriated trade secret. Third, the DTSA immunizes individuals from liability under federal and state law for certain confidential disclosures of trade secret information."[16]

Trade Secret Definition Change

The DTSA provides the owner of a misappropriated trade secret a path for civil action only where the trade secret is "related to a product or service used in, or intended for use in, interstate or foreign commerce."[17] This provision changed the long-standing definition under the UTSA and set a uniform threshold for what may be considered a trade secret under the DTSA. However, this new definitional language should be viewed with caution. As many

8-15 Bill Donahue, *BREAKING: House Passes Federal Trade Secrets Bill*, LINKEDIN (Apr. 28, 2016), http://www.law360.com/articles/788378/print?section=ip.

8-16 Eric Bensen, *Defending Trade Secrets Under the Economic Espionage Act*, LEXIS PRACTICE ADVISOR JOURNAL (Sept. 13, 2016), https://www.lexisnexis.com/lexis-practice-advisor/the-journal/b/lpa/archive/2016/09/13/defending-trade-secrets-under-the-economic-espionage-act.aspx.

8-17 Defend Trade Secrets Act of 2016, Pub. L. No. 114-153, 130 Stat. 376.

recent trade secret cases involve confidential customer information, a hypothetical example involving a local business (i.e., builder, distributor, e-commerce business, or similar entity) and its customers' private information highlights how "the claimant's customer information would be unlikely to be viewed as related to or used in interstate commerce under a reasonable interpretation of Congress's interstate commerce power."

Civil Seizure Provisions

"Unlike the UTSA, the DTSA provides for ex parte seizures of property when necessary to prevent the dissemination of misappropriated trade secrets. However, while Congress was considering the bill, an amendment was added to ensure that ex parte seizures were available only in 'extraordinary circumstances,' that is, where a defendant is expected to attempt to flee the country or planning to immediately disclose the trade secret to a third party, or where a defendant is otherwise not amenable to the enforcement of the court's orders."[18]

The DTSA included several limitations on the ex parte provision. For a seizure application to be granted by a court, it must find that the application meets several facts:[19]

- That an "order issued pursuant to Rule 65 of the Federal Rules of Civil Procedure or another form of equitable relief would be inadequate . . . because the party to which the order would be issued would evade, avoid, or otherwise not comply with such an order."[20]
- "[I]mmediate and irreparable injury will occur if such seizure is not ordered."[21]
- "[T]he harm to the applicant of denying the application outweighs the harm to the legitimate interests of the person against whom seizure would be ordered of granting the application and substantially outweighs the harm to any third parties who may be harmed by such seizure."[22]
- The likelihood of an applicant's success, based on the merits of its claim (i.e., that the information in question is actually a trade secret and that it was misappropriated).[23]
- The defendant has actual possession of the trade secret and any other property to be seized.[24]
- The property to be seized is described with "reasonable particularity"[25] and its location is identified.
- The likelihood that the defendant, upon notice of the application, "would destroy, move, hide, or otherwise make such matter inaccessible to the court."[26]
- "[T]he applicant has not publicized the requested seizure."[27]

8-18 Doc 19, https://www.lexisnexis.com/lexis-practice-advisor/the-journal/b/lpa/archive/2016/09/13/defending-trade-secrets-under-the-economic-espionage-act.aspx
8-19 Defend Trade Secrets Act of 2016, Pub. L. No. 114-153, 130 Stat. 376.
8-20 *Id.*
8-21 *Id.*
8-22 *Id.*
8-23 *Id.*
8-24 *Id.*
8-25 Defend Trade Secrets Act of 2016, Pub. L. No. 114-153, 130 Stat. 376.
8-26 *Id.*
8-27 *Id.*

"The DTSA also sets forth numerous requirements for the seizure order itself. Most are fairly routine. The order must: (1) set forth the court's findings of fact and conclusions of law, (2) provide for the narrowest seizure of the property necessary to achieve the purpose of the order, and to do so with minimal interruption of the business operations of third parties and the legitimate business interest of the defendant, (3) provide guidance to the law enforcement officials that will execute the order, (4) set a date for hearing at the earliest possible time, and (5) require the applicant to provide security for the payment of damages in the event that the seizure or attempt to seize was wrongful or excessive."[28]

Immunity for Individuals

"The DTSA also immunizes individuals from liability under federal and state law for certain confidential disclosures of trade secret information. Three types of disclosure are protected:

- A disclosure made in confidence to a federal, state, or local government official, either directly or indirectly, or to an attorney solely for the purpose of reporting or investigating the suspected violation of law
- A disclosure made in a complaint or other document filed under seal in a lawsuit or other proceeding
- A disclosure to an attorney or in a court proceeding by an individual who files a lawsuit for retaliation by an employer for the individual's reporting of a suspected violation of law, as long as any court rulings are made under seal and the individual does not otherwise disclose a trade secret except pursuant to a court order"[29]

The legal changes over the past few decades have increased the value of trade secrets and decreased the value of patents. As software programs, business methods or processes, devices, and other items become easier to copy or reverse engineer (e.g., cheap labor, increased programming knowledge, the ease with which new ideas or inventions are able to proliferate around the world in short periods of time), the importance of trade secrets as a replacement for patents has increased—as has their value.

Bundling Trade Secrets with Other IP

Trade secrets routinely get bundled with other forms of IP when being licensed. Bundling increases the overall value of the portfolio, a situation where the whole is greater than the sum of its parts. While trade secrets can be bundled with any other type of IP, they are most routinely bundled with patents.

8-28 Doc19, https://www.lexisnexis.com/lexis-practice-advisor/the-journal/b/lpa/archive/2016/09/13/defending-trade-secrets-under-the-economic-espionage-act.aspx.

8-29 Eric Bensen, *Defending Trade Secrets Under the Economic Espionage Act*, LEXIS PRACTICE ADVISOR JOURNAL (Sept. 13, 2016), https://www.lexisnexis.com/lexis-practice-advisor/the-journal/b/lpa/archive/2016/09/13/defending-trade-secrets-under-the-economic-espionage-act.aspx.

"Patents are typically viewed as a cornerstone of intellectual property licensing. The licensing landscape, however, has been changing. In recent years, trade secrets ha[ve] become 'the crown jewels of corporations' and 'workhorse[s] of technology transfer.'"[30] Technology transfers are a great example of the bundling of IP. In the realm of technology transfers, bundling trade secrets with patents in a license agreement is especially common due, in large part, to the intrinsic nature of the two types of IP and the fact that they have become more intertwined in recent years.

> Trade secrets cover 90% of all new technology. . . . Therefore, it is virtually impossible to license a patent without also transferring applicable proprietary knowledge and information. As there is always more to every invention and certain information inevitably escapes a patent application, some commentators asserted that 'a patent [is a] little more than an advertisement for the sale of accompanying know-how.' Some went even further proclaiming that patents should be viewed as merely supplemental to trade secrets.[31]

Case Studies

To conclude this chapter, we have outlined two cases that illustrate some of the methodologies used to value trade secrets. The first case study from 2016 was the largest trade secret misappropriation case in terms of damages. Since all information was made public in the course of litigation, the actual names and dollar values are presented in the case study. In the second case study, we were retained to analyze the value of trade secrets that were misappropriated by a former employee. To protect the confidentiality of our client, all names and numbers have been changed.

Case Study 1: Epic Systems Corporation (Plaintiff) v. Tata Consultancy Services Limited and Tata America International Corporation d/b/a TCA America (Defendants)

Case background: "Epic Systems Corporation asserts a variety of federal and state law claims against defendants Tata Consultancy Services Limited and Tata America International Corporation, respectively; a much larger, India-based company and its smaller U.S. arm. Among other things, defendants provide information technology services to the U.S. healthcare industry, while Epic is a leading provider of software to this industry. Essentially, plaintiff claims that defendants accessed its web portal without authorization while servicing a mutual client, and then used information obtained to help develop their own competitive software product and for other improper purposes."[32]

Trade secret valuation: Epic Systems Corporation (Epic) hired a damages expert (the Expert) to conduct a valuation of the trade secrets and other confidential information (the

8-30 Maxim Tsotsorin, *Practical Considerations in Trade Secret Licensing* (Oct. 1, 2012), https://papers.ssrn.com/sol3/papers.cfm?abstract_id=2334060.

8-31 *Id.*

8-32 *Epic Sys. Corp. v. Tata Consultancy Servs.*, No. 14-cv-748-wmc, 2015 U.S. Dist. LEXIS 176561 (W.D. Wis. Mar. 2, 2015).

Trade Secrets) that were misappropriated by Tata Consultancy Services Limited and Tata America International Corporation (Tata).

The Expert conducted his analysis using an avoided R&D cost (Avoided R&D) methodology. This falls under the cost approach that is one of the mainstays in IP valuation. The Expert used this Avoided R&D cost analysis that attempted to measure the investment Epic made to develop the misappropriated trade secrets and confidential information before Tata stole them. Tata did not dispute the characterization of this confidential information. Instead, defendants contend that there is no evidence of their being misappropriated.

In determining compensatory damages, the Expert began with a comparative analysis that was prepared by Tata and used confidential information obtained illegally through a consultant for Epic for the purpose of determining any differences between the two companies' competing software platforms. The Expert used the Comparative Analysis to "tether specific R&D costs associated with the trade secrets and confidential information implicated in the comparative analysis."[33] The Expert "then provided relative weighting of the various trade secrets and confidential information as they pertain to the overall value of Epic's software"[34] and proceeded to identify "only those trade secrets and that confidential information incorporated into the comparative analysis."[35] He went on to calculate the total R&D expenses that Epic incurred during the development of its software, which resulted in an implied value for the trade secrets and other confidential information of $200 million.[36] "The $200 million figure related specifically to the avoided R&D benefit associated with [Tata's] preparation of the comparative analysis. Using the modified 'X analysis' . . . [the Expert] was able to tether the specific R&D costs associated with the trade secrets and confidential information implicated in the comparative analysis."[37]

The jury in this case awarded a total of $240 million in compensatory damages. The original $200 million in damages determined by Epic's Expert using the Avoided R&D analysis was reduced by 30%, based on Tata's expert's testimony that "rates are generally 30 to 40 percent less [in India] than [in] the U.S."[38] The additional $100 million awarded by the jury as compensatory damages was due to ample evidence that the trade secrets and other confidential information not used in the comparative analysis were used in other ways.

The jury was also entitled to award punitive damages. Under Wisconsin law, punitive damages can be no more than two times compensatory damages. Punitive damages in this case were reduced from the $700 million originally awarded by the jury to $480 million. To be awarded punitive damages, Wisconsin case law requires the court to apply the following six-factor test:

1. "The grievousness of the acts;
2. The degree of malicious intent;

8-33 Brief in Opposition–Document #926. Doc 23. Epic Systems Corporation v. Tata Consultancy Services Limited and Tata America International Corporation dba TCA America, 14-cv-748-wmc.
8-34 *Id.*
8-35 *Id.*
8-36 *Id.*
8-37 *Id.*
8-38 *Id.*

3. Whether the award bears a reasonable relationship to the award of compensatory damages;
4. The potential damage that might have been caused by the acts;
5. The ratio of the award to civil or criminal penalties that could be imposed for comparable misconduct; and
6. The wealth of the wrongdoer."[39]

"Courts are called upon to analyze only those factors which are most relevant to the case. The most important indicium of the reasonableness of a punitive damages award is the degree of reprehensibility of the defendant's conduct."[40] Originally Epic was awarded $240 million in compensatory damages with an additional $700 million in punitive damages, for a total of $940 million. This was ultimately reduced to a total of $720 million.

Case Study 2: Biotech Company v. Former Executive

CONSOR was retained by Biotech Company ("Biotech") to analyze the value of the various processes, formulae, designs, systems, assays, documents and forms, methods, data, techniques, and other proprietary information relating to the manufacture, storage, handling, distribution, and/or use of biological therapy products and services (collectively the Trade Secrets) to which a former executive ("Former Executive") had access and from which he took, without permission, the documents that he deemed most useful.

Case background: Former Executive was president and CEO of Biotech from 2003 until his departure in 2010. While president and CEO, Former Executive had access to Biotech's computer systems and Trade Secrets. Biotech's computer systems store a variety of confidential data and information, which includes the Trade Secrets. Specifically, the entirety of Biotech's methods, procedures, and protocols were included, as well as portions of Biotech's Investigational New Drug (IND) applications, service and sales contracts, studies, presentations, and business plans. When manufacturers of biological therapy products attempt to gain regulatory approval for a product, regulators inspect each method, procedure, and protocol in place in deciding whether to allow the product to proceed or to place the product on clinical hold.

Former Executive resigned from Biotech in 2010 and subsequently formed Former Executive Consulting, Inc., and began providing consulting services for HealthPlus, a company for which Biotech had previously done consulting work. While employed at Biotech, the company provided Former Executive a laptop (the "Laptop") for company use. Biotech's written company personnel policy requires former employees to return company property upon termination of employment. Around the time Former Executive filed a lawsuit against, it was discovered that he had not returned the Laptop upon his resignation. In late 2012, Former Executive returned the Laptop, and Biotech caused a copy of the Laptop to be made for forensic analysis. Biotech received a forensic copy of the Laptop hard drive (the Forensic Copy) days before the end of discovery. It was concluded that the Laptop contained a significant portion of Biotech's, and its customers', confidential and proprietary information and controlled document database library. Moreover, it was discovered that, after the end of

8-39 *Id.*
8-40 *Id.*

Former Executive's employment with Biotech, the confidential information was extensively modified, copied, and/or accessed without authorization. Former Executive transferred the Trade Secrets information to an external hard drive and sent it to personnel at HealthPlus.

Valuation methodology: Based on the context of the situation, we chose to use the relief-from-royalty approach as the most reasonable indication of value for the Trade Secrets. The relief-from-royalty method is a variation of the income approach that establishes the value of the IP as the capitalized value of the royalties that the company is relieved from paying due to its ownership of the assets. This approach provides a measure of the value by determining the avoided cost. This method is appropriate to use when the assets in question have comparable licensing information to use.

Royalty rate research: A key element of the relief-from-royalty approach is to identify appropriate royalty rates for use of the IP. To determine the fair market value of a royalty fee for use of the Trade Secrets, we used the market approach to identify comparable license agreements. Royalty rate transaction data were collected from various sources. Specifically, we used annual royalty rate industry surveys, public documentation from corporate 10-Q and 10-K forms, our internal database of license agreements, and third-party databases that contained tens of thousands of publicly available licensing transactions.

Based on our research, we identified third-party license agreements that focused on licenses with comparable proprietary information, processes, and know-how comparable to the Trade Secrets. Our royalty rate conclusions are presented in Figure 8.3.

Revenue projections and valuation: To determine hypothetical revenues that Biotech would generate in the future, we analyzed their past revenue figures to calculate a compound annual growth rate (CAGR) that could be applied to their most recent revenue figure. We then applied Biotech's 15.0% CAGR to their most recent revenue figure and projected out 10 years of company revenue.

In our analysis, we relied on the average royalty rate of 4.7% from our comparable license agreements. Applying this royalty rate to the Biotech revenue projections generated a hypothetical royalty charge for each year of our projections.

To discount the future hypothetical royalties that were projected in our model, we created a discount rate that was representative of the level of risk involved in an investment in the Trade Secrets. To determine the appropriate rate, we conducted a benchmark analysis of discount rates and weighted average cost of capital calculations for investments in similar asset classes. As the Trade Secrets could not generate a return on investment without the contribution of other assets, an investment in this type of asset should be considered to be of greater risk than investments in an entire corporation. Additionally, processes included in the

Figure 8.3 Comparable License Agreements Summary

Minimum	1.0%
Median	5.0%
Average	**4.7%**
Maximum	8.5%
Concluded Royalty Rate	4.7%

Figure 8.4 Relief from Royalty Calculation

		2014	2015	2016	...	2023	2024
Revenue		**$8,626,720**	**$9,922,706**	**$11,413,387**		**$30,402,235**	**$34,969,542**
CAGR			15.0%	15.0%		15.0%	15.0%
Reasonable Royalty Rate Cap			4.7%	4.7%		4.7%	4.7%
Hypothetical Royalty Charge			$ 466,367	$ 536,429		$ 1,428,905	$ 1,643,568
Less Taxes @	40%		$ 186,547	$ 214,572	...	$ 571,562	$ 657,427
After Tax Hypothetical Royalty Charge			**$ 279,820**	**$ 321,858**	...	**$ 857,343**	**$ 986,141**
Discount Factor (WACC) @	20%		0.91	0.76		0.21	0.18
Present Value of Free Cash Flow			$ 255,440	$ 244,845	...	$ 182,018	$ 174,469

Present Value of Cash Flows	**$2,126,731**

Figure 8.5 Terminal Value Calculation

		Value	Calculation
Terminal Period Cash Flow	(a)	$ 986,141	n/a
Discount Rate	(b)	20.0%	n/a
Terminal Growth Rate	(c)	3.0%	n/a
Terminal Value	(d)	5,974,855	(a*(1+c)/((b–c))
Discount Factor	(e)	0.18	n/a
Present Value of Terminal Value		**$ 1,057,074**	**(d)*(e)**

Trade Secrets are licensed less regularly than patents or trademarks and will therefore inherently carry greater risk. We ultimately determined that a discount rate of 20% was appropriate. Figure 8.4 is a summary of our relief from royalty analysis.

Additionally, because trade secrets have an indefinite life span, a terminal value of the hypothetical royalties generated by the Trade Secrets needed to be calculated. Using the final time period's hypothetical royalty figure, the same discount rate, and a terminal growth rate of 3.0%, we determined the present value of the terminal value cash flows. A summary is presented in Figure 8.5.

The final step in determining the value of the Trade Secrets was to combine the present value of the cash flows with the present value of the terminal value. Figure 8.6 shows our concluded value for the Trade Secrets.

Figure 8.6 Concluded Value for Trade Secrets

Relief from Royalty Valuation	
PV of Free Cash Flows	2,126,731
PV of Terminal Value	1,057,074
Value of Trade Secrets	**$3,183,806**

Conclusions

As the global business landscape continues to evolve in the face of technology and innovation, so too will trade secrets. We have seen how the value and usage of trade secrets has increased over the past few decades. Now, as we attempt to forecast how trade secrets will evolve in the coming decades, we should again look to the past.

Just like the gold rush of 1849, the people who truly became wealthy and laid the foundation for decades of marketplace dominance were the ones who were not interested in searching for gold in dirt and streams. They were the ones who saw the thousands of prospectors in search of tools, supplies, and other materials needed to their dreams of striking it rich. Big-tech companies are giving away, or "open sourcing," some of their most cutting-edge and potentially valuable trade secrets: algorithms. Google has open-sourced its artificial intelligence engine; Amazon open-sourced its algorithm for product recommendations; and Facebook open-sourced parts of its computing framework for machine learning algorithms. Instead of selling the tools, big tech is giving away the pickaxes, shovels, and pans of the digital age in the form of algorithms, software, trade secrets, know-how, and other proprietary information in order to make another trade secret exponentially more valuable: data.

These companies are playing the long game and positioning themselves for potential new sources of revenue, some of which may not even be thought up for years or decades. Companies, both large and small, are collecting any and all data from consumers in the hopes of finding some value within. Looking ahead, data will be the new dirt, the new streams, the new gold rush of the 21st century.

Chapter 9

Copyright Valuation: Trends and Cases

Since the beginning of the new millennium, several developments have impacted both the value of copyrights and how copyright valuations are performed. These include, but are not limited to, technological advancements, as well as changes in copyright law. In some instances, the former was the root cause of the latter.

Copyright laws protect original works of art as well as content in all forms of media including photos, music, videos, literary works, and various website content such as computer programs and databases.[1] The Federal Copyright Act of 1976 specifically defines copyrights as providing protection for "original works of authorship fixed in any tangible medium of expression, now known or later developed, from which they can be perceived, reproduced, or otherwise communicated, either directly or with the aid of a machine or device."[2] Before diving into our more contemporary thoughts on copyright valuation, we will briefly touch on some of the static concepts that remain core to copyright valuation.

Economic analysis of the value of copyrighted works falls into three general categories:

- Financial valuation (e.g., for taxes or financial reporting),
- Transactions (e.g., for determination of a license fee or sales price), and
- Litigation (e.g., damages).

At its core, valuation is the fair market value of the copyrighted work between a willing seller and a willing buyer. A copyrighted work may be valued differently by accountants and other financial professionals in situations that do not involve commercial transactions (e.g., bankruptcy, financial reporting, and taxes). In most cases, one can rely on one or more of the three traditional valuation methods: cost, market, or income/relief from royalty.

This chapter contains a bias toward the music industry since much of the recent activity has occurred in this sector, stemming from disruptive technologies.[3] Here, we will discuss

9-1 17 U.S.C. § 102(a).

9-2 *Id.*

9-3 See, e.g., Williams v. Bridgeport Music, Inc., No. LA CV13-06004 JAK (AGRx), 2014 U.S. Dist. LEXIS 182240 (C.D. Cal. Oct. 30, 2014).

these changes and complement the conversation with relevant case studies from our own experiences as well as important cases within the industry.

Copyright Protection Is Getting Longer

When the United States first passed the Copyright Act (in 1790), copyright protection was only good for a term of 14 years.[4] Today, copyright protection can last for more than 100 years, as protection endures for a term consisting of the life of the author plus 70 years after the author's death.[5] Why does the law keep getting extended? Well, it is widely known within the industry that a little mouse named Mickey has had something to do with it.[6]

Copyright protection was extended under the Sonny Bono Copyright Term Extension Act of 1998 so that material is protected for the shorter of 95 years from the first date of publication or 120 years from the date of creation. These terms of protection were extended because of pressure exerted by the Walt Disney Company (in great fear that Mickey Mouse would fall into the public domain) and other powerful corporate interests in the music, art, and entertainment worlds.

In Europe, the term of copyrights in sound recordings and performers' rights was recently extended from 50 years to 70 years.[7] However, some countries have amended, by EU treaty, longer terms.

U.S. copyright law also gives artists the opportunity to regain ownership of works that were transferred to record labels and music publishers. The Copyright Act of 1976 provides that "termination of the grant may be effected at any time during a period of five years beginning at the end of thirty-five years from the date of execution of the grant."[8] Regardless of the terms of the transfer, any grant of copyright to a third party may be reclaimed by the "author."[9] These so-called termination rights have the potential of being extremely lucrative for artists since income related to the exploitation of reclaimed sound recordings and/or compositions would bypass record labels and/or publishers and flow directly to artists. Because of these financial implications, termination rights have remained shrouded in controversy.[10]

This controversy has been only lightly litigated, particularly as it pertains to sound recordings. The uncertainty of how these issues will play out in court has seemingly deterred many from initiating a lawsuit.[11] Instead of facing the imposing risk, many record labels

9-4 Copyright Act of 1790.

9-5 17 U.S.C. § 302(a).

9-6 Steve Schlackman, How Mickey Mouse Keeps Changing Copyright Law, Artrepreneur, Oct. 18, 2017, https://artlawjournal.com/mickey-mouse-keeps-changing-copyright-law/.

9-7 Glyn Moody, UK Copyright Extension on Designed Objects Is "Direct Assault" on 3D Printing, ArsTechnica, Aug. 8, 2016, https://arstechnica.com/tech-policy/2016/08/uk-copyright-extension-designed-objects-3d-printing/.

9-8 17 U.S.C. § 203.

9-9 *Id.*

9-10 Larry Rother, Record Industry Braces for Artists' Battles Over Song Rights, N.Y. Times, Aug. 15, 2011, http://www.nytimes.com/2011/08/16/arts/music/springsteen-and-others-soon-eligible-to-recover-song-rights.html?mcubz=0.

9-11 Ed Christman, Reversion Rights: Will 2013 Be a Game Changer?, Dec. 27, 2012, http://www.billboard.com/biz/articles/news/1483926/reversion-rights-will-2013-be-a-game-changer.

and artists have entered negotiations to settle termination rights on a case-by-case basis.[12] The late artist Prince was the subject of one such highly publicized negotiation. Rather than pursuing his termination rights, Prince renegotiated ownership of his sound recordings with Warner Brothers Records in 2014.[13] Prince set a new standard. Now, reclaiming ownership has become the industry standard for top-selling artists. As opposed to the simple royalty rate typically paid in accordance with an artist agreement, an ownership interest generally calls for profit sharing.[14] In renegotiation, the most common scenario would be a 50/50 split between the artist and record label.[15]

As copyrights' lives are extended, so too are their values. These were just some of the many considerations our firm took into account when providing an opinion of the fair market value of a Trust owned by the estate of a deceased musician (see case study 1).

Digital Millennium Copyright Act and Fair Use

The Digital Millennium Copyright Act (DMCA) of 1998 was created to protect Internet service providers from liability for copyright infringement by their users (provided that the Internet service provider meets certain statutory requirements). The Internet service provider must take the following steps when it receives notice of infringing material: implement a policy that leads to termination of users who are repeat infringers and accommodate standard technical measures that are used by copyright owners to identify and protect copyrighted works.[16]

Prior to 1998, if an individual uploaded a video with a popular song playing in the background, the owner of the copyrighted song could commence an infringement action against either the hosting website or the parent. Today, however, because of the DMCA, song owners now notify the website of an infringement, and the website would have to subsequently remove the content.

Further, as addressed in *Lenz v. Universal Music Corp.* in connection with 17 U.S.C. Section 512, copyright owners must consider fair use in good faith before issuing a takedown notice for content posted on the Internet. If the owner does not conduct a fair use analysis prior to sending the website a takedown notice, the copyright owner risks being liable for misrepresentation.[17]

9-12 *Id.*

9-13 Ben Sisario, *Years After a Bitter Fight, Prince and Warner Bros. Make a New Deal*, N.Y. Times, Apr. 18, 2014, https://artsbeat.blogs.nytimes.com/2014/04/18/years-after-a-bitter-fight-prince-and-warner-brothers-make-a-new-deal/?mcubz=0.

9-14 Ed Christman & Andrew Hampp, *What Will Upcoming Contract Negotiations Mean for Taylor Swift, Usher, and Justin Timberlake?*, Nov. 21, 2014, http://www.billboard.com/articles/business/6327443/taylor-swift-usher-justin-timberlake-label-contract-negotiations.

9-15 *Id.*

9-16 DIGITAL MILLENNIUM COPYRIGHT ACT, 1998 Enacted H.R. 2281, 105 Enacted H.R. 2281, 112 Stat. 2860, 105 P.L. 304, 1998 Enacted H.R. 2281, 105 Enacted H.R. 2281.

9-17 *Lenz v. Universal Music Corp.*, No. C 07-3783 JF, 2010 U.S. Dist. LEXIS 16899 (N.D. Cal. Feb. 25, 2010) (Fair use is a defense against a claim of copyright infringement. At the core, "fair use is any copying of copyrighted material done for a limited and 'transformative' purpose, such as to comment upon, criticize, or parody a copyrighted work." In these instances, no permission is required from the copyright owner. Lawmakers kept the definition of fair use vague on purpose. Similar to free speech, "they wanted it to have an expansive meaning that could be open to interpretation).

Copyright Valuation in the "Information Age"

From social interactions to E-commerce, the rise of the Internet has changed our day-to-day lives tremendously. This fluid evolution is particularly noticeable in the music industry. From the onset of illegal downloading and music sharing sites to current disputes over streaming services and artist royalties, the Internet continues to raise many questions. The Internet has also had a similar effect on intellectual property (IP) valuation. While artists use social media and websites to promote, sell, and share songs, the IP consultant uses these platforms and their traffic statistics as analytical tools in litigation situations.

Today, the audience for copyrighted content is global, not bound by any geographic location. However, quantifying the audience or viewership of any copyrighted work or related marketing material can be done with careful analysis and accuracy. This provides IP professionals with a plethora of useful information for analyzing the value of a copyright (or damages).

For example, value apportionment of damages attributable to a copyright infringement—predominantly a quantitative process—can be easier today. However, since the "information age" is relatively new, there are few pieces of literature that exist on the topic of value apportionment. A recent copyright infringement case that involved Marvin Gaye's family against rappers Pharrell Williams, Rob Thicke, and Clifford Harris, which also happens to be one of the biggest payouts in music copyright history, illustrates how greater access to discrete information has made value apportionment more easily quantifiable than ever before (see case study 3).

Copyright Value Measured as Damages

More so than not, copyright material is valued because it is in litigation from misuse. Actual and statutory damages are the two approaches used to establish damages during litigation.[18]

Actual Damages and Infringer's Profits

The first approach to value damages is to calculate the copyright owner's actual damages and any additional profits of the infringer.[19] It is our experience that measuring actual damages or establishing an infringer's true profitability is difficult, if not impossible. One reason for this can be situational differences between the infringer and copyright owner (e.g., geographic location, price points, and business models). Sometimes the infringer reports no profits from the infringing sales, or the copyright owner runs into difficulties proving it suffered from actual damages in any form.

The Copyright Act of 1976 provides no guidance on how to calculate "actual damages." However, courts have construed actual damages to be the degree to which the market value of the work has been destroyed by the infringement.[20]

9-18 17 U.S.C. § 504(a).
9-19 17 U.S.C. § 504(b).
9-20 *In Design v. K-Mart Apparel Corp.*, 13 F.3d 559, 563 (2d Cir. 1994).

Another method for determining the damage to the market value of a work is to identify the revenue the plaintiff would have gained, but for the infringement. The plaintiff has the burden of proving the causal connection between the infringement and the loss of revenue.[21] Once this burden is met, the burden of proof shifts to the defendant to try to show that the revenue would not have been received, even if there was no infringement.[22] Plaintiff's damages are usually limited to the profit from the lost revenue.[23]

Because of different manufacturing and sales costs, the profit margin of the plaintiff and defendant on sales of the infringed work are likely to be different. This is important because a plaintiff is entitled to recover not only actual damages but also the infringer's profits, so long as those profits are not already taken into account in a recovery of plaintiff's lost profits (to avoid double recovery).

Further, in determining plaintiff's lost profits, it is necessary to deduct the increase in costs, if any, that the plaintiff would have incurred if the sales had been made.[24] By contrast, when establishing the infringer's profits, "the copyright owner is required to present proof only of the infringer's gross revenue, and the infringer is required to prove his or her deductible expenses and the elements of profit attributable to factors other than the copyrighted work."[25]

Statutory Damages

The other approach to value damages is to calculate statutory damages. "[T]he copyright owner may elect, at any time before final judgment is rendered, to recover, instead of actual damages and profits, an award of statutory damages for all infringements involved in the action, with respect to any one work, for which any one infringer is liable individually, or for which any two or more infringers are liable jointly and severally, in a sum of not less than $750 or more than $30,000 as the court considers just."[26]

"If a party so demands, a jury must determine the actual amount of statutory damages under § 504(c) in order to preserve 'the substance of the common-law right of trial by jury.'"[27] If the copyright owner proves that the infringement was willful, the court has discretion to increase the award of statutory damages to an amount up to $150,000. Likewise, "[i]n a case where the infringer sustains the burden of proving, and the court finds, that such infringer was not aware and had no reason to believe that his or her acts constituted an infringement of copyright, the court in its discretion may reduce the award of statutory damages to a sum of not less than $200."[28]

The fact finder considers several factors when determining statutory damages: the infringer's knowledge, profits of the infringer, the magnitude of the infringement, and revenues lost by the plaintiff (this list is nonexclusive).[29] Moreover, if multiple works are infringed, the

---

9-21 *Montgomery v. Noga*, 168 F.3d 1282, 1294–95 (11th Cir. 1999); *Data Gen. Corp. v. Grumman Sys. Support Corp.*, 36 F.3d 1147, 1171 (1st Cir. 1994).

9-22 *Harper & Row, Publishers, Inc. v. Nation Enters.*, 471 U.S. 539, 567 (1985).

9-23 *Id.*

9-24 *Taylor v. Meirick*, 712 F.2d 1112 (7th Cir. 1983).

9-25 17 U.S.C. § 504(b).

9-26 17 U.S.C. § 504(c).

9-27 *Feltner v. Columbia Pictures Television, Inc.*, 523 U.S. 340, 345 (1998).

9-28 17 U.S.C. § 504(c)(2).

9-29 *See N.A.S. Import, Corp. v. Chenson Enters., Inc.*, 968 F.2d 250, 252 (2d Cir. 1992); *Video Cafe, Inc. v. De Tal*, 961 F. Supp. 23, 26–27 (D.P.R. 1997).

Figure 9.1 Copyright and File Sharing Cases Between 2010 and 2017

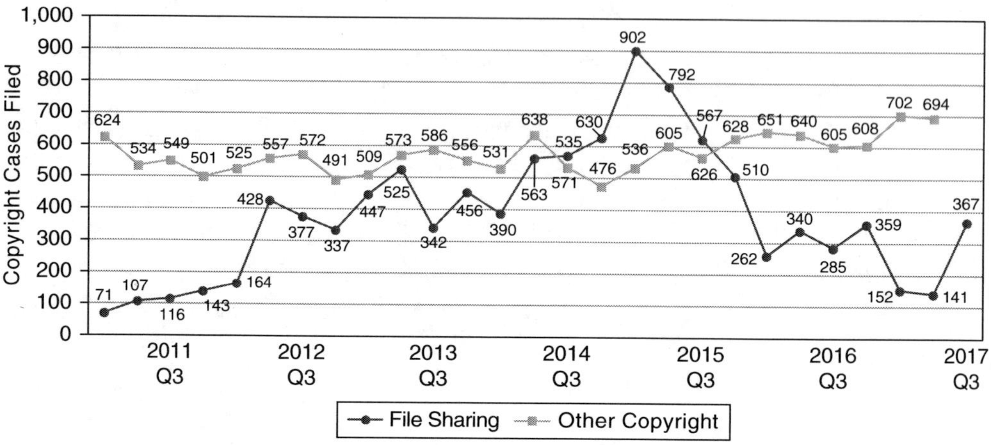

Source: IP Watchdog.[30]

applicable statutory damages can be multiplied by the number of infringed works and can lead potentially to very high damages figures.

This was the situation in a recent copyright damages case that our firm worked on. We assessed the statutory damages caused to a publication company as a result of willful infringement from one of its customers. The case ultimately settled prior to the defendant being at the mercy of the jury (see case study 2).

Recent Trends in Copyright Litigation

Digital technology has expanded the scope and frequency of copyright infringement litigation. The Internet is used regularly, e.g., to pirate software, music files, and videos, leading to actions under the Digital Millennium Copyright Act. The performing rights organization Broadcast Music, Inc. and Sony/ATV filed the most copyright cases, with 1,124 cases and 623 cases, respectively, between 2009 and 2016.

Figure 9.1 demonstrates file sharing cases and all other, more traditional cases. "From its apogee in Q1 of 2015 at over 900 cases, the number of file sharing cases filed each quarter declined steadily and rapidly until Q2 of 2016, which saw only 262 cases. Since then, the number of cases has been less predictable—Q4 2017 (367 cases) returns to the levels seen in late 2016, after two low quarters of around 150 cases."[31]

Textile lawsuits have also been on the rise in recent years.[32] These cases typically take form as copyright trolls "salt" textile patterns in China and India. Subsequently, these

9-30 Steve Brachmann, *Copyright Litigation in 2016 Saw Rise in Textile Plaintiffs, Decline in File Sharing Cases*, IPWatchDog, Feb. 15, 2017, http://www.ipwatchdog.com/2017/02/15/copyright-litigation-textile-plaintiffs-decline-file-sharing-cases/id=78287/.

9-31 Brian Howard, *Lex Machina Q4 2017 End of the Year Litigation Update*, LEXMACHINA, Jan. 16, 2018, https://lexmachina.com/lex-machina-q4-litigation-update/.

9-32 Steve Brachmann, *Copyright Litigation in 2016 Saw Rise in Textile Plaintiffs, Decline in File Sharing Cases*, IPWATCHDOG, Feb. 15, 2017, http://www.ipwatchdog.com/2017/02/15/copyright-litigation-textile-plaintiffs-decline-file-sharing-cases/id=78287/.

Figure 9.2 Cases Terminated Between 2009 and 2016

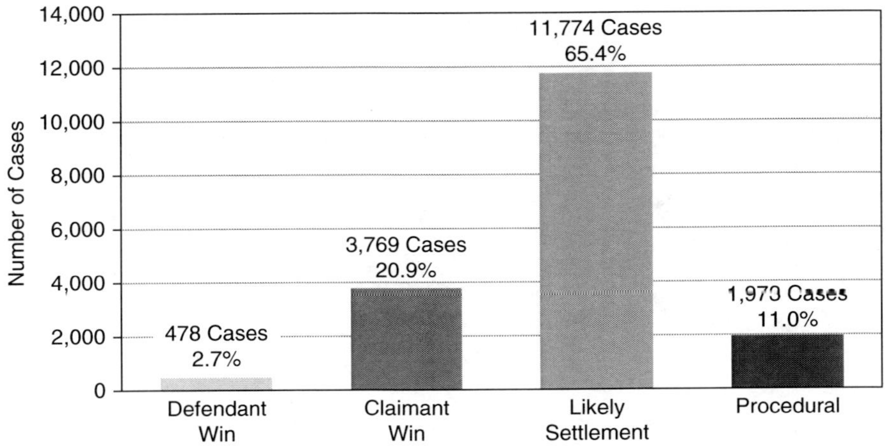

Source: IPWatchDog.[33]

patterns show up a year or two later as finished products on racks of retailers such as Macy's, which ultimately become the target of a copyright infringement suit by the actual copyright holder/troll.

In legal proceedings from 2009 to 2016, fair use findings were a much more likely resolution when resolved in a pretrial summary judgment; cases that did reach trial were much more likely to end with a finding of no fair use (Figure 9.2).[34] Further, default judgment rates are much higher in copyright litigation given the ease of duplicating a copyright versus a patent, for example. "It's a lot easier to manufacture something in a fly-by-night operation that runs afoul of copyright or trademark laws than patent laws. Often, it's people from other countries who choose not to come to the United States and fight a suit or, at a minimum, decide to ignore the court process. That's a lot easier to do when you're a small-time operator instead of a large manufacturing company infringing a patent."[35]

Of the cases resolved, the most likely scenario was settlement, which accounted for 11,774 cases, or almost two-thirds of all case resolutions in copyright litigation.[36]

Of the $608 million worth of damages awarded in default judgments from 2009 to 2016, a significant portion may not get collected, as many parties will refuse to respond to court procedures. Interestingly, Disney Enterprises, Inc. received the greatest total damages from all copyright suits between 2009 and 2016, with $296 million in damages awards through 50 cases. Statutory damages for willful copyright infringement resolved through consent judgments, default judgments, judicial actions, and jury accounted for $26 million, $373 million, $43 million, and $52 million, respectively (Figure 9.3).[37]

9-33 Steve Brachmann, *Copyright Litigation in 2016 Saw Rise in Textile Plaintiffs, Decline in File Sharing Cases*, IPWATCHDOG, Feb. 15, 2017, http://www.ipwatchdog.com/2017/02/15/copyright-litigation-textile-plaintiffs-decline-file-sharing-cases/id=78287/.

9-34 *See* Brian Howard, *Lex Machina Q4 2017 End of the Year Litigation Update*, LEXMACHINA, Jan. 16, 2018, https://lexmachina.com/lex-machina-q4-litigation-update/.

9-35 *Id.*

9-36 *Id.*

9-37 *Id.*

Figure 9.3 Judgment Types Between 2009 and 2016

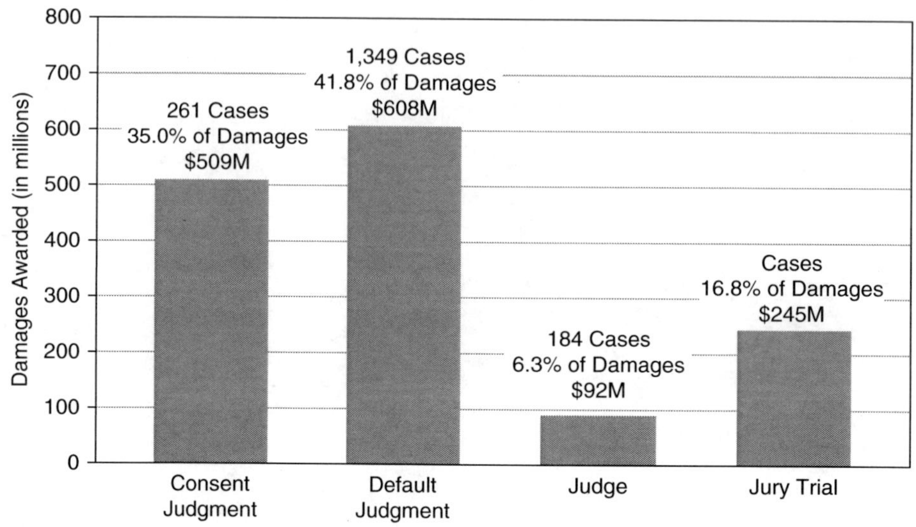

Source: IPWatchDog.[38]

Case Study 1: Valuation of a Musician's Estate (Released Songs Only)

Our firm was retained by an institution to provide an opinion of the fair market value of a Trust owned by the estate of a deceased musician. In dispute for estate tax purposes, the analysis is always conducted as of the date of death. In other words, only information available prior to the musician's death can be used.

Also, the analysis should be conducted under the fair market value standard, which assumes a rational hypothetical buyer or investor (Rational Investor) has the means and motivation to maximize its investment value by fully exploiting the IP rights in the future. We therefore assume a Rational Investor would have the motivation, knowledge, skill, and infrastructure to maximize the exploitation of the asset.

For simplicity, the analysis will be limited to the artist's songs that had been released domestically (the Released Songs) over the course of his/her lifetime.

Key Considerations

Copyright Reversion

Given the uncertainty surrounding copyright reversion (mentioned above), we assumed any song with a significant royalty stream would be recaptured domestically at the earliest possible time. Internationally, copyright reversion is not universally acknowledged.

9-38 *Id.*

Figure 9.4 Annual Percentage Change in Sales After Death

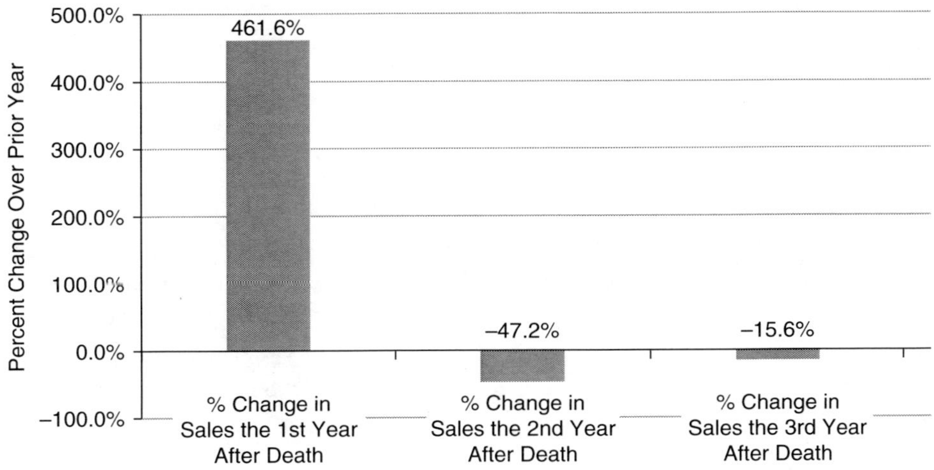

Postmortem Sales Spike

Historically, musicians have experienced a short-term spike in album sales following their death. Numerous factors could be responsible for this sales spike, including increased media coverage and the emotional response among consumers. To fully capture this phenomenon in our analysis, we reviewed the album and digital track sales of seven comparable musicians.[39] On average, album sales increased roughly 462% in the first year after death (Figure 9.4). Subsequently, sales declined at an average rate of 47% in the second year and 16% the third year.

Often, an artist will have music that is released posthumously. Postmortem releases can even be some of their most successful, such as The Notorious B.I.G.'s *Life After Death*, published just days after he was fatally shot in 1997.

Qualitative factors must also be considered as they can greatly impact the magnitude of the spike in sales after a celebrity's death. Some of these factors include:

- The nature of the celebrity's death (i.e., accidental or natural),
- The celebrity's age when he/she died,
- To which demographics an individual celebrity appealed (e.g., the genre of music, average age of fan base, the cultural diversity of the fan base),
- Public perception of the celebrity prior to death (local, national, and global popularity),
- Depth of celebrity performer portfolio (to include, but not limited to, quantity of songs, albums, movies, and similar components), and
- The economic climate at the time of the celebrity's death.

9-39 "Nielsen compiles data from more than 39,000 retail outlets globally to help record labels, publishers, artists, artist management and performance rights organizations understand what albums, singles and music videos people are buying, and where they're buying them."

Valuation Methodologies

When valuing IP, we consider each valuation methodology—the income approach, the cost approach, and the market approach. However, since we had the historical earnings for the assets contained in the Trust and sales data of comparable artists, we felt confident the income method was most appropriate.

Valuation of the Released Songs

At the time of death, the Trust included 150 songs written by the artist. All of the songs were written after 1978. According to the U.S. Copyright Office, "[a] work that was created (fixed in tangible form for the first time) on or after January 1, 1978, is automatically protected from the moment of its creation and is ordinarily given a term enduring for the author's life plus an additional 70 years after the author's death." Therefore, the Released Songs have been valued with a remaining life of 70 years from the date of death. We did not anticipate any reversion or recapture rights since the artist's heirs inherited the copyrights after death.

In the immediate years following the artist's death, we projected royalties to increase based on the postmortem sales spike experienced by other reasonably comparable artists. We were provided with consolidated data regarding the historical royalties generated by the Released Songs for the two-year period prior to the artist's death. Average annual royalties generated by the Released Songs for this two-year period equaled $1,000,000.

After taking the postmortem sales spike into account, we projected royalties to decline toward the level of royalties generated in the 12 months prior to the artist's death. In the second year after death, comparable celebrities saw a higher percentage decline in sales than the third year after death. We assumed annual sales would continue this trend and gradually return to pre-death levels over a 10-year horizon.

We estimated an annual decline of 10% in years 4 through 6 and 5% in years 7 through 10. This decline in sales aligns with the trend identified in our postmortem sales spike analysis and gradually brings sales to the level they were at prior to the artist's death (Figure 9.5).

For years 11 through 70, we projected royalties to decline at a rate of 2.8% annually. This represents the compound annual growth rate in domestic recorded music revenues for the 15 years prior to the artist's death. Historical industry revenues are summarized in Figure 9.5. A discount rate of 9.72% was used to reflect the long-term low-risk stability of this asset class.

Figure 9.5 U.S. Recorded Music Revenues (Millions of Dollars)

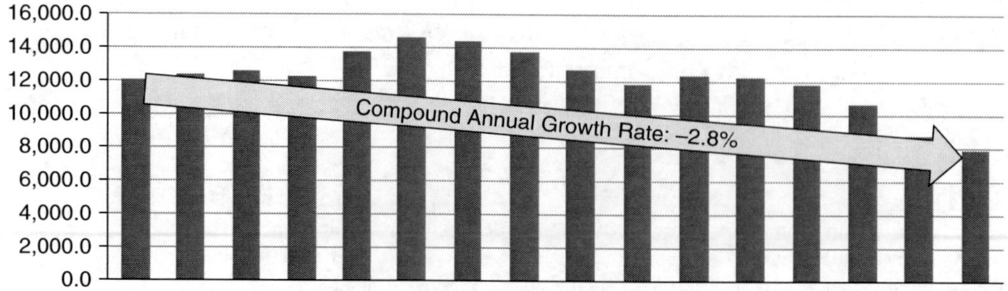

Figure 9.6 Discounted Cash Flow Analysis of the Released Songs

	Year	1	2	3	4	5	6	7	8	9	10	11 ...	69	70
Projected Royalties		561,620	296,550	250,339	225,305	202,774	182,497	173,372	164,703	156,468	148,645	144,420	27,127	26,356
Revenue Growth		461.6%	–47.2%	–15.6%	–10.0%	–10.0%	–10.0%	–5.0%	–5.0%	–5.0%	–5.0%	–2.8%	–2.8%	–2.8%
Discount Period (midpoint)		0.5	1.5	2.5	3.5	4.5	5.5	6.5	7.5	8.5	9.5	10.5	68.5	69.5
Discount Factor @	9.72%	0.955	0.870	0.793	0.723	0.659	0.601	0.547	0.499	0.455	0.414	0.378	0.002	0.002
Present Value of Royalties		**536,177**	**258,045**	**198,544**	**162,866**	**133,599**	**109,592**	**94,893**	**82,165**	**71,145**	**61,602**	**54,552**	**47**	**42**

Value of the Released Songs	**2,184,918**

Conclusion

Using the forecasts outlined above, we calculated the net present value of reportable royalties from the artist's Released Songs to be $2,184,918. This became the basis of our concluded value of $2.2 million, as the revenue projections included terminal value at 70 years, as seen in Figure 9.6.

Case Study 2: Statutory Copyright Damages

Our firm was retained by a leading provider of research, analysis, and data in the energy sector to provide consulting services in relation to litigation against a private equity firm illegally utilizing and disseminating one of their popular publications (the Publication). For this analysis, we will refer to the plaintiff as ABC Corp. and the defendant as XYZ LP.

Background

ABC Corp. has been producing energy sector–related publications, reports, analyses, and data for more than 50 years. The people and businesses that follow ABC Corp.'s publications have a strong interest in the oil and gas industries; these include bankers, investors, stock market analysts, traders, and other industries.

An employee at XYZ LP purchased a single subscription of the Publication. For approximately 10 years (the Infringement Period), the employee either had a single-copy subscription to the Publication or was part of a group consisting of XYZ LP employees, managers, senior management, and officers who purchased the Publication subscription at a group rate. Throughout this time period, the employees at XYZ LP routinely forwarded copies of the Publication via email or shared login information. During the Infringement Period, there were more than 1,500 known instances of illegally forwarding or distributing copies of the Publication.

In addition to forwarding copies of the Publication to individuals without paid subscriptions within XYZ LP, employees at the private equity firm forwarded copies of 500 issues to third parties. Despite numerous notices, in an effort to avoid detection, XYZ LP employees altered the copyright management information of 400 of those 500 issues by changing the file name of the Publication pdf. The minimum statutory damages that ABC Corp. would be eligible for is $1,216,500. This was calculated by multiplying the non-willful

Figure 9.7 Number of Infringing Publications Forwarded

Year	Issues Published	Approximate Instances of Electronic Forwarding	Instances of Electronic Forwarding as a % of Issues Published
2005	251	5	2%
2006	248	34	14%
2007	251	222	88%
2008	252	171	68%
2009	254	206	81%
2010	256	214	84%
2011	257	213	83%
2012	254	227	89%
2013	252	237	94%
2014	97	93	96%
Total	**2,372**	**1,622**	**68%**

minimum damages per infringement ($750) by the number of known issues that were forwarded (1,622). Conversely, the maximum statutory damages that ABC Corp. would be eligible for is $243,300,000. This was calculated by multiplying the willful maximum damages per infringement ($150,000) by the number of known issues that were forwarded (1,622) (Figure 9.7).

To determine a reasonable damages amount, we analyzed the key facts and value drivers pertaining to the case, such as the infringer's knowledge, profits of the infringer, the magnitude of the infringement, and revenues lost by the plaintiff.

Key Considerations

- XYZ LP had a subscription to the Publication for 10 years. During the Infringement Period, there were numerous infringements of the copyrighted publications that XYZ admitted to.
- ABC Corp. had wide-ranging copyright notices, warnings, and disclaimers that explicitly stated that their content is copyrighted and outlined the uses that were prohibited.
- XYZ LP tried to circumvent the copyright terms to avoid detection by modifying them when forwarding and/or distributing the Publication to third parties.
- Furthermore, during the Infringement Period, XYZ LP successfully managed multiple energy-related funds. The XYZ LP Funds outperformed the S&P 500 from 2 times to 7 times and from 2 times to 4 times on an annual basis. The firm also cumulatively collected roughly $600 million in investment management fees. The management fees grew at a compound annual growth rate of 34% during the 10-year Infringement Period.
- In light of the willful copying and distribution of the Publication and its valuable copyrighted sister publications, and the exceptional performance of the XYZ LP Funds, we reasonably selected a lower bound of willful damages per infringement ($30,001) and applied it to the 1,622 known instances of forwarding. This results in calculated damages of approximately $49 million (Figure 9.8).

Figure 9.8 Range of Possible Statutory Damages

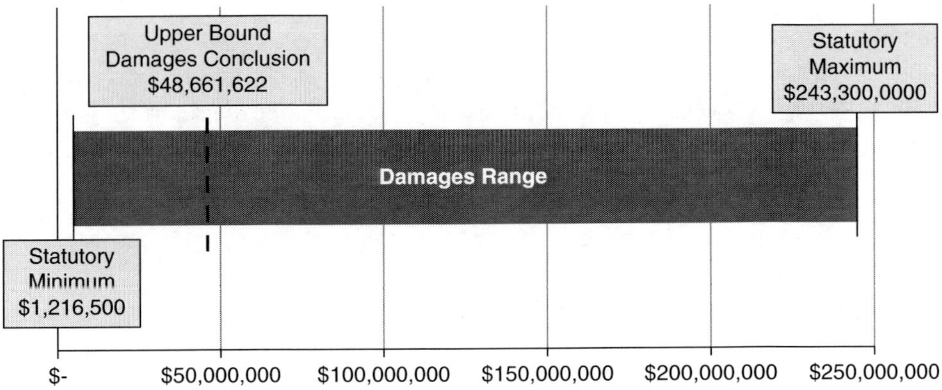

- Potentially, there are additional statutory damages under the Digital Millennium Copyright Act, up to $10 million. These stem from XYZ LP's attempt to circumvent copyright protection by altering and/or modifying copyright management information in order to avoid detection.

We also calculated actual damages to ABC Corp., which amounted to slightly more than $2 million. ABC Corp. elected to pursue statutory damages, which was logical. In the final event, a settlement was reached before the legal process ran its full course.

Case Study 3: Value Apportionment—Marvin Gaye[40]

In the case *Williams et al. v. Bridgeport Music Inc. et al.*, the main issue from an expert witness point of view was not if copyright infringement occurred, rather what portion of the damages was attributable to the infringement and what portion was attributable to other factors (such as the heavy promotion and marketing and the infamous music video). As is the case in many value apportionment cases, the alleged infringer expended both human and financial capital in combination with the infringed IP.

Case Background

The birth of the case was the result of publicized charges by the Gaye family, alleging that the song "Blurred Lines" resembled certain musical elements of Marvin Gaye's 1977 "Got to Give it Up." The three artists—Pharrell Williams, Robin Thicke, and Clifford Harris, Jr.—then went on the offensive and filed a complaint stating that, "by alleging that their work had the same feel or sound as the earlier song, the Gaye family was trying to claim ownership of an entire genre rather than a specific work."[41] Ultimately, the case would go to trial.

9-40 Doug Bania, *Apportioning Copyright Damages: The Case of "Blurred Lines,"* JOURNAL OF INTELLECTUAL PROPERTY & LAW PRACTICE, 2015, http://www.experts.com/content/articles/Nevium1-Doug-Bania-Journal-Intellectual-Property.pdf.

9-41 *Id.*

Between March 2013 and August 2013, the music videos and the single for "Blurred Lines" were released, and sales peaked. A lot of the media attention that the hit song received was regarding the raciness of the accompanying music videos. Moreover, public appearances, live performances on popular shows, and provocative social media marketing by the artists also added to the notoriety. Universal Music Group (UMG)—a global leader in music recording, publishing, and merchandising—also started promoting the song. More than 90% of sales of "Blurred Lines" had occurred by the end of January 2014.

Key Considerations[42]

Williams' and Thicke's team argued that the following noncopyright factors directly contributed to the success of "Blurred Lines":

- *Awareness created by the music video:* A positive correlation between the number of viewer reviews of the video on iTunes and the SoundScan sales data indicates that the video made a substantial contribution to the success of "Blurred Lines" (Figure 9.9)
- *Marketing activities:* UMG allegedly invested $3.6 million in marketing efforts. For example, after the company arranged a performance of the song on *The Voice*, sales increased from 70,000 to more than 200,000 units.
- *Radio play and media attention:* When the radio history for "Blurred Lines" is compared to SoundScan data, it appears that initial radio spins were quickly followed by sales growth.

Figure 9.9 Correlation Between Marketing Events and SoundScan Sales Data

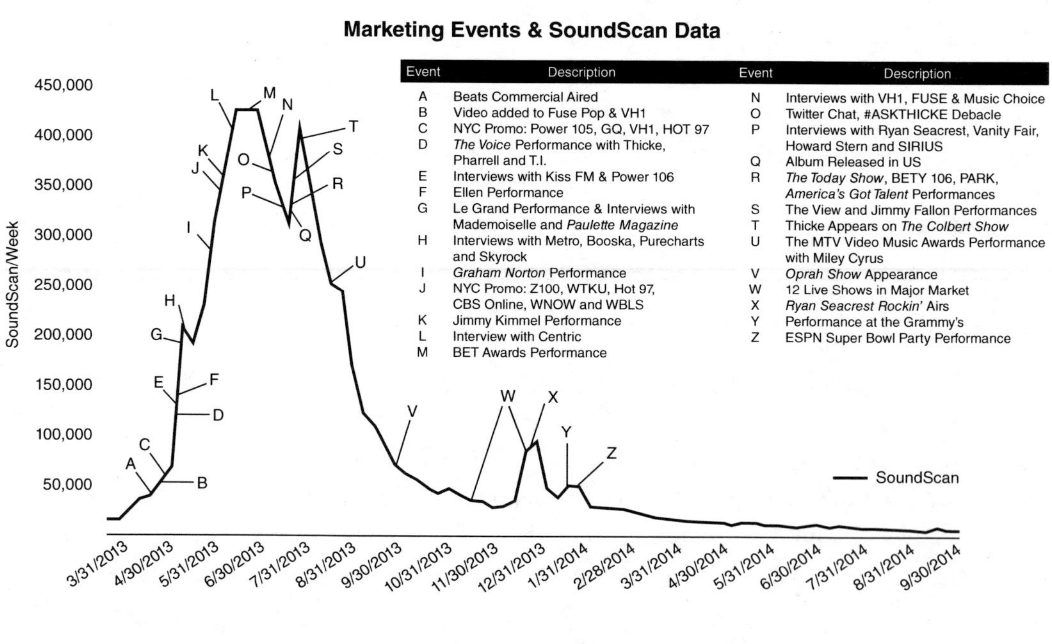

9-42 *Williams v. Bridgeport Music, Inc.*, No. LA CV13-06004 JAK (AGRx), 2014 U.S. Dist. LEXIS 182240 (C.D. Cal. Oct. 30, 2014).

Figure 9.10 Correlation Between Social Media Activity and Volume of Sales

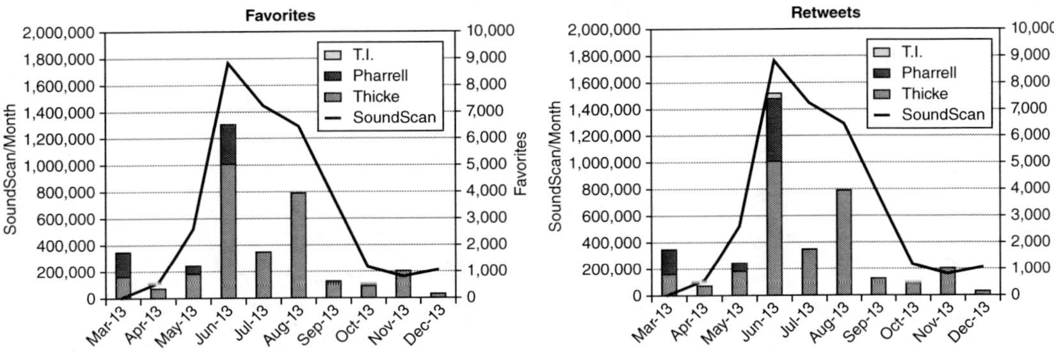

- *Social media activities:* There was a strong correlation between social media activity related to "Blurred Lines" and the volume of sales on SoundScan (Figure 9.10).
- *Awards and promos:* Sales increased as a result of Thicke's and Williams' efforts on events such as the BET awards.

Outcome

In spite of the defendant's counter claims and in spite of the time and promotional dollars they spent, the defendants had a basic problem: their song sounded much like Marvin Gaye's earlier song "Got to Give It Up."

In the end, a jury found Thicke and Williams guilty of unlawfully copying "Got to Give It Up" and ordered the pair to pay the Gaye family \$7.3 million (but the judge later decreased the figure to \$5.3 million, while awarding the Gaye family 50% of the song's future royalties).[43]

While it would be impossible to quantify with perfect accuracy the contributions of all noncomposition copyright factors to the success of the song, the above analysis does illustrate that the Gaye family should only be entitled to a portion of the financial success of "Blurred Lines" since the musical elements of the song's composition played only one part in its success. According to the expert on the case, this was perhaps why the judge decided to reduce the damages to \$5.3 million.

Conclusion

In today's digital world, copyrights are playing a bigger role in our daily lives. Copyright law in the developed world has extended the lives of creative works and is more rigorous today than ever before. This has resulted in higher values for copyrights and greater emphasis and importance on performing accurate valuations. We don't expect these trends to change any time soon with the emergence of virtual reality and artificial intelligence technologies that will affect copyright configurations, usage, value, and litigation over the next few decades.

9-43 *Id.*

Chapter 10

Trademark Litigation: Trends and Cases with Contributions from Pierce Urban

In this chapter we first discuss the trends in global trademark applications as well as litigation. We then continue with an overview of sensory trademarks, trademark layering and brand extension, and how these strategies directly affect value. Case studies follow to conclude the chapter.

Registration and Litigation Activity

Trademark applications have seen a constant increase over the past 26 years. Globally, from 1990 to 2016, there was an increase of 135% in trademark applications.[1] As the number continues to rise, the once static definition of a trademark is gradually adapting to the advances in technology and the creativity of the human mind. Figure 10.1 summarizes the number of trademark applications by direct residents of each country.

The China Effect

Recently, China has been rapidly increasing its trademark activity. From 2008 to 2015, China increased its trademark applications by 1.4 million, or 238%.[2] As mentioned in chapter 6, the useful life of most patents is significantly less than 20 years. As innovation continues, older patents often become obsolete quickly, especially in this era of technological advancement. Trademarks, however, have an indefinite life span (if they are in use), and as trademarks

---

10-1 The World Bank, *Trademark Applications, Total,* https://data.worldbank.org/indicator/IP.TMK.TOTL?end=2016&start=1990.

10-2 The World Bank, *Trademark Applications, Direct Resident,* https://www.data.worldbank.org (based on internal calculations).

Figure 10.1 Trademark Applications by Direct Resident

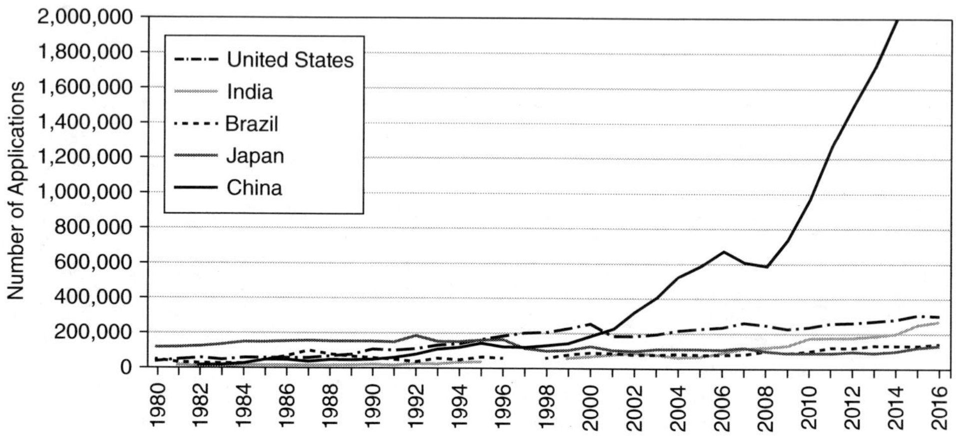

Source: The World Bank. https://www.data.worldbank.org.[3]

age, their value often increases, which is a major factor in China's shift to trademark applications. Figure 10.2 illustrates China's recent emphasis on trademarks.

In China, there is "growing evidence of the brand value that can be created by registering trademarks. . . . Awareness of the rising value of Chinese brands is growing in all sectors of society and the economy. In 2012, just one Chinese brand appeared in global consulting firm Millward Brown's list of the world's top 100 brands. In 2017, 13 Chinese companies are featured."[4] China's enormous increase in trademark applications is promoting an innovative and competitive environment for brand development and financial growth.

The number of trademark litigation cases is also rising as the number of trademark applications increases. From 1993 to 2017, the number of contested trademark cases increased by 223%.[5] If this trend continues to increase at a compound annual growth rate of 5.5% per year (based on data for 1993–2017), the expected number of contested trademark cases in 2020 will be just under 3,800.[6] Figure 10.3 shows the number of contested trademark cases filed from 1993 to 2017.

Figure 10.2 Patent and Trademark Applications in China

	2015	2016	Growth (%)
Patent Applications	2,887,300	3,127,900	8.30%
Trademark Applications	6,013,200	6,997,600	16.40%

Source: World Intellectual Property Organization. http://www.wipo.int/pressroom/en/articles/2017/article_0013.html.[7]

10-3 *Id.*

10-4 World Intellectual Property Organization, *Trademarks and China's Business Reform Agenda,* http://www.wipo.int/wipo_magazine/en/2017/04/article_0005.html.

10-5 U.S. Patent and Trademark Office, *USPTO Annual Reports,* https://www.uspto.gov/about-us/performance-and-planning/uspto-annual-reports (based on internal calculations of USPTO data).

10-6 *Id.*

10-7 World Intellectual Property Organization, *China Tops Patent, Trademark, Design Filing in 2016,* http://www.wipo.int/pressroom/en/articles/2017/article_0013.html.

Figure 10.3 Number of Contested Trademark Cases Filed, from 1993–2017

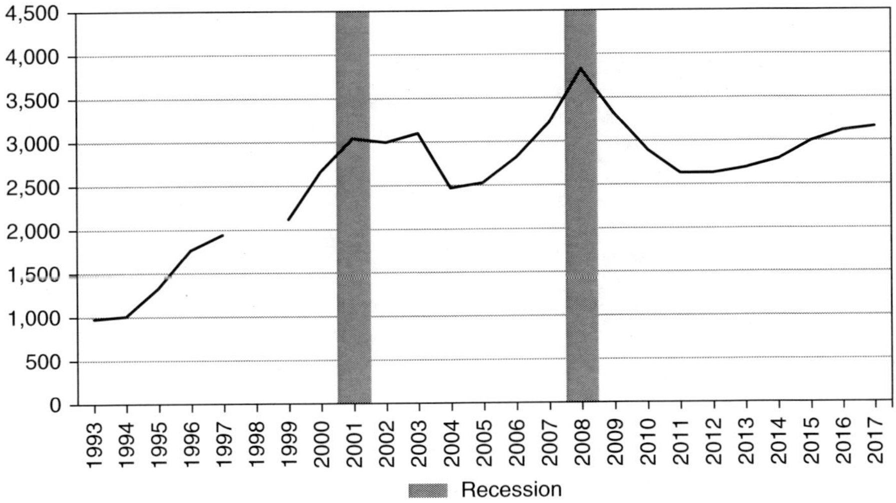

Source: USPTO.[8]

Statutory Damages

For cases that involve the use of a counterfeit trademark "in connection with the sale, offering for sale, or distribution of goods or services, the plaintiff may elect, at any time before final judgment is rendered by the trial court, to recover, instead of actual damages and profits under subsection (a), an award of statutory damages for any such use in connection with the sale, offering for sale, or distribution of goods or services in the amount of—

1. not less than $1,000 or more than $200,000 per counterfeit mark per type of goods or services sold, offered for sale, or distributed, as the court considers just; or
2. if the court finds that the use of the counterfeit mark was willful, not more than $2,000,000 per counterfeit mark per type of goods or services sold, offered for sale, or distributed, as the court considers just."[9]

In trademark litigation, "default judgments happen frequently, often result[ing] in findings of a Lanham Act violation, which account for 68.0% of all Lanham Act violation findings. Consent judgments are less frequent, but account for another 19.5% of all Lanham Act violation findings."[10]

10-8 *Id.*

10-9 Cornell Law School, *Legal Information Institute,* https://www.law.cornell.edu/uscode/text/15/1117.

10-10 Lex Machina, *Lex Machina Trademark Litigation Report 2016,* http://pages.lexmachina.com/rs/098-SHZ-498/images/LexMachina%202016%20TM%20Litigation%20Report.pdf.

Figure 10.4 Top Parties by Damages Won: January 2009–March 2016 in Cases Filed and January 2005–March 2016 Damage Awards

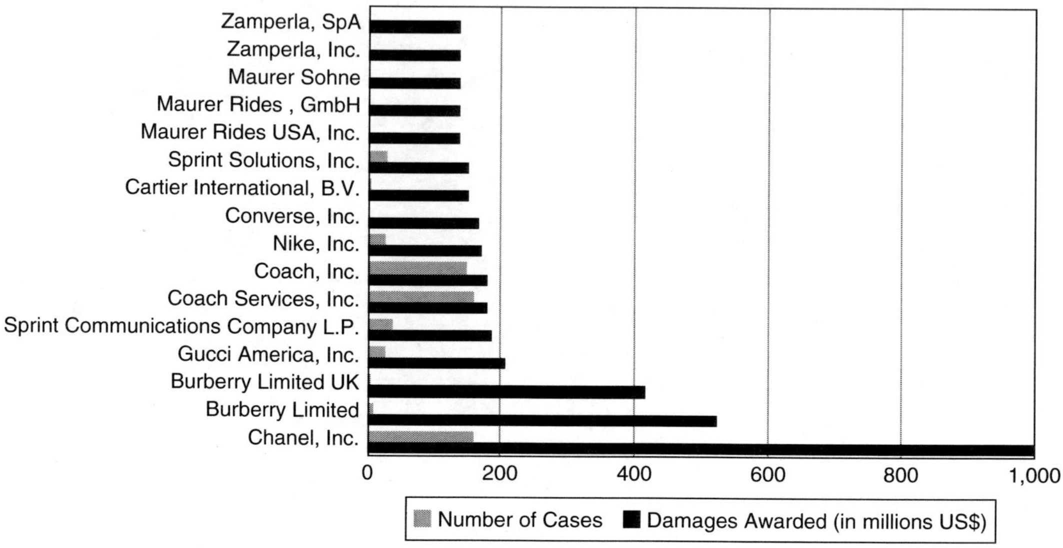

Source: Lex Machina Trademark Litigation Report 2016.[11]

Trademark ownership/validity (the party enforcing the valid trademark or trade dress and owns the right to do so) is frequently "resolved on consent judgment (30.0% of those findings), while no ownership/validity was most found on summary judgment (62.2% of those findings)."[12] Figure 10.4 shows the parties with the highest cumulative damages awards.

"Damages in trademark litigation come almost entirely from default judgments, and a majority of the rest come from consent judgments. Of damages resulting from decisions on the merits, juries have awarded more damages than judges. Chanel has won the most damages ($1 billion) followed by Burberry Limited ($523 million), and Gucci ($208 million)."[13] When consent and default judgments are omitted, the damages awarded substantially decrease, as evidenced by the awards given to the parties as shown in Figure 10.5.

Trademark Evolution: Sensory Marks

New types of trademarks are beginning to appear, which we believe has a direct connection to the increasing prevalence of trademark litigation. As trademarks evolve and new categories and uses of trademarks emerge, specifically sensory trademarks, trademark litigation is well positioned to continue its upward trend.

10-11 *Id.*
10-12 *Id.*
10-13 *Id.*

Figure 10.5 Top Parties by Damages Won (Omitting Consent and Default Judgments), January 2009–March 2016 in Cases Filed January 2005–March 2016

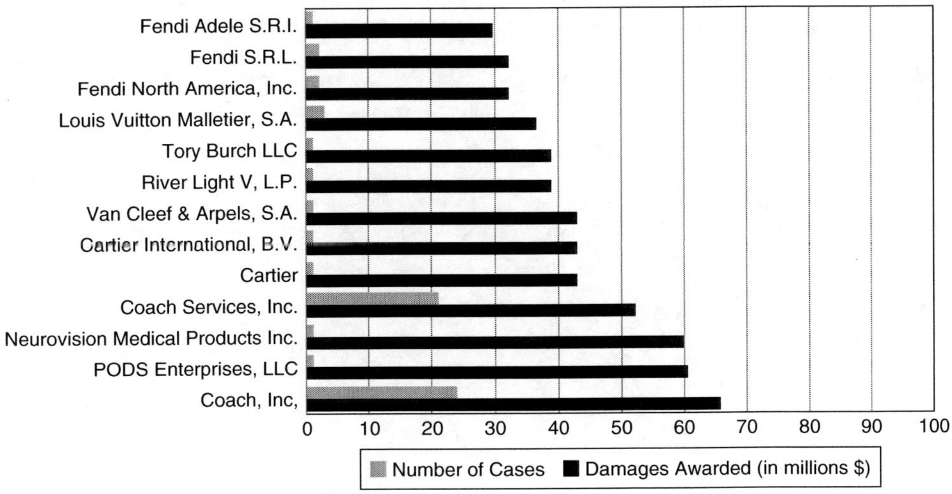

Source: Lex Machina Trademark Litigation Report 2016.[14]

Over the years, trademarks have developed beyond printed and visual presentation and now entail:

- Smells,
- Textures, — Sensory Marks
- Sounds,
- Colors, and
- Three-dimensional shapes.

Scent marks, color marks, and sound marks must prove nonfunctionality and identify the source of the product.

To register a sensory mark, one or more of the following must be provided (depending on the country of registration):

- Proof of distinctiveness (measured by "secondary meaning" criteria);
- A visual drawing of the mark (graphic representation);
- A written, detailed description of the mark; and
- A sample of the product using the distinguished mark.

Scent Marks: Fresh Cut Grass

Olfaction is almost entirely subjective, making it challenging to trademark a specific scent, as each person has the ability to interpret a smell in their own way. The process of trademarking

10-14 *Id.*

a smell requires a thorough description of the smell itself. In 1999, the tennis ball "fresh cut grass" scent failed to gain recognition as a trademark. Although the fresh cut grass smell is a distinct, familiar scent, the European Union Intellectual Property Office mandated a graphical representation. In this case, the "drawing" of the fresh cut grass scent was demonstrated through a chemical formula. It was decided that the graphic representation was not adequately intelligible and therefore could not be trademarked.[15]

Color Marks: Louboutin

As mentioned briefly in chapter 2, Louboutin's red sole shoe gained recognition as a registered color trademark, limited, however, to the red lacquer on the soles of the shoes. Aside from the clear distinctiveness of the red soles, proving identity of the source, Louboutin satisfied multiple factors in determining secondary meaning including millions in advertising costs and a large volume of sales.

Sound Marks: NBC

NBC holds one of the original sound trademarks, a sequence of chimes, applied for in 1970 and registered in 1971. Sound marks are either graphically represented by musical notation or concise description, such as stomping a foot twice on concrete. NBC's trademark utilizes musical notation for their chime.

Texture Marks: Louis Vuitton

Fashion designer Louis Vuitton trademarked a textured pattern for its line of handbags and other leather-related products. The texture is described as a "pebble grained texture."[16] A common obstacle in texture trademarking is that the applied mark cannot be an ordinary feature of the good, for instance, a basketball.

Trademark Sub-Brands and Brand Extension

As trademarks extend into additional classes, the owner assumes more control of the overall brand name and decreases the risk of future infringement and litigation. Revenue from sub-brands increases the value of the parent brand, in turn, increasing the value of the overall trademark portfolio. Nevertheless, if a sub-brand is unsuccessful, it begins to dilute the parent brand, lowering perceived value and potentially harming the overall value of the trademark portfolio.

There are three main questions that determine whether a trademark holds value. First, is the trademark unique, does it differentiate itself from surrounding names, logos, products, and similar items within the same class? Second, do people express interest in using the trademark and, if so, how much? Third, are other parties willing to license or purchase the name

---

10-15 Luca Escoffier & Arnold Jin, *To Scent, or Not to Scent, That Is the Question: A Comparative Analysis of Olfactory Trademarks in the EU and US as Good Brand Opportunities for SMEs*, WORLD INTELLECTUAL PROPERTY ORGANIZATION.

10-16 International Trademark Association, A Nontraditional Spectrum, http://www.inta.org/INTABulletin/Pages/ANontraditionalPerSpectrum.aspx.

for a product in a different trademark class? Each question adds more value than the last; a yes to all three questions potentially indicates a very valuable trademark.

As an example of positive responses to those three questions, a brand extension strategy can add significant value to trademarks. A brand portfolio consists of a single parent brand and one or more sub-brands under the parent brand. When companies add additional successful sub-brands to their brand portfolio, the value of the IP and the company often increases in unison.

Ralph Lauren and Disney demonstrate brand extension strategies. These two companies take full advantage of the ability to register trademarks in multiple classes. Both companies hold numerous trademark registrations for related and sub-brands attached to their core brand name. Ralph Lauren alone has more than 15 sub-brands that cover multiple products and trademark classes with various consumer price points. Figure 10.6 lists many of the current Ralph Lauren brands.

Disney also continues to expand their core business and brand to many sub-brands including those listed in Figure 10.7.

Expansion into multiple products and services or different price points within the same industry allows companies to capture a wider customer base or increase market share. Rather than having sales be isolated to a single item or industry, diversification and brand extension allow companies to generate revenue from various sources while simultaneously increasing value of their brand portfolio. Companies not only earn additional income from their sub-brands, they also gain trademark value from increased revenue, recognition, and reputation of the goods or services being provided.

How do you value Ralph Lauren's and Disney's intellectual property? Do you value only the parent brand or each sub-brand? Most importantly, how do you value a sub-brand without incorporating the core brand, and which methods are used specifically for this purpose?

Figure 10.6 Ralph Lauren Sub-Brands

Men	Women	Men and Women
• Polo Ralph Lauren	• RL Collection	• RLX A
• Black Label	• RL Black Label	• RRL
• Purple Label	• RL Blue Label	• RL Tennis
• Polo Golf	• Lauren by Ralph	• Pink Pony
• Polo Jeans Co.	• RL Golf	• RL Denim Supply
• Polo Denim	• Lauren Jeans Co.	• RL Home
• Lauren by Ralph Lauren		
• Ralph by Ralph Lauren		

Source: http://www.ebay.com/gds/A-Guide-About-The-Ralph-Lauren-Brands-/10000000010098354/g.html.[17]

10-17 http://www.ebay.com/gds/A-Guide-About-The-Ralph-Lauren-Brands-/10000000010098354/g.html.

Figure 10.7 Disney Sub-Brands

Media Networks
- Disney ABC Television Group
  - Disney Channels
    - Disney Junior
    - Disney XD

Parks and Resorts
- Disneyland & Walt Disney World
- Disney Cruise Line

Consumer Products
- Disney Licensing
- Disney Publishing Worldwide
- Disney Store

Studio Entertainment
- Walt Disney Motion Pictures
- Walt Disney Animation Studios
- Lucasfilm/Disney
- Pixar Animation Studios/Disney
- Disney Theatrical Group
  - Disney Theatrical Production
  - Disney on Ice
- Disney Music Group
  - Walt Disney Records
  - Disney Music Publishing

Interactive
- Disney.com
- Disney Infinity

Source: Walt Disney–Unstoppable Media Conglomerate.[18]

The most common methods to value the overall brand portfolio and how to apportion value to each sub-brand are covered in chapters 3 and 4.

Trademark Layering

Trademark layering occurs when multiple trademark owners are using and/or licensing their rights together to build consumer interest in a product. This typically occurs in team sports and with entertainment properties in a co-branding situation, such as a major movie or music event. Examples include:

- The National Football League (NFL),
- NASCAR, and
- Harry Potter movies.

NASCAR handles IP differently than any other sport. In NASCAR, each trademark holder manages their own individual trademarks. The NFL, by contrast, tries to control the IP of the team logos, current players, and even retired players, but each has central points of contact for licensing deals. Note, however, that in today's changing environment in professional sports, most NFL athletes retain at least some authority over their own rights of publicity.

NASCAR manages the use of their trademarks through each layer of the driver, the team, sponsors, the car manufacturer, and NASCAR. Someone who wishes to license one or more

10-18 *Walt Disney–Unstoppable Media Conglomerate,* https://storify.com/sdereje2/disney.

of these trademarks must approach and secure license rights individually, and each license requires a different royalty rate to be paid. "Each race team will typically deliver its own team rights and the rights for its drivers, which are usually secured with the driver's services agreements."[19] Other rights must be negotiated with NASCAR and other trademark holders.

The following case studies demonstrate trademark infringement and how damages are apportioned to the trademark owner for valuation and mediation purposes.

Case Study 1: Chevron Corporation v. Steven Donziger et al.

Our firm was retained on behalf of the Chevron Corporation to provide an opinion regarding the value of the Chevron, Texaco, Havoline, URSA, and other trademarks (collectively the Chevron Trademarks) that had been subject to an embargo order in Ecuador. The Chevron Trademarks were predominantly being used in Ecuador for the sale of automotive and other industrial lubricant products.

Our analysis was limited to use within the country of Ecuador and did not address the global value of the Chevron Trademarks. Chevron had recently been assessed an $18.2 billion judgment by Ecuador based on a verdict in the Lago Agrio case.[20]

At the time of our analysis, Ecuador's economy was heavily dependent on the oil industry, which had accounted for more than half of the country's export earnings and more than 40% of its public-sector revenues in recent years. Sales of finished lubricants were concentrated among major suppliers. At the time of the analysis, the top 10 companies accounted for approximately 88% of total sales. Figure 10.8 shows the estimated market share of finished lubricant sales in Ecuador by company.

Figure 10.8 Estimated Market Share of Finished Lubricant Sales in Ecuador, 2011

Supplier	% of Total
Chevron	23%
Gulf	14%
Exxon Mobil	11%
PDVSA	8%
Valvoline	7%
Golden Bear	6%
BP	6%
Shell	5%
Amalie	4%
Pennzoil	4%
Other	12%

10-19 International Trademark Association, *NASCAR and the Fast Lane of Trademarks,* http://www.inta.org/INTABulletin/Pages/NASCARandtheFastLaneofTrademarks.aspx.

10-20 *Chevron Corp. v. Donziger*, 974 F. Supp. 2d 362 (S.D.N.Y. 2014).

Lubricants sold under Chevron Trademarks led in all three primary lubricant market segments:

- Commercial automotive,
- Consumer automotive, and
- Industrial oils and fluids.

Valuation Approach

To calculate the value of the Chevron Trademarks in Ecuador, we used the income approach to establish the enterprise value of Chevron's Ecuadorian lubricant business. We then allocated a portion of that value to the Chevron Trademarks. The income approach is used to calculate the present value of future income streams specifically attributable to the IP asset. This method utilizes forecasted financial results based on factors such as historical financial results, industry trends, and the competitive environment.

We obtained market size data for the finished lubricant industry in Ecuador. Using outlook information and consumption data from industry sources, we developed a 10-year market forecast. Based on the lubricant pricing data and Chevron Corporation's subsidiaries' historical market share in Ecuador, we projected revenues derived from the sale of lubricants using the Chevron Trademarks.

After establishing the total finished lubricant consumption (in gallons) in Ecuador from 2011 to 2022, we took the total finished lubricant consumption and multiplied it by the average price per gallon in Ecuador to solve for the total revenue of finished lubricant. The total revenue of finished lubricant was then multiplied by Chevron's market share in Ecuador (23%) to find the revenue of lubricants using the Chevron Trademarks.

To discount future earnings, we used a discount rate representative of the level of risk involved in an investment in the Chevron Trademarks. As the trademarks could not generate a return on investment without the contribution of other assets, an investment in this type of asset should be considered a greater risk than investments in an entire corporation. However, given the extensive operating history and widespread recognition of the trademarks, the risk involved was partially mitigated. For that reason, we applied a discount rate of 10%. As the Chevron Trademarks were expected to earn future income throughout each forecast period, we used mid-period discounting.

Industry Asset Value Allocations

To properly value the Chevron Trademarks, we needed to ascertain their relative contribution to the total earnings generated by the sale of lubricants using the Chevron Trademarks in Ecuador. Chevron generated earnings through use of both tangible and intangible assets. As the Chevron Trademarks were used in conjunction with other assets, only a portion of the past and expected future earnings were directly attributed to use of the Chevron Trademarks. The contribution of a given trademark varies based on a range of factors, including customer recognition, history of usage, business performance, market conditions, and brand opportunities.

To establish a range of values attributable to trademarks in the oil and gas industry, we reviewed mergers and acquisitions data from public financial statements. When public companies merge or acquire other companies, they are required to make disclosures regarding the nature of the transaction. Generally, the level of detail correlates to the size of the transaction, as it would be impractical to disclose extensive information for many small transactions. Overall, the values allocated to acquired trademarks ranged from 4% to 16% of the overall purchase price.

We used our VALMATRIX® analysis to measure the relative strength and strategic value of the Chevron Trademarks across several dimensions. The trademarks were analyzed and rated on a scale of 0 (weak) to 5 (very strong) to arrive at an overall measure of their contributions to earnings. This analysis allowed for a direct comparison of the Chevron Trademarks to other trademarks, even those in different markets.

The Chevron Trademarks scored 44 out of a possible 60, or 73%, in the VALMATRIX analysis. At the time, Chevron Trademarks were globally recognizable due to Chevron Corporation and its affiliates' extensive international operations and consistent marketing efforts. In 2012, Chevron Corporation ranked number nine on Forbes' The World's 25 Biggest Oil Companies list. Chevron Corporation also achieved superior profitability with an earnings before interest, taxes, depreciation, and amortization margin of 21.8% in 2012, compared to the peer group median of 10.2%.

Within Ecuador, Chevron products marketed under the Texaco brand were active for more than 50 years. Chevron Corporation's affiliates were also the market leaders in Ecuador for all three primary lubricant market segments: commercial automotive, consumer automotive, and industrial oils and fluids. Overall, competition in the finished lubricant industry was expected to remain fierce. However, global demand for oil and oil derivatives was expected to continue growing along with the world's population and the industrialization of China and other developing countries.

Allocation of Value to Chevron Trademark

Compared to the trademarks reviewed in the industry asset value allocation analysis and the VALMATRIX analysis, the Chevron Trademarks had a more extensive history of usage and were far more recognizable. Lubricants sold under the Chevron Trademarks were also market share leaders in Ecuador. As a result, the value attributed to the Chevron Trademarks was above the industry median. We estimated that the use of the Chevron Trademarks contributed 10% to the total enterprise value of lubricant sales operations that used the Chevron Trademarks in Ecuador.

Net Present Value

To find the net present value (NPV), we discounted the projected cash flows from 2013 to 2022 (as mentioned above) and applied mid-period discounting to reach the present value of projected cash flows. A summary of our calculations and findings can be seen in Figure 10.9.

We found the NPV of cash flow to be $125,788,546.

Figure 10.9 Summary of Calculations and Findings of Net Present Value

		Forecast 2013	2014	2015	2016	2017	2018	2019	2020	2021	2022
Free Cash Flow		$15,538,580	$16,460,601	$17,437,331	$18,472,019	$19,568,103	$20,729,225	$21,959,245	$23,262,252	$24,642,576	$26,104,805
Discount Period (midpoint)		0.5	1.5	2.5	3.5	4.5	5.5	6.5	7.5	8.5	9.5
Discount Factor @	10%	1.0	0.9	0.8	0.7	0.7	0.6	0.5	0.5	0.4	0.4
PV of Free Cash Flow		$14,815,455	$14,267,788	$13,740,366	$13,232,441	$12,743,292	$12,272,225	$11,818,571	$11,381,686	$10,960,952	$10,555,770
Net PV of Cash Flow	**$125,788,546**										

Figure 10.10 Summary of Calculations and Concluded Value

Terminal Value	
Terminal Period Cash Flow (2022)	$ 26,104,805
Discount Rate	10%
Terminal Growth Rate	3.0%
Terminal Value	$384,113,554
Discount Factor	0.40
PV of Terminal Value	**$155,320,623**

Terminal Value

Assuming a 3% growth rate, we discounted the 2022 projected revenue by 10% and applied a discount factor of .40 to determine the present value of terminal value. Figure 10.10 shows a summary of our calculations and concluded value.

We calculated the present value of terminal value to be $155,320,623. Figure 10.11 combines both the net present value of cash flows and the present value of terminal value to arrive at the final enterprise value.

We concluded the final enterprise value in Ecuador of operation selling lubricants using the Chevron Trademarks to be $281,109,169.

Brand Value

Based on the income approach, we used the enterprise value and multiplied it by 10%, the allocation of value to Chevron Trademarks. The final value of the Chevron IP Trademarks in Ecuador is shown in Figure 10.12.

We determined the fair market value of the Chevron IP Trademarks in Ecuador to be $28,110,917.

Figure 10.11 Combined Net Present Value of Cash Flows and Present Value of Terminal Value

Enterprise Value	
PV of Free Cash Flows	$125,788,546
PV of Terminal Value	$155,320,623
Enterprise Value in Ecuador of Operation Selling Lubricants Using the Chevron IP Trademarks	**$281,109,169**

Figure 10.12 Final Value of the Chevron IP Trademarks in Ecuador

Trademark Allocation	
Enterprise Value in Ecuador of Operation Selling Lubricants Using the Chevron IP Trademarks	$281,109,169
Allocation of Value to the Chevron Trademarks	10%
Chevron IP Trademarks Value in Ecuador	**$ 28,110,917**

Case Study 2: AOP Ventures, INC. v. Steam Distribution, LLC et al.

AOP Ventures is a Delaware corporation engaged in the sale of electronic cigarette (e-cigarette) liquids branded under THE MILKMAN Mark, and their products include The Milkman and The Milkman E-Liquid Churrios. AOP Ventures is also the owner of the registered DRIP CLUB Mark for goods and services that include flavored e-cigarette liquid (e-Liquid) comprised of flavorings in liquid form used to refill e-cigarette cartridges. The defendants, Steam Distribution, LLC, and One Hit Wonder, Inc., sell E-Liquids through a variety of platforms including physical locations, direct sales and distribution, via telephone and electronic mail, and in person.[21]

AOP Ventures filed THE MILKMAN Mark with the US Patent and Trademark Office (USPTO) on May 4, 2015, and first used it in commerce on January 5, 2015. On March 3, 2015, more than two months after AOP Ventures began selling E-Liquid under THE MILKMAN Mark, defendant Anthony Tellez III filed a trademark application with the USPTO for "Milk Man." On June 24, July 8, and July 24, 2015, the infringing nature of Tellez's use of the name "Milk Man" for the sale of E-Liquids was conveyed via cease-and-desist letters by counsel. However, Tellez's infringing actions remained ongoing. In addition, Tellez used AOP Ventures' DRIP CLUB Mark without authorization to divert actual and potential customers to their knockoff product.[22]

We were asked to provide an opinion regarding the damages sustained by AOP Ventures, as measured as the unjust enrichment of Tellez, resulting from their alleged trademark infringement of ("THE MILKMAN Mark" and the "DRIP CLUB Mark"); and to value THE MILKMAN mark after reviewing the report of the opposing expert, it was apparent that he used a nonstandardized method of valuation. Without reasonable basis, he stated the key value drivers of THE MILKMAN mark were:

- The "One Hit Wonder" umbrella brand,
- The premium classification of the "One Hit Wonder" product line,
- High-quality flavors that resonate within the vape community,
- Volume pricing model,
- Robust social media marketing strategy through Facebook and Instagram,
- Curating relationships with industry influencers,
- Strong relationships with distributors and wholesalers, and
- ShareAsale trademark affiliate network.

Based on his professional opinion, and with no outside research to back up his claim, he specified that no more than 10% of the net profits should be attributable to THE MILKMAN Mark. In a rebuttal report to counter this claim, we used two standard methods of valuation—the relief-from-royalty method and unjust enrichment (based on gross profits). Here, we demonstrate how the two valuation methodologies were applied.

10-21 *AOP Ventures, Inc. v. Steam Distribution, LLC et al.* No. 5:15-cv-01586.
10-22 *Id.*

Figure 10.13 E-Cigarette Sales Data

	(Actual) (Industry Estimate)							
	2011	2012	2013	2014	2015	2016	2017	2018
E-Cigarette "Packs" Sold	89,000,000	164,000,000	433,000,000	754,000,000	1,211,000,000	1,601,000,000	2,046,000,000	2,500,000,000
E-Cigarette "Pack" Price	$2.81	$3.05	$3.23	$2.88	$2.54	$2.70	$2.86	$3.03
Revenue	**250,090,000**	**500,200,000**	**1,398,590,000**	**2,171,520,000**	**3,075,940,000**	**4,322,700,000**	**5,851,560,000**	**7,575,000,000**
Revenue Growth		**100%**	**179.6%**	**55.3%**	**41.6%**	**40.5%**	**35.4%**	**29.5%**

Revenue Projections

During the course of our analysis, we were provided with historical financial data for products sold under THE MILKMAN Mark. To project future revenues generated by products sold under THE MILKMAN Mark, we reviewed industry data and projections developed by numerous third parties. While sales of e-cigarettes and E-Liquids have rapidly increased in the last five years, there remains a high level of competition in the industry. Many of the large publicly traded tobacco companies have expanded their product offerings to include e-cigarettes and accessories. In addition, there are uncertainties regarding the long-term regulation of the industry.

For the first two years, we projected revenue growth to be in line with data reported by financial services company Canaccord Genuity. In a tobacco industry research report, Canaccord Genuity projected revenues from the sale of e-cigarettes to increase 35.4% in 2017 and 29.5% in 2018. Complete industry projections are presented in Figure 10.13.

As the e-cigarette industry approaches maturity, it is unlikely to continue to experience the high year-over-year revenue growth experienced over the last five years. Due to the low level of revenue volatility in the broader tobacco industry, we projected that from 2019 to 2022, revenues would increase at the same rate as the long-term U.S. average rate of inflation, approximately 3.2%. For the remainder of the 10-year forecast period, we projected zero revenue growth. As a terminal growth rate, we projected negative 0.5% based on estimates from IBIS World that the broader tobacco industry will contract over time.

Royalty Rate Analysis

Establishing appropriate market-based royalty rates for use of THE MILKMAN Mark was critical in the analysis on this assignment. In accordance with accepted valuation and damages analysis methodology, we used the market approach to identify appropriate royalty rates based on what others have paid to use similar intangibles. Royalty rate transaction data were collected from various sources. Specifically, we used industry data, annual royalty rate industry surveys, and public documentation from corporate 10-Q and 10-K forms.

We identified three agreements in which IP comparable to THE MILKMAN Mark were licensed in an arm's-length transaction (the Comparable Agreements). Based on our research, we concluded that a reasonable market-based royalty for THE MILKMAN Mark was 3%, the median royalty for the Comparable Agreements. See Figure 10.14 for royalty rate summaries of the Comparable Agreements.

Figure 10.14 Royalty Rate Summaries of the Comparable Agreements

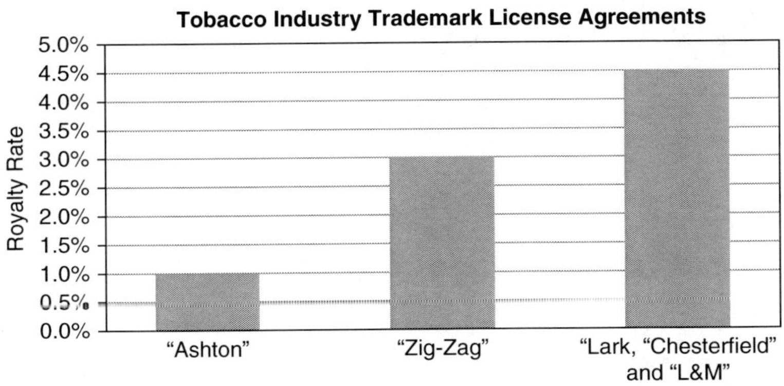

Discount Rate Analysis

To calculate the present value of future royalty streams, we used a discount rate that was representative of the level of risk involved in an investment in THE MILKMAN Mark. To determine the appropriate rate, we conducted a benchmark analysis of discount rates using the Duff & Phelps capital asset pricing model (CAPM) and weighted average cost of capital (WACC) calculations for investments in similar asset classes.

We relied on the WACC for standard industrial classification composite 21 of 6.46%. SIC Code 21 is comprised of companies that manufacture tobacco products. The WACC of 6.46% incorporates the SIC composite CAPM + size premium. A size premium reflects the historical tendency for the stocks of firms with smaller market capitalizations to outperform the stocks of firms with larger market capitalizations.

We used the relief-from-royalty valuation approach, which is a hybrid of the income and market approaches, to calculate the value of THE MILKMAN Mark. As products sold under THE MILKMAN Mark were expected to earn future income throughout each forecast period, we chose to use mid-period discounting to determine the present value of the hypothetical royalties that THE MILKMAN Mark would generate. In the full analysis, projected earnings are spread until 2026; for readability purposes, the additional calculations are cut off. Figure 10.15 provides a summary of our analysis and our concluded value of THE MILKMAN Mark.

Figure 10.15 Summary of Analysis and Concluded Value of THE MILKMAN Mark

"THE MILKMAN Mark" Trademark Valuation—Relief from Royalty Method	2015	*Historical* 2016 (Jan 1–June 20)	*Forecast* 2016 (June 21–Dec 31)	2017	2018	2019	2020
Revenue from Sales of Products Under "THE MILKMAN Mark"	4,437,210	2,592,514	**4,109,337**	**9,072,173**	**11,744,169**	**12,122,332**	**12,512,671**
Revenue Growth			40.5%	35.4%	29.5%	3.2%	3.2%
Reasonable Royalty Rate			3.0%	3.0%	3.0%	3.0%	3.0%
Hypothetical Royalty Charge			123,280	272,165	352,325	363,670	375,380
Discount Period (midpoint)			0.27	1.03	2.03	3.03	4.03
Discount Factor @	6.46%		0.98	0.94	0.88	0.83	0.78
PV of Royalty Income			121,252	255,170	310,280	300,837	291,681
Net PV of Cash Flow	**2,665,088**						

Figure 10.16 Calculations and Concluding Value

Terminal Value	
Terminal Period Cash Flow	399,943.81
Discount Rate	6.46%
Terminal Growth Rate	–0.5%
Terminal Value	5,717,588
Discount Factor	0.55
PV of Terminal Value	3,154,579

Figure 10.17 Total Value of THE MILKMAN MARK

Total Value of THE MILKMAN Mark	
PV of Forecast Cash Flows	2,665,088
PV of Terminal Value	3,154,579
Value of "THE MILKMAN Mark"	5,819,667

We concluded the net present value of cash flow to be $2,665,088. In addition, because THE MILKMAN Mark can be used in perpetuity, we also found the present value of terminal value. Figure 10.16 shows our calculations and concluding value. The present value of terminal value was found to be $3,154,579. Figure 10.17 shows that these two concluding values were added up to realize the full value of THE MILKMAN Mark.

Using the relief-from-royalty approach, we concluded the value of THE MILKMAN Mark to be $5,819,667.

Unjust Enrichment

While historical revenue data regarding the Defendant's unauthorized sale of E-Liquid under the "Milk Man" name was provided, no information was provided detailing the expenses incurred by the Defendant to generate those sales. To estimate the gross profits benefit attained by the Defendants as a result of their allegedly infringing actions and in order to be conservative, we accepted data for cost of goods sold from the opposing side, since they had access to additional information that we were not able to obtain. The gross profits relating to the Defendant's unjust enrichment are summarized in Figure 10.18.

The gross profits benefit attained by the Defendants as a result of their allegedly infringing actions was $6,052,232.

Figure 10.18 Summary of Gross Profits Relating to the Defendant's Unjust Enrichment

Defendant's Unjust Enrichment from Sales of Allegedly Infringing "Milk Man" Products				
	Retailer 1	**Retailer 2**	**Retailer 3**	**Total**
Revenue	$2,620,696	$6,080,039	$1,182,693	$9,883,428
Less: Cost of Goods Sold	$1,177,607	$2,435,145	$ 218,444	$3,831,196
Gross Profits	$1,443,089	$3,644,894	$ 964,249	$6,052,232

Summary of Opinions

After reviewing the documentation provided and performing extensive research and analysis, we arrived at the following opinions in this case:

- The value of THE MILKMAN Mark was $5,819,667.
- Damages as a result of the Defendant's alleged infringement of THE MILKMAN Mark and the DRIP CLUB Mark was $6,052,232.

Case Study 3: Celebrity Guitarist v. World Renowned Artist

Our firm was asked to provide an opinion on the damages incurred by an artist, arising from the alleged trademark infringement and related claims against a guitarist. The calculation of damages is based on the assumption that the Guitarist was unjustly enriched through the unauthorized use of the artist's trademarked band logo (Band Logo) on band merchandise (Accused Products). The artist designed the Band Logo for the Guitarist, but *only* to be used on an album cover, not for merchandise or other uses.

In this mediation case, apportionment plays a big role. The defendant is an award-winning celebrity guitarist (Guitarist) with numerous successful albums and a Billboard Lifetime Achievement Award. The plaintiff is an artist (Artist) who is experienced in freehand airbrush, hand-drawn, and digital illustration. He has years of experience living and working at the intersection of music and fashion, creating distinctive looks for new tours and merchandise, and focusing on image branding. He has created artistic works for Mötley Crüe, Linkin Park, Red Hot Chili Peppers, Jimi Hendrix's estate, Bob Dylan, Billy Idol, Bon Jovi, the Beatles, KISS, and more.

We had to determine the profits earned from merchandise earned sold by the Guitarist that were directly attributable to the Band Logo. The calculation of damages was based on the assumption that the Guitarist was unjustly enriched through the unauthorized use of the Band Logo on various Accused Products. To calculate any profits achieved by the Guitarist, we looked at the net sales of Accused Products and deducted the cost of goods sold (COGS), and selling, general, and administrative expenses (SG&A) to arrive at the net profits. Figure 10.19 provides a summary of our calculations.

We determined the net profits from the Accused Products were $210,369.

Figure 10.19 Guitarist Sales and Profits Summary

	Sales	COGS	Gross Profits	SG&A	Net Profits
2012	N/A	N/A	N/A	N/A	$ 82,392
2013	N/A	N/A	N/A	N/A	$ 78,545
2014	$ 51,201	$ 6,032	$45,169	$23,387	$ 21,782
2015	$ 25,423	$ 3,532	$21,891	$ 6,237	$ 15,654
2016	$ 23,522	$ 1,242	$22,280	$10,284	$ 11,996
	$100,146	**$10,806**	**$89,340**	**$39,908**	**$210,369**

Trademark Apportionment

To determine the profits that were directly attributable to the Band Logo, multiple apportionments had to be applied to the net profits earned by the Guitarist from the sale of Accused Products. The first apportionment applied was based on the value driven by the trademarked elements of the Band Logo. We looked at the relationship between the art/trademark and the Guitarist's right of publicity (ROP) and how each drives value in order to determine a reasonable percentage of value that each portion represents within the Band Logo.

The Band Logo, which represents the branding on the Accused Products, is comprised of two elements that drive value. The first element is the ROP of the Guitarist and the second is the trademarked artwork within the Band Logo design. In analyzing the relationship between artwork and celebrity ROP, we reviewed average royalty rates for the licensed use of both a celebrity's ROP, and of artwork to determine the value that each brings. As the average royalty rate for celebrity ROP licensing is 10.5% and the average royalty rate for artwork is 6.3%, we determined that a reasonable portion of value for the Band Logo is 37.5%.[23] Figure 10.20 provides a summary of our first apportionment.

Merchandise Apportionment

In 2013, Euromonitor International (Euromonitor) conducted a survey of approximately 250 of its own analysts to better understand how consumers shop for clothes and what ultimately drives their purchasing decisions. Euromonitor administers its surveys online and distributes them to in-house analysts and consumers through leading panel providers who abide by the International Chamber of Commerce/European Society for Opinion and Market Research code for ethical market research.

Euromonitor asked the respondents what drove their garment-purchasing decisions and then graphed the results. Figure 10.21 shows the average percent of respondents who report that the factors listed in the figure are among the top four determinants of their apparel-purchasing decisions.

Figure 10.20 Licensing Royalty Rates Apportionment Analysis

Property Type		Average Royalty 2015	Portion of Value to Subject Artwork
Art (Art and Artists)	a	6.3%	37.5%
Celebrities (Entertainers)	b	10.5%	62.5%

Notes:
Portion of value calculated as: a/(a+b) and b/(a+b).

10-23 Average Royalty Rate, By Property Type, 2006–2015. The Licensing Letter. 2016.

Figure 10.21 Garment Purchasing Factors—Average Response Percentage

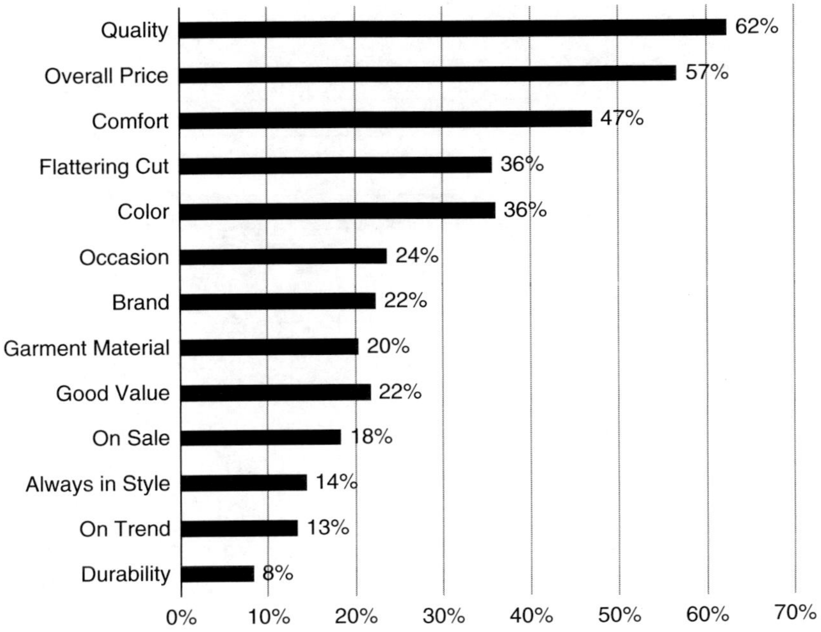

Many factors drive a consumer's purchasing decision. Of the approximately 250 people surveyed, 13 factors fell among the top four apparel-purchasing determinants, with quality and overall price being the only two factors that achieved a response percentage of at least 50%. The brand, or branding, on a garment encompasses various IP elements. This is no different than the IP elements that a company's logo on a shirt or food product would represent. By incorporating the Band Logo into the design of the Accused Products, the Band Logo becomes the branded elements of the product (the Branded Elements).

We chose to establish a range for our apportionment relating to the Branded Elements of the Accused Products. In the Euromonitor survey, branding is 1 of 13 factors. By dividing 1 by 13, we established a lower-bound apportionment amount of 7.7%. An average of 22.3% of respondents chose branding as one of their top four apparel-purchasing factors. Some portion of respondents considered branding as their most important factor when choosing to purchase a garment. To be conservative, however, we chose 22.3% as the upper-bound apportionment amount relating to a consumer purchasing an Accused Product due to the Branded Elements.

To calculate the range of Accused Products profits attributable to the Branded Elements, we first applied the lower- and upper-bound apportionment amounts of 7.7% and 22.3% due to the Branded Elements, respectively, to the total Accused Products profits of $210,369. Figure 10.22 provides a summary of the profits derived from the Branded Elements.

Figure 10.22 Accused Product Apportionment Range and Profits Summary

Apportionment Range Due to Branded Elements	7.7%	–	22.3%
Apportionment Due to Trademark Elements		37.5%	
Total Apportionment Range:	2.9%	–	8.4%
Accused Products Profits		$210,369	
Range of Merchandise Profits Attributable to Trademark Elements:	$6,074	–	$17,592

We found the range of merchandise profits attributable to the art/trademark elements to be between $6,074 and $17,592. As a reasonableness check, we compared the total range of profits attributable to the trademarked elements of the Band Logo to comparable art purchased by the Guitarist during his career (Comparable Art). In 2004, the Guitarist paid $19,000 for an exclusive, worldwide, perpetual license for commercial use of a piece of artwork from a different artist. Then, in 2008, the Guitarist again paid for an exclusive, worldwide, perpetual license for commercial use of another piece of artwork from a different artist, for a total of $6,000. The range of payments for the Comparable Art is presented in Figure 10.23.

Our range of profits attributable to the trademarked elements of the Band Logo provides an indication that our calculations are conservative, grounded in the value the market-places on art for commercial use, and eminently reasonable. As a result, after reviewing the documentation provided, performing research and analysis, and based on our professional knowledge, we arrived at the opinion: that the range of total profits attributable to the Artists' elements was $6,000–$18,000.

The moral of the story: value allocation is becoming more important in every context of trademark analysis and valuation. We are entering a period when more sophisticated and insightful analysis of value such as this simplified case represents will be the norm.

Figure 10.23 Market Comparables/Reasonableness Check Summary

Range of Payments for Comparable Art:	$6,000	–	$19,000

Chapter 11

Right of Publicity Analysis and Valuation

This is an unique chapter because it brings together two phenomena. The first is based on a complex legal system of intellectual property (IP) rights, i.e., right of publicity (ROP) protection and exploitation, which is increasingly being utilized under a patchwork of states' rights protection. The second phenomenon, which is cultural and business based, is the growth of celebrity usage of their branding rights via licensing, promotion, and endorsement. Celebrities, athletes, and other persons of interest are using not only their ROP but their other rights including trademarks and copyrights, together known as name and likeness rights.

These two phenomena are brought together in this chapter. From both points of view, ROP fuels the following three fast-growing areas of law, marketing, and valuation:

- One of the fastest areas of change in IP law,
- One of the fastest changing areas of marketing and branding, and
- One of the fastest growing areas of licensing, merchandising, and therefore valuation.

In fundamental terms, a person's ROP is based on a person's use of their IP and intangible assets in a promotional or commercial environment. This can involve anything from a five-year licensing agreement on a product, to a one-time promotion, to a short-term advertising campaign, to a long-term endorsement and any other marketing effort. These are examples of a celebrity's ROP being commercialized. This is not substantially different from other traditional brands' use of licensing and promotion. Whether it's Marvel Entertainment, Ford Motor Company, Spider-Man toys, or official Mustang apparel, each has scores of licensing and promotional deals in place.

Consider this, 10 years ago when we wrote the *Intellectual Property Primer on Valuation*, ROP wasn't even mentioned. The concept of ROP was, and continues to be, a stepchild in the family of IP. As recently as 2008, the industry tracking service for trademark licensing, *The Licensing Letter*, did not even record data for celebrity licensing or ROP. The International Trademark Association did not form an official ROP committee until 2014. Even today, the American Intellectual Property Law Association does not have a section or a committee devoted to ROP.

Nonetheless, ROP activities have grown at a relatively rapid pace. In 2017, *The Licensing Letter* estimated that retail sales for ROP licensed products were $5.92 billion on an international basis.[1] This is up 2.2% from 2016 and represents only a part of the picture as it does not include activity or revenue from endorsements, promotions, and other ROP usages.

The Origin of Rights of Publicity

A very brief review of ROP history is necessary in order to understand this area of IP. ROP sprang from the concept of right of privacy in the United States, which really did not exist until the dawn of the 20th century. In its simplest form, ROP can be defined as "the inherent right of every human being to control the commercial use of his or her identity."[2] This can include one's voice or one's personality quirk or signature. ROP is, in fact, often thought of as a subset of rights of privacy.[3] In broadest terms, ROP is an individual right to control how any other third party uses one's name, image, voice, likeness, and even personal characteristics in *any* type of public setting or media. These rights are controlled differently by each state, and in some jurisdictions, the right is applied much more broadly than in others.

It is also important to understand that ROP falls outside the stricter parameters of the three main types of IP, copyrights, trademarks, and patents, where most valuation experts (and most attorneys) typically spend their time. Most importantly, there's no federal law that protects ROP. As mentioned above, these rights are protected by various state statutes or by common law in other states. Even then, a dozen states have not formally recognized ROP.

However, as one expands ROP in its broadest sense of all uses of name and likeness, one begins to encompass a person's trademarks if they have registered them, as well as copyrights, licensing rights, and other related IP rights. Where copyrights and trademarks are involved, protection can be sought under federal copyright laws as well as under the Lanham Act for trademark protection.

Historically, however, ROP and the right to protect one's good name and reputation has always been recognized. We can go all the way back to Shakespeare's *Othello* where the character Iago talks about the importance of his good name:

> Who steals my purse steals trash; 'tis something, nothing;
> 'Twas mine, 'tis his, and has been slave to thousands;
> But he that filches from me my good name
> Robs me of that which not enriches him
> And makes me poor indeed.[4]

11-1 "Retail Sales of Licensed Merchandise, By Property Type, U.S./Canada, 2016–2017." *The Licensing Letter.* May 2018 Vol XLII, No. 5.

11-2 *ETW Corp. v. Jireh Publ'g, Inc.*, 332 F.3d 915 (6th Cir. 2003).

11-3 *Id.*

11-4 WILLIAM SHAKESPEARE, OTHELLO, act 3, sc. 3.

However, the phrase "right of publicity" did not come into usage until 1953 when Judge Frank, in *Haelan Laboratories, Inc. v. Topps Chewing Gum, Inc.*, coined the phrase.[5] From that point forward, ROP law began to grow. Subsequently, professor of law Melville B. Nimmer wrote a landmark article on the topic,[6] which was to become the foundation for ROP. Here is a timeline:

- 1902–1905: Legal recognition of "privacy." The 1902 recognition of common law privacy rights in New York in the Roberson case[7] and the 1903 New York statute creating a limited statutory right.[8] The 1905 Pavesich decision of the Georgia Supreme Court[9] accepting a common law right of privacy. These developments were the first steps taken to extend the "right of privacy" to the legal recognition of the affront to dignity and mental distress caused by the unpermitted advertising or other commercial use of a person's identity. The concept of invasion of "privacy" as a tort continued to be dealt with by the courts over several decades, creating a somewhat disorganized and inconsistent body of law.
- 1953–1954: Creation of a "right of publicity." The ruling in the 1953 Haelan case[10] of a "right of publicity" and the 1954 article by Professor Nimmer[11] that built a legal framework for the "right of publicity." These two landmark cases were the beginning of explicit recognition of the commercial impact and injury caused by unpermitted commercial use of a person's identity, using the label "right of publicity."
- 1960: Privacy law organized. In his 1960 article, Professor Prosser[12] divided all "privacy" rights into four different torts. Prosser's four torts of privacy proved to be immensely influential. His theory was embodied in the Restatement of Torts and has been uniformly accepted by the courts.
- 1970s: The "codification of parts of privacy era." This codification was in response to a wide variety of social concerns, loosely clustered together as invasions of "privacy." Congress passed a spate of laws directed at such disparate problems as electronic eavesdropping, government computerized record keeping, confidentiality of credit and educational records, and intrusive acts by bill collectors. While these statutes are outside the scope of this book, they represent an important development, which most people view as including "privacy" rights. They illustrate that "privacy" is no longer a single, unified body of law. Rather, it has been subdivided into a series of discrete parts, each addressing a specific social concern.
- 1972–2000: The era of state codification of ROP. Starting with California in 1972, a number of key states enacted statutes codifying ROP. By the turn of the century, other states including Illinois, Indiana, Nevada, Ohio, Texas, and Washington had enacted ROP laws.

11-5 *Haelan Labs., Inc. v. Topps Chewing Gum, Inc.*, 202 F.2d 866 (2d Cir. 1953).
11-6 Melvin B. Nimmer, *The Right of Publicity*, 10 LAW & CONTEMP. PROBS. 203 (1954).
11-7 *Roberson v. Rochester Folding Box Co.*, 171 N.Y. 538, 64 N.E. 442 (1902).
11-8 N.Y. Civ. Rights Law § 50.
11-9 *Pavesich v. New England Life Ins. Co.*, 122 Ga. 190, 50 S.E. 68 (1905)
11-10 *Haelan Labs., Inc. v. Topps Chewing Gum, Inc.*, 202 F.2d 866 (2d Cir. 1953).
11-11 Melvin B. Nimmer, *The Right of Publicity*, 10 LAW & CONTEMP. PROBS. 203 (1954).
11-12 William L. Prosser, *Privacy*, 48 CALIF. L. REV. 383 (1960).

- 1979: U.S. Supreme Court decision *Zacchini v. Scripps-Howard Broadcasting Co.*[13] In that case, a Scripps-Howard television station broadcast an entire performance of a circus performer. The Ohio Supreme Court, although recognizing a performer's right to the publicity value of his performance under Ohio law, nevertheless held that the company's broadcast was privileged and entered judgment for the television station. The U.S. Supreme Court then granted certiorari and reversed. The Court found that while the press is protected by the First Amendment to report on the performer's act, they are not free, to take the entire performance for which people pay money and show it on television for free and they cannot "get free some aspect of the plaintiff that would have market value and for which you would normally pay."[14] Since 1979, curiously there have been no other ROP cases that have come before the U.S. Supreme Court.
- 2013: Remembering Marilyn Monroe. A court decision[15] was handed down on the status of Marilyn Monroe's postmortem ROP. Although Ms. Monroe lived the majority of her life in California and died there, the court ruled that because she had for many years been paying taxes in New York State, her ROP was to be decided under New York State law. Thus, there were no postmortem ROP rights attached to her estate, and obviously they were not assignable to her heirs. As a consequence, any rights to Ms. Monroe's images rest with photographers and not with the estate.

Current Status of Protections

While a lot of ROP protections arise under state statute or state common law, there is protection under federal law as well. An extensive body of federal case law deals with ROP issues, but these cases generally arise either as diversity matters or Section 43a of the Lanham Act.

It is indeed a patchwork of laws, precedents, and protections that one must turn to when looking for guidance for protection of his own or a client's ROP. The word "patchwork" is appropriate because each state has variations in its laws both in terms of the breadth of protection and the range of remedies. Finally, it's important to understand that postmortem, protection for celebrities and the time of protection can run from 2 years up to 100 years, or no protection at all as in New York.

Thirty-eight states have common law and/or statute protection. However, it's important to understand that only 20 of the 38 have some form of postmortem protection. You need to look carefully at Table 11.1 in order to understand that some states that have common law protections also have statutory protections; so there is a good deal of overlap. As a final note of caution, the figures presented here were updated in 2017; of course, states pass new and interesting statutes all the time.

Coverages vary from state to state, with all states covering both name and likeness. Many others cover photographic imagery, voice, and signature as additionally protected elements.

11-13 *Zacchini v. Scripps-Howard Broad Co.*, 433 U.S. 562 (1977).
11-14 *Id.* at 576.
11-15 *Milton H. Greene Archives, Inc. v. Marilyn Monroe Ltd. Liab. Co.*, 692 F.3d 983 (9th Cir. 2012).

Penalties for misuse can be severe, ranging from as little as $50, e.g., in Virginia, to treble the provable damages. As a final note, as indicated in Figure 11.1, many states have a media exemption that does provide the media a "fair use" exemption. However, each statute needs to be read individually in order to understand what that fair use exemption really means.

Figure 11.1 State Statute Provisions

State	Original Enactment Date of Most Current Revision	Aspects of Identity Included (See Code)	Express Post-mortem Statutory Rights?	Post-mortem Duration	Statutory Remedies (See Codes)	Statutory News Media Exemption?
Arizona	2007	N, L, P	Yes		I, P, A, 3X Two statutes, both apply to members of the military only. For the purpose of the statute "a 'soldier' is defined as any active duty member or former member of the armed forces of the United States, including any member who was killed in the line of duty." This act was passed as an emergency measure to preserve public peace, health, and safety.	Yes
California	1985; 2008	N, L, P, V, S	Yes	70 years	D, P, A Also provides for $750 minimum award for damages or actual damages and profits. Postmortem rights are retroactive to include those who died prior to January 1, 1985.	Yes
Florida	1967	N, L, P	Yes	40 years	I, D, P Damages may include reasonable royalty.	Yes

(Continued)

State	Original Enactment Date of Most Current Revision	Aspects of Identity Included (See Code)	Express Post-mortem Statutory Rights?	Post-mortem Duration	Statutory Remedies (See Codes)	Statutory News Media Exemption?
Hawaii	2009	N, L, P, V, S	Yes	70 years	D, I, A Damages are greater of $10,000 or actual damages plus profits; impounding.	No
Illinois	1999	N, L, P, V, S	Yes	50 years	I, D, P, A Damages may include actual, profit, or both.	Yes
Indiana	1994; 2012	N, L, P, V, S Includes a person's distinctive appearance, gestures, or mannerisms. The statute specifically does not cover anyone who has formed a personality solely on the basis of being charged or convicted of a crime. Postmortem rights are retroactive to include those who died prior to June 30, 1994.	Yes	100 years	I, D, P, A, 3X Provides for recovery of whichever is greater, $1,000 or actual damages including profits and for impoundment and destruction orders.	Yes
Kentucky	1984	N, L	Yes	50 years		No
Massachusetts	1974	N, L	Yes	70 years	I, D, 3X Language states "any person," without using "living" as a modifier.	No

(*Continued*)

State	Original Enactment Date of Most Current Revision	Aspects of Identity Included (See Code)	Express Postmortem Statutory Rights?	Postmortem Duration	Statutory Remedies (See Codes)	Statutory News Media Exemption?
Nebraska	1979 1998	N, L	No		Merely says a person has a "legal remedy."	Yes News Media: Incorporates all Constitutional defenses.
Nevada	1989	N, L, P, V, S	Yes [C]	50 years	I, D, P Also provides for minimum damages of $750. Postmortem rights require a transfer and registration with the secretary of state.	Yes
New York	1903; 2000	N, L, V	No		I, D, P Someone who violates this statute will be criminally guilty of a misdemeanor.	No
Ohio	1999 2009	N, L, P, V, S Includes distinctive appearance.	Yes	60 years	I, D, P, A, 3X Damages include profit, are set at a minimum of $2,000 and a maximum of $10,000, and impoundment and/or destruction of goods may also be ordered.	Yes
Oklahoma	1955; 1986	N, L, P, V, S	Yes Deceased personalities include "any such natural person who has died within 50 years prior to January 1, 1986."	100 years	I, D, P, A Remedies can include profit.	Yes

(*Continued*)

State	Original Enactment Date of Most Current Revision	Aspects of Identity Included (See Code)	Express Post-mortem Statutory Rights?	Post-mortem Duration	Statutory Remedies (See Codes)	Statutory News Media Exemption?
Pennsylvania	2003	N, L, P, V, S	Yes	30 years	I, D Aspects of identity include "voice or a substantially similar imitation of one or more there.	Yes
Rhode Island	1956; 1980	N, L	No Language states "any person," without using "living" as a modifier.		I, D, A	No
Tennessee	1984	N, L, P	Yes	10 years Postmortem: 10 years and longer if commercial use continues.	I, D	Yes
Texas	1987	N, L, P, V, S	Yes Postmortem: Available to anyone who died before September 1, 1987 but was alive before January 1, 1937.	50 years $2,500 minimum or actual damages, whichever is greater as well as profits.	D, P, A [C]	Yes
Utah	1953; 1981	N, L	No		I, D, P, A Statutory liability only if there is a false implication of approval or endorsement.	Yes

(*Continued*)

State	Original Enactment Date of Most Current Revision	Aspects of Identity Included (See Code)	Express Post-mortem Statutory Rights?	Post-mortem Duration	Statutory Remedies (See Codes)	Statutory News Media Exemption?
Virginia	1950; 1977	N, L	Yes	20 years	I, D, P The unauthorized use of the name or picture of any person is deemed a misdemeanor and a fine of $50 to $1,000 will be assessed.	No
Washington	2008	N, L, P, V	Yes 75 years for persons whose identity "has commercial value"; 10 years for those whose identity does not have "commercial value."	10 OR 75 [C]	I, D, P Damages are calculated from $1,500 or actual damages, whichever is greater and may also include profits. While the statute is still good law, sections regarding domicile and choice of law were found unconstitutional under *Experience Hendrix, L.L.C. v. HendrixLicensing.com, LTD.*	Yes
Wisconsin	1998	N, L	No		I, D, A	Yes Incorporates by reference all media defenses.

Notes: Aspects of identity column: L, likeness (including "picture"); N, name; P, photograph; S, signature; V, voice.
Statutory remedies column: 3x, treble damages; A, reasonable attorney's fees; D, damages; I, injunction; P, punitive/exemplary damages.

Now we come to the more complex part of state law coverage, which is the state common law ROP and the precedents that have brought about the common laws. Each state's common law has come into existence as a result of some precedent that was set specifically in each state (Figure 11.2). These cases are complex and diverse and take time to understand. Some are tied to the right of privacy and precedent concept, others are tied to the right of identity, while others are based on the misappropriation of likeness. The one commonality that you will find is that they all cover name and likeness. Also, of the 38 states that do have common law coverage, 13 have additional coverage via state statutes.

Figure 11.2 Common Law Precedents

State	Important Precedent	Aspects of Identity	Postmortem Rights	Remedies	Defenses/Exceptions	State Statute
Alabama	2004	N, L		D [C]	Consent, newsworthiness	No
Arizona	1945	N, L, V, S	[C]	D, I [C]	Consent, statute of limitations, incidental use	Yes
Arkansas	1962; restatement second torts*	N, L,		D	Consent, First Amendment	No
California	1992 [C]	N, L [C]	No [C]	D, I	Statute of limitations, First Amendment [C]	Yes
Colorado	2001; restatement second torts	N, L		D	First Amendment	No
Connecticut	1982; restatement second torts	N, L, V, S [C]		D, I	Newsworthiness, statute of limitations	No
Delaware	2001; restatement second torts			D		No
Washington, DC	1985; restatement second torts	N, L		D [C]	First Amendment [C]	No
Florida	1944	N, L [C]	No	D [C]	Consent, statute of limitations, First Amendment [C]	Yes
Georgia	1982	N, L	Yes	D, I, P [C]	Consent, statute of limitations, First Amendment [C]	No
Idaho	1998[C]	N, L		D [C]	Consent, First Amendment	No
Indiana	1949; restatement second torts	N, L [C]		D, I [C]	Consent, statute of limitations, First Amendment [C]	Yes
Iowa	1977; restatement second torts	N, L		D	First Amendment	No

(*Continued*)

State	Important Precedent	Aspects of Identity	Postmortem Rights	Remedies	Defenses/Exceptions	State Statute
Kansas	1975; restatement second torts	N, L		D	First Amendment	No
Kentucky	2001 [C]	N, L		D	First Amendment	Yes
Louisiana	1979; restatement second torts	N, L		D	First Amendment	No
Massachusetts	1977; restatement second torts	N, L		D	First Amendment	No
Maine	1996 [C]	N, L		D		No
Michigan	1983 [C]	N, L	Yes [C]	D, I [C]	First Amendment [C]	No
Minnesota	1998 [C]	N, L		D, I	[C]	No
Mississippi	2008 [C]	N, L		D		No
Missouri	2003 [C]	N, L		D [C]	Consent, First Amendment	No
New Hampshire	2003; restatement second torts	N, L, V		D		No [C]
New Jersey	1967; restatement second torts	N, L, V	Yes [C]	D, I [C]	Consent, incidental use, First Amendment	No
New Mexico	1975 [C]; restatement second torts	N, L		D	Newsworthiness	No
Nevada	1995 [C]	N, L		D, I	Consent, transformative use [C]	Yes
North Carolina	1938 [C]	N, L		D, I [C]	Consent [C]	No
Ohio	1970; restatement second torts	N, L	No	D, I	Incidental use	Yes
Oregon	1986	N, L		D	First Amendment	No
Pennsylvania	1985 [C]	N, L [C]	Yes	[C]	First Amendment, newsworthiness, public figure	Yes
South Carolina	1999 [C]		Yes [C]	D		No
Tennessee	1987 [C]	N, L	Yes [C]	D	First Amendment	Yes
Texas	1999 [C]	N, L	No	D, P [C]	First Amendment, consent	Yes
Utah	1997 [C]; restatement second torts	N, L		D	First Amendment	Yes

(*Continued*)

State	Important Precedent	Aspects of Identity	Postmortem Rights	Remedies	Defenses/Exceptions	State Statute
Vermont	1990; restatement second torts	N, L		D	First Amendment	No
Washington	2010 [C]			D [C]	Consent, First Amendment	Yes
West Virginia	restatement second torts	N, L		D	Consent, First Amendment	No
Wisconsin	1979 [C]	N, L [C]		D		Yes

Notes: Code: [C], comment.

Aspects of identity column: L, likeness (including "picture"); N, name; P, photograph; S, signature; V, voice.

Remedies column: D, damages; I, injunction; P, punitive/exemplary damages.

*Restatement second of torts requires a person's name or likeness to have commercial value.

There's one final table that is of importance to everyone who is involved in ROP valuation work. Figure 11.3 includes a summary of postmortem ROP protection. This information is important because today, more and more ROP cases involve dead celebrities or "delebrities." It is important that valuation analysts and the representatives of the dead celebrity be clear on the client's postmortem rights.

Figure 11.3 ROP Postmortem Rights

State	Duration	Transferability/ Dependability	Registration	Common Law/ Statutory	Continuing Use Requirement
Arizona	Statute of limitations, rights terminate if not transferred in writing; 5 years	Yes: S/No: CL	No	S	None specified
California	70 years	Yes	Yes	S	None specified
Florida	40 years	Yes	No	S	None specified
Georgia	Statute of limitations, rights terminate if not transferred in writing; 2 years	Yes	No	CL	No
Hawaii	70 years	[C]	No	S	None specified
Illinois	50 years	Yes	No	S	Yes [C]

(*Continued*)

State	Duration	Transferability/ Dependability	Registration	Common Law/ Statutory	Continuing Use Requirement
Indiana	100 years	Yes	No	S	None specified
Kentucky	50 years	Yes	No	S	None specified
Massachusetts	70 years; as of publication, the Massachusetts state Senate passed a bill to begin the process to create postmortem ROP interest for 70 years after death for those personalities domiciled in Massachusetts at the time of death; the bill must now pass the Massachusetts House				
Michigan	[C]	Yes	No	CL	None specified
Nevada	50 years; statute requires a person bring the claim within six months after the date he becomes aware or should have become aware of the use	Yes	Yes	S	None specified
New Jersey	Statute of limitations, rights terminate if not transferred in writing; 6 years	Yes	No	CL	None specified
Ohio	60 years	Yes	No	S	None specified
Oklahoma	100 years	Yes	No	S	None specified
Pennsylvania	30 years; there has been no common law statute of limitations determined, but it would likely be governed by the state's two-year catchall statute of limitations, although misappropriation claims have a one-year statute of limitations	Yes	No	Both	None specified

(Continued)

State	Duration	Transferability/ Dependability	Registration	Common Law/ Statutory	Continuing Use Requirement
South Carolina	NA	Yes	No	CL	None specified
Tennessee	10 years; can be extended beyond 10 years and will be terminated if not used for any 2-year period following initial 10-year period	Yes	No	Both	Yes [C]
Texas	50 years	Yes	Yes	S	None specified
Virginia	20 years	Yes	No	S	None specified
Washington	10/75 years; 75 years for a person whose identity has "commercial value" and 10 years for a person whose name does not have "commercial value"	Yes	No	S	None specified

International Protection and Valuation

While there's minimal harmonization among the various U.S. states, there's even less harmonization or protection outside the country. Even when a jurisdiction recognizes ROP, there is no commonality from country to country. For example, there is no such thing as an EU ROP concept or protection. Each country's practices and protections have to be looked at individually. As a result, ROP is rarely valued on its own outside the United States. Instead, a firm engaged in valuing a celebrity's trademarks and copyrights outside of the United States rarely considers the component value for ROP in and of itself.

For example, when one looks at a cross section of international jurisdictions in Europe, Asia, and Latin America, it becomes quickly obvious that ROP is still a developing legal theory. Unlike other forms of IP such as copyrights and trademarks, no international bodies are unifying the law in this area, and there are no international treatises or conventions governing ROP. Each country or jurisdiction has variations in what aspects of an identity are protected (if any). Thus, one must be cautious when measuring and assigning value to ROP outside of the United States. One caveat is important: there is the commencement of a noticeable commonality in the right of privacy theory. The impact of the European Human Rights Convention has been considerable in many international jurisdictions. We believe that recognition of the common human right to privacy will continue to expand globally.

The Parallel Between Traditional Brands and Celebrity Brands

Today, a celebrity's ROP and name and likeness has become the equivalent of a celebrity's brand. In that regard, a celebrity's individual brand is little different from a traditional brand. It has many of the same components of value. Many well-known celebrities have developed a critical mass around their ROP and name and likeness assets that reflect lifestyle, ideals, and values that consumers resonate with. As with other brands, these lifestyles and values go a long way to developing the value of a celebrity brand. Within a celebrity brand, one can find the following assets:

- Core brand name/celebrity brand/celebrity's name,
- Trademarks,
- Likeness of the celebrity,
- Photographs and images,
- Line art,
- Nicknames or sub-brands,
- Theme music (if any),
- Distinctive trade dress,
- Signature or tag line graphics, and
- Current marketing themes, such as a tour or movie campaign.

All of these become known as the brand bundle, which we briefly discussed in earlier chapters on valuation methodologies. The assets within the brand bundle form the basis of value that is offered when inducing a licensee or sponsor to enter a partnership or merchandising deal with a celebrity. There can be stability with celebrities, but more often there are changes in value. As proof of this, one needs to review the annual surveys published in *Forbes*, which annually analyzes income for celebrities and celebrity brands. There are three main surveys: top earning celebrities, top earning athletes, and top earning dead celebrities. Figure 11.4 provides a comparison of the 2015 *Forbes* survey on athletes with the 2016 *Forbes* survey. It's fascinating to see how great the differences are when the data are compared side by side. With the top athletes, one can see not only a clear increase in the value of ROP and name and likeness assets but also many changes in the people at the top.

2015 Top Paid Athletes	
Name	**Earnings**
Floyd Mayweather	$300 million
Manny Pacquiao	$160 million
Cristiano Ronaldo	$79.6 million
Lionel Messi	$73.8 million
Roger Federer	$67.0 million
LeBron James	$64.8 million
Kevin Durant	$54.1 million
Phil Mickelson	$50.8 million
Tiger Woods	$50.6 million
Kobe Bryant	$49.5 million

2016 Top Paid Athletes	
Name	**Earnings**
Cristiano Ronaldo	$88.0 million
Lionel Messi	$81.4 million
Lebron James	$77.2 million
Roger Federer	$67.8 million
Kevin Duant	$56.2 million
Novak Djokovic	$55.8 million
Cam Newton	$53.1 million
Phil Mickelson	$52.9 million
Jordan Spieth	$52.8 million
Kobe Bryant	$50.0 million

Success comes down to the following four drivers of value, plus one that we refer to below:

- Level of celebrity,
- Level of endorsement,
- Level of actual usage, and
- Level of connection.

There is one other key factor related to these drivers and that is a lack of negative publicity. Celebrities can be famous or they can be notorious. While their fame can generate substantial positive buzz and great Twitter and Facebook activity, there's a line that they cannot cross. It is that invisible line between being famous and garnering unacceptable bad publicity. It's hard to see the line, but we all know when it has been crossed.

Finally, we developed an equation that we think expresses celebrity ROP value. It is:

$$(C + T) + (P \times G) = V$$

The equation simply reflects the following: the context of the usage plus the amount of time involved, plus the product or service to which the celebrity is adding its name, times the geography. This leads to a value conclusion as you engage in a rational valuation calculation.

Case Study 1: Tiger Woods—Valuation of ROP in a Litigation Environment

A decade ago, we were retained on behalf of Tiger Woods (TW) as the plaintiff in a litigation to provide our conclusion as to valuation and damages in the area of ROP. The case involved TW's purchase of a luxury motor yacht from a defendant Christensen Shipyards, Ltd. (CSL).[16]

As a major part of the purchase contract, there was to be no advertising, promotion, or other mention of TW as the owner of the yacht. That requirement was memorialized in the purchase contract in some detail.

Overview and Background

In February 2004, a corporation owned by TW and known as Privacy, Ltd., contracted with CSL to purchase a 155-foot custom motor yacht (Yacht). Among other items such as the payment schedule, build specifications, and other contract clauses, the contract with CSL contained stipulations about photographs and promotions associated with the Yacht: "Although Builder reserves the right to use or show the name of the Motor Yacht, it agrees not to disclose Customer's name or the name of Customer's principal or any member of his family (except as permitted under paragraph 18.5) without Customer's consent." The disclosure of TW's interest in the Yacht was revealed by CSL soon after the purchase contract was signed.

11-16 *Woods v. Christensen Shipyards, Ltd.*, No. 04-61432-CIV-ZLOCH, 2005 U.S. Dist. LEXIS 42994 (S.D. Fla. Sep. 23, 2005).

One month later, a picture of the Yacht under construction was published in the Sailing Magazine, *Columbian,* under the title "Tiger's Toy" in large bold-faced font.[17]

Summary of Facts Relevant to the Analysis

We considered several facts relevant to the damages analysis. TW was the top-ranked golfer in the world at the time and had been among the top-ranked golfers since shortly after turning professional in 1996. He had won 66 tournaments, including 48 on the PGA tour.[18] Ten of the wins were for major tournaments,[19] including four times at the Masters, and he is the only golfer to be the defending champion of all four majors at the same time.

TW had one of the highest awareness scores among celebrities, with an awareness E-score[20] of 93% on his name and 73% on his face.[21] In comparison, Phil Mickelson, the most recent Masters Tournament champion at the time, had an awareness E-score of 28% on his name and 17% on his face. Other top ranked golfers, such as Vijay Singh, Ernie Els, and Retief Goosen, did not even appear in the awareness charts.

As a result of his high awareness, positive image, and professional success, TW had been in demand as an endorser for a wide variety of products and services, including golf apparel and equipment (Nike), motor vehicles (Buick), management consulting services (Accenture), timepieces (Tag Heuer, Rolex), laser surgery centers (TLC Laser Eye Centers), financial services (American Express), video games (Electronic Arts), and collectibles (Upper Deck).

TW did not sign short-term endorsement deals or engage in one-off promotional activity on behalf of endorsement partners. The preferred relationship was one that covered roughly five to six years and featured a well-planned marketing campaign. Ideally, the endorsement relationship was one that portrayed and enhanced TW's likeable personality and competitive effectiveness.[22]

It is not unusual for popular athletes and celebrities to be well compensated for the use of their name, image, and likeness. At that time, retired boxer Muhammad Ali had recently sold 80% of the rights to his name and likeness for $50 million.[23] In 1999, George Foreman was paid $137.5 million for the worldwide rights to use his name on the now-famous George Foreman® grill over a five-year period.[24]

Calculation of Damages

The heart of the matter is that CSL systematically publicized the fact that TW was the owner of the Hull 026 yacht through the corporation Privacy, Ltd. The methods used by CSL to

11-17 David Yowell deposition dated March 14, 2006, Exhibit 8.
11-18 www.tigerwoods.com.
11-19 The Masters, PGA Championship, US Open, and British Open are considered to be the major tournaments in golf.
11-20 E-score is a celebrity rating service that provides complete personality profiles. There are more than 2,300 celebrity profiles available in the database. It shows how well known a celebrity is and provides details on the attributes associated with him/her.
11-21 www.epoll.com.
11-22 Interview with Mark Steinberg, agent for TW.
11-23 Associated Press news release dated April 12, 2006.
11-24 Celebrity Endorsements Reach for the Stars, (June 2, 2003), www.brandchannel.com.

accomplish the unauthorized association of TW with CSL's products were in direct violation of their contractual obligations. In essence, what CSL enjoyed at the expense of the plaintiff is a de facto free endorsement of their products.

The effects of these actions on TW's earning capability and financial well-being are twofold. Detailed explanations of each damages category are presented below.

Free Endorsement Damages

Free endorsement damages encompass the fair market compensation for CSL's actual use of the TW name. The damages in this category are determined by reviewing the costs a typical licensee would bear in order to have TW associated with their product. It is important when conducting this analysis to match the CSL activities as closely as possible with the terms of TW's actual endorsement contracts.

Damages were calculated by ascertaining the most likely hypothetical contract terms that would have prevailed had CSL actually paid market value for the free endorsement they enjoyed. The resulting damages are based on compensation levels found in existing TW endorsement deals and portray the foregone income TW would have enjoyed had the free endorsement activity been fully compensated.

TW's endorsement deals typically feature a five-year life span.[25] In fact, more than 80% of his endorsement deals are for five years or longer. It is therefore reasonable to assume that any new endorsement deals signed by TW would also be negotiated for multiple-year periods, with the most likely term being five years.

The best comparable for the CSL free endorsement situation is one in which the demands on TW personally are minimal.[26] As it happens, one of the legitimate TW endorsement deals, the TLC Laser Eye Centers agreement, requires no services of TW whatsoever.[27] Another agreement with limited requirements is TW's endorsement agreement with Tag Heuer.[28] Because the requirements on TW in these two agreements are in line with the CSL free endorsement situation and the product categories are non-golf–related products, these two TW endorsement agreements were selected as the best comparables for the CSL agreement template.

Accordingly, the annual compensation assumption for the free endorsement situation is $2,000,000. This is a conservative choice for this analysis since we assumed annual compensation to be well below the $5.1 million average annual compensation in TW's endorsement agreements.[29] The endorsement fees are assumed to be paid in a lump sum at the end of the year rather than accrued throughout the year.

After applying the 20% discount rate to the final three years of the hypothetical contract and a 5% interest rate to the first two years, the overall damages related to the free

11-25 The average life span of current TW endorsement deals is actually 5.33 years.

11-26 TW has never spoken with anyone at CSL and has never visited the shipyard (Eldrick "Tiger" Woods deposition dated January 19, 2006, pages 76 and 153). Also, there have been no photography sessions for CSL at which TW was present.

11-27 TLC Laser Eye Surgery Centers endorsement agreement as amended January 28, 2005, paragraph 8, Bates number Plaintiffs 003194.

11-28 Tag Heuer agreement as amended November 26, 2004.

11-29 The $5.1 million average annual endorsement deal compensation does not include figures from the Nike deal.

Figure 11.4 Damages Suffered by TW as a Result of CSL's Actions

Year	Periods to Discount[1]	De Facto Endorsement Fees	PVIF	PV of Endorsement Fees
2004	(1.5000)	$2,000,000	1.0759	$2,151,860
2005	(0.5000)	2,000,000	1.0247	2,049,390
2006	0.5000	2,000,000	0.9129	1,825,742
2007	1.5000	2,000,000	0.7607	1,521,452
2008	2.5000	2,000,000	0.6339	1,267,876

Total Endorsement Value: $8,816,320

Valuation Date	June 30, 2006
Discount Rate	20.00%
Interest Rate	5.00%

1 - Assumes an end-of-year payment. 2004 and 2005 are future valued at 5% simple interest, 2006 and beyond are present valued at a 20% discount rate.

endorsement activity are $8.8 million. This is the appropriate measurement for the free endorsement category of damages suffered by TW as a result of CSL's actions, as shown in Figure 11.4.

Reduced Future Earning Capability

This analysis is concerned with the damages that result from the loss in leverage when negotiating contract renewals and future endorsement deals that TW has suffered as a result of the inappropriate association of TW's name with CSL's products.

A good portion of the value of TW's endorsement appeal to licensees is related to its "scarce" nature and/or the presence of an "exclusive" clause in his contracts. Existing endorsement partners may well perceive the value of their investment as diminished if commercial use of TW's name can be had for no charge in some cases. The impact on TW's negotiating leverage resulting from the CSL free endorsement activity is estimated to be a reduction of 15% to 20% of the endorsement fees associated with each consummated contract.[30] For the purposes of this analysis, we have conservatively estimated the impact to be a reduction of only 10%.

Allowing free use of TW's name for commercial purposes will significantly dilute his earning capacity as a paid endorser. For example, where TW may have been able to negotiate an annual endorsement fee of $6 million in the past, he may now only be able to negotiate a $5.4 million fee. This is due to the legitimate concerns that a prospective endorsement licensee may have in relation to the CSL free endorsement situation. The $600,000 annual difference in this example is illustrative of the damages involved.

This diminished negotiating leverage will have an impact on both renewals of existing contracts and any new endorsement deals considered. However, we have conservatively limited the calculation of damages related to this category to include only the potential impact

11-30 Kel Devlin declaration dated April 14, 2006.

Figure 11.5 NPV of Reduced Future Earnings

Year	Periods to Discount[1]	Impact of Reduced Negotiating Leverage			PVIF	PV of Earnings Reduction
		2006 Contract Expirations[2]	2007 Contract Expirations[3]	Earnings Reduction		
2006	0.5000	$18,512,500	$ –	$1,851,250	0.8944	$1,655,808
2007	1.5000	37,025,000	3,000,000	4,002,500	0.7155	2,863,956
2008	2.5000	37,025,000	6,000,000	4,302,500	0.5724	2,462,895
2009	3.5000	37,025,000	6,000,000	4,302,500	0.4579	1,970,316
2010	4.5000	37,025,000	6,000,000	4,302,500	0.3664	1,576,253
2011	5.5000	18,512,500	6,000,000	2,451,250	0.2931	718,427
2012	6.5000	–	3,000,000	300,000	0.2345	70,341

NPV of Total Future Earnings Reduction: $ 11,317,995

Valuation Date	June 30, 2006
Discount Rate	25.00%
Earnings Reduction on Renewals	10.00%
Annual Fees subject to 2006 Expiration	$37,025,000
Annual Fees subject to 2007 Expiration	$ 6,000,000

1 - Utilizes end-of-year payment convention.
2 - At risk endorsement fees due to contracts that expire in 2006. Average renewal point is assumed to be mid-year.
3 - At risk endorsement fees due to contracts that expire in 2007. Average renewal point is assumed to be mid-year.

on the renewal of existing endorsement contracts due to expire in the next two years, or $43.3 million.

The minimum annual endorsement fees associated with TW contracts expiring in 2006 are $37,025,000. The minimum annual endorsement fees associated with TW contracts that expire in 2007 are $6,000,000. None of TW's endorsement deals currently set to expire past 2007 are included in this analysis.

Applying the 10% reduced earning capacity impact to these renewal opportunities leads to an effective aggregate impact of $21,512,500 over five years. This reflects an initial five-year renewal period for each of the expiring contracts, which is the average length of an endorsement contract for TW.

Since the projection of lost endorsement income in this analysis has a lower perceived risk of occurring than that presented in the free endorsement analysis, a higher premium is added to the risk-free rate when determining an appropriate discount rate. Accordingly, the discount rate in this analysis is 25%.

Applying the discount rate to the projections of reduced endorsement income associated with TW's diminished negotiating leverage leads to $11.3 million in present value damages over the next six years (Figure 11.5).

As we see, damages can take two forms. One is the benefits gained by the defendants, in this case, the builder of the yacht, which amounts to $8.8 million. The second measure is the reduced future earning potential for TW, which in this case amounts to $11.3 million. The total damages therefore were $20.1 million.

The case settled before trial. A "black box" deal was negotiated by the defendant's insurance carrier.

Case Study 2: Right of Publicity Valuation in a Transaction Environment

We were retained to value the IP of a deceased celebrity by the management of her estate and her heirs. This is a confidential assignment, and the identity of the person involved must remain confidential. The woman has been dead for two decades, but she nonetheless is an iconic, timeless persona with a transatlantic and international following and remains a recognizable force on a global basis even today. She was both an actress and a "face" that is instantly recognizable in the United States, Europe, Japan, and in markets around the world. While she has this type of global recognition, her IP has been underused and underleveraged.

The management of the estate, which provides both licensing and endorsement management of her film rights, engaged our firm to analyze and value all of her intellectual property assets. The heirs of the estate asked for this analysis to be conducted so that they could use it to gauge whether they should continue to own and manage the assets themselves or consider a sale or other financial event. Under consideration by the heirs was whether to prepare for a possible acquisition or joint venture with suitors such as LVMH, Disney, or one of the large talent agencies such as CAA. Another option was to reexamine their approach to the utilization of her assets on an internal basis and expand that usage.

Our valuation conclusions were to be done on the basis that we would consider only the income streams as they currently existed without consideration of other income opportunities. In other words, we were not to examine revenue streams that might occur from pending deals or other proposals that had been received. Finally, the valuation was also being provided to the heirs so they could formally reorganize the ownership of the rights into a corporate structure that was more favorable for tax purposes since the current ownership was being held individually by the heirs, rather than collectively as shareholders in some form of a corporate entity. Licensing and film rights activities were being managed through sub-agents and overseas IP attorneys, scattered among the various key markets where the celebrity had substantial audiences. It was believed that a more efficient structure should be established.

The Celebrity's IP

There were several components to the IP held by the celebrity's estate through the heirs. First were film participation rights. There were 10 major films in which the celebrity had appeared. All were major releases to global markets; all but one had been substantial box office successes; and all had been rereleased more than once. Several had been the basis for spin-offs and merchandising programs.

Another component was the celebrity's U.S. ROP and associated name and likeness rights, which included copyrights and a substantial library of still photography and movie and video photography.

Third, were trademarks, both domestic and international. The primary trademarks were the celebrity's name and signature. In addition, registrations had been done of both her full image and her silhouette image. Trademark coverage was substantial, with registrations in the United States, Europe, Japan, Korea, China, and a number of other key markets.

The management of the estate had been diligent in its registration and maintenance of trademark rights in the time since her death.

Fourth, given her global presence while she was alive, both a major agency of the United Nations as well as the State of New York had recognized her good works and established humanitarian awards that continue to exist and to raise funds for children around the world.

Valuation Approaches for the Celebrity IP

This assignment called for valuation based on revenue streams as they currently exist. In preparing to analyze the financial data, we considered the four most generally accepted approaches to value as outlined in chapters 4 and 5 (Figure 11.6). Because we had a substantial amount of information on the celebrity's past income and because we wanted to take an approach that most closely reflected value as of the valuation date, without regard to future potential income, we elected to use the income approach.

As we look at the historical financial results in Figure 11.7, a careful examination reveals two things. First is that over the six-year period for which we have actual results, one sees a steady decline in overall net revenues. Second, on careful examination of background information, we found that in 2009, there were two very large, single-event licensing deals that accounted for $2.35 million of revenue in that year that were not reoccurring events. When the impact of those events is removed from the financial results, the pattern of a slow but steady decline in net revenues further reveals itself. That decline over time amounts to between 5% and 10% per year on a going forward basis.

Having examined the financials, we charted the pattern of an annual decline in revenue. Otherwise, there is a pattern of relatively high stability in the estate's portfolio given the twin sources of income from both film and licensing. We were able to conclude to a discount rate

Figure 11.6 Four Most Generally Accepted Approaches to Value

Method	Description	Relevance for Analysis
Cost Approach	Amount a potential buyer would pay to replace or create an asset himself or herself	**Not Used in This Analysis:** As the celebrity IP has been used for many decades, not feasible to recreate the asset in a reasonable time frame
Market Approach	Value based on observed transactions involving comparable or similar assets	**Not Used in This Analysis:** Similar assets identified are not of comparable size (e.g. Monroe, Presley, Ali)
Relief from Royalty Approach	Present value of expected royalty compensation from observed licensing transactions involving comparable or similar assets	**Not Used in This Analysis:** Further information on the sales of all current Licensee's would be necessary to determine a value of the Hepburn IP under this approach
Income Approach	Present value of future economic benefits received from ownership of an asset	**Applied in This Analysis:** Normalized income related to licensing use and monetization of the Hepburn IP

Figure 11.7 Historical Financial Results

Normalized Revenue Calculation								
Year	**2006**	**2007**	**2008**	**2009**	**2010**	**2011**	***Q1 & Q2 2012***	***Q3 & Q4 (Proj.)***
Net Film PP Revenue	469,688	548,443	535,953	489,556	339,376	460,440	364,361	117,757
Net Licensing Revenue	3,666,800	1,700,250	1,327,755	1,481,085	603,826	1,465,707	194,583	1,306,975
Adjustments[1]	(2,005,000)	-		-				
Adjusted Licensing Revenue	1,661,800	1,700,250	1,327,755	1,481,085	603,826	1,465,707	194,583	1,306,975

Average	**1,391,712**
Median	**1,481,085**

1 2006 licensing revenue included a $1.25 million deal with GAP and a $1.1 million deal with Mitsui Bank; as these deals are not anticipated to occur again in the future, we have removed the revenues for our calculation

of 20%, which we established through a benchmarking process. Using the historical financial data and the 20% discount rate, it was a fairly simple matter to get to a valuation based on the declining revenue scenario, as shown in Figure 11.8.

As one can see from the calculations in Figure 11.8, under this declining revenue scenario, the value of the celebrity's IP is a very conservative $6.25 million. In this case, the heirs and the estate management asked us to establish a value based on an "as-in where-is" basis without regard to future potential pending deals. This value is appropriate and represents the lower parameter of value.

It is also appropriate to set up a second parameter of value for an as-is where-is valuation. Consequently, we did a valuation based on a no-growth scenario using an average

Figure 11.8 Declining Revenue Valuation

Discounted Cash Flow Valuation - Declining Revenue Scenario											
Summary Financial Results	**2012**	**2013**	**2014**	**2015**	**2016**	**2017**	**2018**	**2019**	**2020**	**2021**	**2022**
Revenue	2,970,161	2,747,399	2,524,637	2,301,875	2,079,113	1,856,351	1,633,589	1,410,826	1,188,064	965,302	742,540
Commissions Paid	986,485	912,499	838,512	764,526	690,540	616,553	542,567	468,580	394,594	320,608	246,621
as % of Revenue	*33%*	*33%*	*33%*	*33%*	*33%*	*33%*	*33%*	*33%*	*33%*	*33%*	*33%*
Net Revenue	1,983,676	1,834,900	1,686,125	1,537,349	1,388,573	1,239,798	1,091,022	942,246	793,470	644,695	495,919

Present Value of Forecast Revenue											
Period		1	2	3	4	5	6	7	8	9	10
Discount Factor @ 20%		0.83	0.69	0.58	0.48	0.4	0.33	0.28	0.23	0.19	0.16
PV of Cash Flow		**1,529,084**	**1,170,920**	**889,670**	**669,644**	**498,247**	**365,381**	**262,964**	**184,536**	**124,946**	**80,094**

Net PV of Cash Flow	**57,75,484**

Terminal Value	
Terminal Period Cash Flow	495,919
Discount Rate	20%
Terminal Growth Rate	0%
Terminal Value	2,975,514
Discount Factor	0.16
PV of Terminal Value	**480,562**

Declining Revenue Scenario Valuation	
PV of Forecast Cash Flows	5,775,484
PV of Terminal Value	480,562
Value	**6,256,046**

Figure 11.9 Constant Revenue Valuation

Discounted Cash Flow Valuation - Constant Revenue Scenario Based on Average Earnings	
Summary Financial Results	**2012**
Normal celebrity IP Earnings	1,400,000
Discount Rate	20%
Terminal Growth Rate	0%
Total Value of Constant Earnings	**7,000,000**

revenue model, as shown in Figure 11.9. You see that we calculate the average and median revenue streams for the celebrity's historical IP licensing activities and found that $1.4 million had been the normalized revenue stream. Using that as the basis of the going-forward revenue stream and using the same 20% discount rate, it is a fairly straightforward step to establish value for the estate at $7.0 million.

This then becomes the second parameter of value for an as is where is valuation in this case.

Conclusions of Value

To briefly recap the work on this case, we provided the client with two pieces of analysis. One in which we calculated value based on a declining-revenue scenario for the celebrity's IP. The second conclusion of value was based on a normalized constant stream of licensing revenue at $1.4 million annually. Based on those calculations, our conclusions of value are as follows:

- The declining revenue basis conclusion of value is $6.25 million.
- On a constant revenue basis going forward, the conclusion of value is $7.0 million.

An interesting footnote to this particular assignment is that within a year of providing this valuation to the clients, they successfully concluded a substantial deal for use of their dead celebrity's ROP. This was a five-year deal with an option to renew that can generate up to $22 million in revenue for the estate. At a 20% discount rate, this would add in excess of $12 million to the estate's value calculation. It is an illustration of how a celebrity's ROP value can change dramatically in a relatively short period of time.

Chapter 12

International Arbitration Valuation and Case Studies

International arbitration brings a new environment to the process of litigating differences, whether they involve intellectual property (IP) valuation or not. In fact, whether they involve the issues of any asset valuation or not, the environment varies quite substantially between U.S. or U.K. litigation and international arbitration. The conditions under which the proceedings are held are vastly different. Differences are not just procedural, they are also professional and cultural.

Sovereign disputes, most often referred to as bilateral investment treaty (BIT) disputes, are settlements over foreign direct investments that are signed by two countries. BITs are international agreements that provide companies and individuals with special rights and legal protection when they invest in a foreign country, typically known as a host state. Each BIT sets out the terms and conditions for investment in one country by the private companies and individuals of the reciprocating country. Obviously, a BIT is intended to promote direct investment while at the same time protect the investment of the foreign national. Virtually every country benefits from inward foreign investment, at least in principal. Whether we are dealing with Albania, Zimbabwe, or the former democratic Venezuela, each has concluded more than one BIT that provides for substantive and meaningful procedures and legal protections to investors. Most of these investments, which are in the territory of another state, provide a number of guarantees, including fair and equitable treatment, protection from expropriation, free transfer of profits, and full protection and security. Most BITs call out the freedom of an investor to bring arbitration in any meaningful forum such as those named below and are usually identified in the specific treaty. In return, the host state is required to submit to the jurisdiction of that arbitration institution.

There are some parallels between international arbitration and a U.S. Judicial Arbitration and Mediation Services, Inc. (JAMS) proceeding. Even then, a JAMS proceeding reflects U.S. litigation rules and procedures more than it has any resemblance to an international arbitration.

What Are the Key Arbitration Institutions?

There are 12 main international arbitration bodies along with three emerging ones. Among those listed below, the most important are the United Nations Commission on International Trade Law, Singapore International Arbitration Centre, International Chamber of Commerce, Swedish Arbitration Association, and International Center for Settlement of Investment Disputes. They represent a broad geographic distribution. Any one of the 12 are a suitable venue depending on where the parties are located and what geographies the dispute may affect. Also, the timing and availability of suitable arbitrators in the geographic area, not only of the arbitration but also of corporate headquarters, may be a factor.

1. World Intellectual Property Organization

The World Intellectual Property Organization is 1 of the 17 specialized agencies of the United Nations. It is a global forum for IP services, policy, information, and cooperation.

2. United Nations Commission on International Trade Law

This is the core legal body of the United Nations system in the field of international trade law. It is a legal body with universal membership that has specialized in commercial law reform worldwide for more than 40 years.

3. Belgian Centre for Arbitration and Mediation

Since its foundation in 1969, the Belgian Centre for Arbitration and Mediation's (CEPANI's) reputation has steadily grown, and it is now the center for dispute resolution in Belgium. CEPANI assists parties in disputes with all their arbitration and mediation proceedings by creating the right legal and administrative framework.

4. China International Economic and Trade Arbitration Commission

Formerly known as the Foreign Trade Arbitration Commission, the China International Economic and Trade Arbitration Commission (CIETAC) was set up in April 1956 under the China Council for the Promotion of International Trade. CIETAC is also known as the Arbitration Court of the China Chamber of International Commerce. The commission has made prominent contributions to the legislation of Chinese arbitration law and the development of arbitration practices in China. It has maintained positive relations and cooperation with major arbitration institutions around the world and has gained a reputation at home and abroad as an independent, impartial, and efficient arbitration institution.

5. Singapore International Arbitration Centre

The Singapore International Arbitration Centre (SIAC) is an independent, neutral, nonprofit global arbitration institution that provides case management services to the international business community. In terms of its internationally administered caseload, SIAC is among the top five institutions in the world.

6. International Chamber of Commerce

The International Chamber of Commerce (ICC) is a world business organization that helps businesses of all sizes and in all countries operate internationally and responsibly. The ICC represents business interests at the highest level of intergovernmental decision-making, whether at the World Trade Organization, the United Nations, or the G20, ensuring that the voice of business is heard.

7. London Court of International Arbitration

The London Court of International Arbitration (LCIA) is one of the world's leading international institutions for commercial dispute resolution. The LCIA provides efficient, flexible, and impartial administration of arbitration and other alternative dispute resolution proceedings, regardless of location and under any system of law. The international nature of the LCIA's services is reflected in the fact that, typically, more than 80% of parties in pending LCIA cases are not of English nationality.

8. Arbitration Institute of the Stockholm Chamber of Commerce

The Arbitration Institute of the Stockholm Chamber of Commerce (SCC) was recognized in the 1970s by the United States and the Soviet Union as a neutral center for the resolution of East–West trade disputes. The high number of international cases, nearly 50%, is clear evidence of the SCC's strong position as a preferred venue for dispute resolution among the international business community.

9. Swedish Arbitration Association

Sweden has been a long-standing center for international arbitration, and the Swedish Arbitration Association (SAA) seeks to promote the interest in and knowledge of arbitration as a dispute resolution method. The SAA arranges conferences and seminars, training for arbitrators, and is involved in publication projects.

10. JAMS (Mediation, Arbitration, ADR Services)

JAMS, formerly known as Judicial Arbitration and Mediation Service, includes mediators and arbitrators who successfully resolve cases that vary in size, industry, and complexity. JAMS typically achieves results more efficiently and cost effectively than through litigation.

11. American Arbitration Association

A nonprofit organization with offices throughout the United States, the American Arbitration Association (AAA) has a long history and experience in the field of alternative dispute resolution. The AAA's role in the dispute resolution process is to administer cases, from filing to closing. The association provides administrative services in the United States, as well as abroad, through its International Centre for Dispute Resolution.

12. International Center for Settlement of Investment Disputes

The International Center for Settlement of Investment Disputes (ICSID) is the world's leading institution devoted to international investment dispute settlement. It has extensive experience in this field, having administered the majority of all international investment cases. States have agreed on ICSID as a forum for investor–state dispute settlement in most international investment treaties and in numerous investment laws and contracts.

Emerging Venues

Dubai International Arbitration Centre

The Dubai International Arbitration Centre (DIAC) offers high-caliber arbitration services and facilities on an international scale. The DIAC is an autonomous, permanent, nonprofit institution.

Mumbai Centre for International Arbitration

The Mumbai Centre for International Arbitration (MCIA) is a first-of-its-kind arbitral institution in India. It was established as part of a joint initiative between the government of Maharashtra and the domestic and international business and legal communities. The MCIA aims to be India's premier forum for commercial dispute resolution.

Korean Commercial Arbitration Board

The Korean Commercial Arbitration Board (KCAB) assists international parties in resolving disputes encountered in the course of commercial activities. The KCAB recognizes the paramount need to be a neutral, independent, and internationally minded administrator in order to deliver the most reliable, efficient, and world class dispute resolution services.

Unique Cultural, Procedural, and Professional Conditions

The environment of an international arbitration is completely different from that of litigation. It is both more conciliatory and more adversarial at the same time. All parties are present for virtually the entire proceeding. Attorneys, experts, fact witnesses, and translators pack into one room for days on end, accompanied by boxes of files, reels of tape, and stacks of computers. It is an environment that is different from even the most hectic court scene.

The primary differences in the arbitration environment can be summed up in seven short statements:

- The audience in an arbitration is different; one is speaking to a three-person panel.
- Discovery is different, and the rules of discovery are vastly more simplified.
- The evidence brought forward is different; in a nutshell, it is simple and sparser.
- Reports and valuation dates are different; there are multiple reports and often multiple valuation dates.

- Testimony is different. Sometimes the expert is allowed to have an opening prepared statement. Sometimes experts from both sides deliver a joint statement or joint report.
- Various types of experts can be heard, including tribunal-appointed experts.
- There is a high standard of professionalism and credibility required from experts and from their valuation analytics and reports.

The Audience

In international arbitration, the audience is usually composed of three arbitrators, rather than a jury or a single judge. Usually there is an option by each side to appoint one arbitrator. In turn, the third arbitrator is appointed either by the sanctioning body or by the other two arbitrators. In general, this audience is much more sophisticated and analytical and will have greater knowledge of the issues at hand than one would find in U.S. or U.K. litigation. In addition, they are usually far more prepared than a judge would be (and certainly far more prepared than a U.S. jury). Most arbitrators will have read all of the materials ahead of time and certainly will have read the reports of the experts in the case—and will have read them carefully.

Experts should structure their presentations and arguments accordingly. In other words, one should be prepared to have a logical and sophisticated presentation and be prepared to refer to documents and financial analyses in some detail. Also, it is important for an expert in arbitration to be not only credible but very transparent in their presentation and, more importantly, appear not to be playing the role of an advocate so much as the role of a fact presenter. Finally, because the audience is well prepared and typically knowledgeable about the topic, clarity is a must.

Discovery

Generally, there is far less discovery that goes on in domestic litigation. Two contributing factors to this are the fact that depositions are very rarely held in arbitration. Also, no interrogatories are presented in international arbitration (at least not typically, unless a prior agreement has been reached between the parties). As a result of these two procedural items, there is more limited document discovery both beforehand and during the arbitration. The expert is working with less information from the opposing party and must build their analysis based on what they and their client know to be factual, as opposed to what they learned from the opposing party.

In these proceedings, expert/counsel communications are generally not discoverable. Thus, the expert is free to work with counsel in a very open manner without fear of discovery of communications or earlier work product. Also, there is some room to expand the process of discovery because that is a negotiated element in arbitration, and discovery is determined by the parties upon the tribunal's approval. However, tribunals are somewhat loath to extend discovery to make it an open-ended "fishing expedition."

Evidence

Because discovery rules are more circumscribed than in other litigation environments, there is much more flexibility in evidence. In fact, arbitration tends to lack clear evidentiary rules.

The arbitrators can essentially change the rules of evidence as the hearing proceeds, admitting additional evidence during arbitration that might not have originally been ruled in at the beginning of the process. There is always concern about the admittance of evidence during the process. As a consequence, there is more flexibility in referring to external sources of evidence from books, journals, and third-party analysis.

This results in the appearance of what can best be described as "surprise" evidence during the experts' testimony. Therefore, one must be ready to react to new evidence during the arbitration hearings. This also means that there will often be responsive revisions to experts' work during the arbitration. It is up to the expert or valuation analyst to ensure that they assemble all of the evidence that is needed to support the valuation process and report within the body of work being submitted. The valuation experts' report must be self-contained; referrals to outside evidence not physically presented can be a mistake. Everything that the valuation expert needs for their analysis and report has to be contained in their submittal, even if this means substantial additional appendices and lists of documents.

Experts' Reports and Valuation Dates

The experts' reports are generally more important in an international arbitration than in litigation. Unlike litigation, where experts' reports are often not seen by judge or jury, they are typically submitted to and thoroughly read by the arbitrators.

Remember that expert reports essentially take the place of depositions that are not used during arbitration. More important, the experts' reports are often used by members of the tribunal as the basis upon which they draft monetary awards, putting the expert valuation reports directly in the spotlight when it comes to the calculation of damages. In addition, arbitrators often call for two reports, an initial report and then a subsequent report after the arbitrators have done their preliminary examination. In addition, because there are various dates on which valuation can be undertaken, multiple reports may be written. In other words, valuation can be calculated at what is known as the "date of taking," or at the date of the tribunal, or the valuation can be calculated on an intermediate date that the two parties may or may not agree upon. As a consequence, the valuation analysis reports can be submitted on two or more dates.

Therefore, expert reports may have financial models in Excel format that will have alternative calculations that may be made at multiple points in times. Finally, many arbitrators are sophisticated at financial analysis, thoroughly understand Excel formats, and are able to manipulate the calculations. The expert report should be submitted with the full Excel files attached so that the arbitrators can recalculate values using alternative inputs such as discount rates or growth rates.

Testimony

Because international arbitration takes place in a more informal setting than litigation, the form of testimony can be quite different. For example, you have the possibility of multiple testifying experts on each side and from each firm of experts. Thus, one needs to consider who will sign the report on behalf of each firm of experts. Testimony can often be more grueling because the time devoted to the testifying expert can be substantial, running on for several hours or even days. Without question, testimony will be more substantive, and inquiries from the three arbitrators will be much more incisive and continue for much longer periods of time than any voir dire from the bench in a U.S. litigation.

There is also the option of having the expert open with a direct 20- or 30-minutes presentation where their entire discussion on valuation is provided in a prepared statement and PowerPoint Presentation. If this is to occur, it is extremely important because it is a one-time opportunity to tell the arbitrators in detail precisely how the expert has arrived at their conclusions. This must be coordinated closely with counsel. Remember that the tribunal usually asks in-depth questions. One must remember who the audience is—it is the three members of the tribunal. Respectfulness is absolutely required and, again, credibility is an issue.

Finally, there is the possibility that witnesses will present together during cross and be seated in the witness box at the same time; with the tribunal peppering the witnesses and asking for answers from each of them in turn.

Experts' Opinions and Reports

Experts may be asked to present their reports in draft form to the opposing party. The arbitration panel can then look at the differences between the two reports and ask for a supplemental or final report in the hope of narrowing the differences between the two parties before final reports are submitted to the tribunal. They can also order a so-called conferencing or, so-called "hot tubbing," session where the experts meet and attempt to come to an agreement on a valuation number or range of numbers. If the experts on the opposing sides cannot reach an agreement, they at least tell the tribunal the issues upon which they can't agree, as well as those parts of the analysis where they have different assumptions and metrics. It is the hope that this type of conferencing brings the two sides closer together.

The tribunal can also appoint its own expert, the neutral tribunal expert, to present their own analysis as to valuation. When this is done, that tribunal expert will typically be brought in to comment on specific valuation issues. For example, the tribunal expert may be brought in to comment on discount rates or the effects of expropriation on a country discount rate or on specific tactical matters of the expropriation.

Several of the most popular arbitration bodies authorize the use of these experts. However, there are issues, and cost is one of them. The second more important issue is the concern that this tribunal-appointed expert will become a de facto "fourth" arbitrator. Therefore, it is imperative that the arbitrators ensure that the parties have a full and fair opportunity to be heard and be allowed some input on the selection of the tribunal-appointed expert. Background, training, certification, and knowledge of the case should be considered before the tribunal appoints this expert. The arbitrators may be resolving the valuation dispute simply by appointing a certain expert who is a proponent of one school of thought vis-à-vis the specific valuation.

Standards of Professionalism

There is a much higher standard of professionalism that is needed in these tribunals. Credibility with the tribunal is an absolute key to success. Equally important, one must appear evenhanded and forthright throughout the process. While working in an arbitration, an expert is much less of an advocate and much more of a presenter of facts and positions. Transparency goes hand in hand with credibility, and transparency is always a positive in front of a tribunal. Finally, proficiency and high technical skills are a key requirement for an expert to be successful in presenting a meaningful and justifiable valuation position.

The cultural, procedural, and professional conditions in which an international arbitrator operates are substantially different from litigation. How do we best summarize these conditions? The following list says it all:

- Expert witness credibility is more critical.
- Testimony is more detailed.
- Report clarity is more necessary.
- Transparency is imperative.
- Professional presentation and technical proficiency are critical.
- Experts are, theoretically at least, working together to come to a common conclusion.
- Technical science and methodologies must remain constant.

With that said, it nonetheless remains an adversarial environment—an environment that presents issues not found anywhere else.

Valuation Issues Unique to International Arbitration

While conditions both procedural and professional are different, so too are many of the issues faced in the process of valuation and analysis. Most of what is discussed below is in the context of sovereign arbitrations; however, most of these issues also affect commercial international arbitrations. What we see from the following is that some of these issues are specific to IP, and some are specific to the forum of arbitration itself.

Legal Standard of Value

The legal standard of value is represented by a question that the arbitrators have to ask themselves at the very beginning. At arriving at a valuation decision, particularly in a sovereign arbitration, they face both a question of law and a question of fact.

The arbitration panel must settle on a legal standard that is most applicable to the valuation case.

- Full compensation,
- Adequate compensation,
- Full reparations,
- Restitution,
- Actual loss,
- Fair market value,
- Fair value,

- Reasonably equivalent value, and
- Lost profits.

Because each of these standards of value is different, it is incumbent upon the arbitrators to give instruction to counsel and to their valuation professionals ahead of the valuation process. Therefore, the arbitrators need to engage in advance planning to make sure that the valuation experts have sufficient time to work toward an appropriate valuation in order to meet the legal standard of value as established by the arbitration panel. If the panel is not certain of the standard of value, the valuation experts must first come to an agreement upon what the legal standard of value is.

Methodologies

There is general agreement on methodologies among experts in the valuation of IP and intangible assets. Those methodologies are much the same as the ones used in litigation. In international arbitration methods include the following:

- The income-based approach, which includes methods that convert anticipated economic benefits into a single discounted present value.
- The market-based approach, which uses methods to compare assets to other assets.
- The asset-based approach, which uses methods based on current market value, net of liabilities.

This last asset-based approach can also be thought of as the cost approach. Naturally, the income approach, uses the discounted cash flow approach for a premium pricing analysis, cost advantage analysis, or relief of royalty analysis. The market approach uses comparable sales or other comparable transactions. In essence, the methodologies are similar to those found in litigation in the United States and the United Kingdom.

The market multiples approach is used often in arbitration because it is easier to state the factual analysis and because there are fewer assumptions. It is also easier to understand, and it is more likely to reflect the current marketplace since it measures relative value not absolute or intrinsic value. It is particularly useful when measuring value based on stock values or IP values. The only danger is when a market continues on a strong upswing because the market multiples method might overstate the value of an asset, particularly in comparison to an income approach such as a discounted royalty stream.

This last comment speaks directly to a key element in valuation and arbitration; multiple valuation methods should be used whenever possible in arbitration. These valuation techniques should be complimentary tools. If values reached using two methodologies are widely inconsistent with each other, we can be certain that something is wrong with the underlying analysis. On the other hand, if two or three valuation methodologies are used to reach relatively consistent results, the arbitration panel will take great comfort from the expert's work. The moral of the story is that whenever possible in valuing IP (not just in an arbitration), the experienced analyst will always use two or more methodologies to arrive at a value.

Valuation Date

One lever of efficiency that the arbitration panel has is advanced planning. Through such planning, the arbitration panel can reduce costs and time, as well as help clarify the evidence and the focus for each side and their respective valuation experts. Of key importance is to establish, prior to the panel sitting in session, which valuation date will be used. In sovereign arbitrations, this is often a point of great dispute because the question is, what is the right date?

- The date of taking?
- The date of the award?
- The date of valuation?
- The date of the notice of expropriation?
- The date of the first government edict that began to restrict the commercial interests of the expropriated asset?

If the valuation date is not determined prior to the seating of panel, the valuation expert is faced with calculating value on two or more valuation dates—a situation that has been presented to us on more than one occasion. What then ensues is an unnecessary battle over which valuation date is the correct one. Rather than focusing on the valuations themselves, the experts and the lawyers spend time battling over a date, all of which could have been avoided by having the panel rule on this issue before the arbitration began.

Currency and Exchange Rates

Here are two key questions: First, in what currency are we calculating value? Second, at what exchange rate and on what date? The answer as to the currency is determined on a case-by-case basis. In cases where the location of the taking of the asset has a stable currency, that currency may be selected for use. However, the more frequent case is that the currency will be of the investing party's home currency. For example, if a Dutch company invests in Argentina and their investment is expropriated, damages calculations will be in euros rather than in Argentine pesos. If, however, a U.S. company's investment in Switzerland were expropriated for some reason, the valuation could likely be done in Swiss francs, although the same calculation could be done in U.S. dollars. Thus, currency selection is situational in each case, with the preponderance of valuations being done in the currency of the investor's home country. As to exchange rates, these are typically set as of the valuation date. Thus, we can see the importance of the valuation date throughout the valuation exercise.

Discount Rates

Much debate occurs, particularly in sovereign arbitration, since the calculation of the discount rate between the claimant whose property has been expropriated and the respondent sovereign entity can have wildly divergent conclusions. It is not unusual to see a claimant come forward with a discount rate, e.g., in the 8% to 12% range and the respondent country coming forward with a discount rate in the +20% range, reflecting their very divergent views of value and risk.

There are two basic approaches to setting a discount rate. One is the buildup approach and one is the weighted average cost of capital (WACC) approach. It is our experience, and that of many valuation experts in arbitration, that the WAAC approach is finding more acceptance in international arbitration. A typical WACC is established based on the weighted average cost of capital for comparable companies. Essentially, this approach considers the calculation that investors or lenders would reach if they were asked to make new investments in the entity that was taken at the valuation date. The WACC takes into account both the cost of equity and the cost of borrowing as of the date of valuation. This discount rate considers the balance between risks and benefits that the third-party investor or lender would reach if they were making a new equity investment and new loans to the company. The valuation analyst then proportionally weighs the cost of the new debt and the cost of the new equity based on the subject company's debt structure to determine the WACC.

One interesting question, which is established on a case-by-case basis, is what country risk premium may or may not be added? Should a country risk premium be added specifically to reflect social conditions, such as civil unrest, that exist in the country where the unlawful taking occurred? The answer is that while normal business risks of operating in a country will be built into the discount rate analysis, abnormal risks such as unexpected political and civil unrest should not be added as a country risk factor. Adding these abnormal risks would raise the discount rate unnecessarily and, therefore, indirectly benefit the sovereign state in calculating value. It would lower the ultimate calculation of damages and thus benefit the sovereign state in the discounted cash flow (DCF) calculation, resulting in a lower value conclusion.

Tax Issues

Because international arbitration invariably deals with cross-border issues, multiple tax rates typically are in play. Because of the many variables in these situations, most valuation experts use pretax valuation conclusions, although there is no universal agreement on whether a pretax or after-tax approach should be used. We believe it is incumbent upon the arbitration panel to provide instruction to the two sides at the beginning of the tribunal, so that each valuation expert is working toward the same goal.

Without such direction, one might consider doing a post-tax calculation such that the valuation is done so that it shows the corporate and personal taxes that would be imposed on the valuation to the recipient—the original owners of the expropriated investment. However, there is an important caveat. In doing so one must then take that after-tax conclusion and gross it back up to a pretax number such that the award will be sufficient to compensate the owners of the expropriated asset. Otherwise, an award given to the owners of the expropriated asset that is only equivalent to their after-tax basis would penalize the recipient. Why is this? Because the recipient would get their award from the sovereign entity via the tribunal after tax and then still be responsible for paying tax on that award. In other words, they would be doubly penalized—once in the award based on after-tax dollars and again when they have to pay taxes on that same award.

Also, arbitrators need to pay close attention to which tax rates are being used. In after-tax valuations and conclusions, the valuation experts will be making their own assumptions about which tax rates will be used. There is no guarantee that both sets of valuation experts will make the same tax assumptions. In fact, it's almost certain that they will have different assumptions as to taxes. In that case, the arbitrators have to make a decision as to how to bring clarity and consistency between the two valuation experts.

"Creeping Expropriation"

General observations are needed regarding an important issue that is raised often in these arbitrations. The issue is when does expropriation actually begin?

- First, the actual act of expropriation tends to be a messy affair. As a result, records are sketchy and memories are hazy and often self-serving. The valuation experts needs to be able to discern truth from fiction as they work through documentation and expert affidavits.
- Second, as a corollary to the above, there tends to be little cooperation from the sovereign party in an expropriation, which means less documentation and less evidentiary discovery.
- Often, government controls and edicts have been issued by the sovereign party in the time preceding the actual taking of the assets. These edicts can have a substantial impact on operating results of the expropriated assets in the years prior to the actual taking.
- Enforced revenue reductions might have occurred prior to the taking of the asset because of government sales controls (e.g. price ceiling or floors), important controls (e.g. tariffs or import quotas) and, on other regulations.
- With IP, one has to also be aware of controls over the use of IP and possible controls over the remittance of royalties, thus artificially depressing the value of the IP prior to the taking of the assets.
- Currency controls and currency exchange rates may also affect preliminary evaluation analyses, as the economy and its currency may have been artificially manipulated prior to the expropriation.
- Social conditions in the country of expropriation may have been deteriorating and issues of civil unrest may have arisen, which may also have led to unnaturally depressed levels of demand or artificially lowered price levels and/or price controls may have been in place.
- There may also have been political risks in play that the owners of the expropriated asset may have considered and that may have caused postponement of expansion or full utilization of the assets that were expropriated.
- The question of "actual state conduct" in the period leading up to the taking of the assets is one that often raises its head in sovereign arbitration cases. The question of whether the government was encouraging its various agencies to artificially and or arbitrarily diminish the value of the assets needs to be carefully examined.

All of these have an impact on the valuation experts' work. For example, when one considers interest to be applied to the award, these considerations come into play. However, interest will be paid on the award so that the respondent sovereign country is not unjustly enriched by using the asset during the period between the actual taking and the date of the award. This will ensure that the claimant is fully compensated not only for their initial loss but for their time and the value of money during the period when they are waiting to collect on the award that's finally agreed to. Most typically, interest is awarded at the prime rate in the country where the claimant resides.

Case Study 1: Latin American Company v. Government X

A Latin American command economy company (the LACE Company) needed expert valuation services in connection with a claim for monetary relief against the government (Government X). Specifically, we were asked to value the business in response to the implementation of government regulations that had negative implications on the LACE Company's business. Above we spoke of issues and differences in international arbitration, many of which came into play in this case, including the following:

- The venue of the arbitration,
- Government controls,
- Currency fluctuations,
- Social conditions and civil unrest,
- Actionable state conduct,
- Discount rate issues,
- Expert witness creditability,
- Date of valuations,
- Country risk premiums, and
- Methodologies used.

Parties and Issues in the Arbitration

The LACE company first began business in 1960 as a corporate successor to a family business with a long history of making coffee and related products. It subsequently grew into one of the best-known brands in its country and adjacent markets. The business continued to grow and expand, and by the time of its taking, it had several trademarks and brands and held number one or number two market positions in premium and popular priced products throughout the country. In about 1990, its parent company, based among the founding European Union countries, had entered a BIT agreement with Country X in South America. This treaty protected the interest in shareholdings of the owners of LACE Company against any claims arising out of the unlawful taking of its investment in Country X. Under the provisions of the BIT treaty and also under the laws of Country X, LACE Company's sole owners are entitled to receive compensation for the taking of its investment.

The issues then became very clear and simple. What amount shall the European owners of LACE Company be compensated for the taking of their enterprise in Country X? Secondly, as of what date shall that compensation be calculated? As of the date of taking, or as of the arbitration hearing, or some other date? These are the primary issues that we were asked to address in arbitration. There was a subtext to this entire dispute caused by the actions of Government X. After the expropriation in 2009, the government, under its own regulations, was required to provide compensation. The country actually has a law on expropriation dating back to the turn of the millennium that specifically says that the expropriating government entity must follow a process. In the later part of 2009, the ministry of agriculture commenced an appropriate procedure and appointed a three-person expert appraisal panel of economists, all from Country X, who were then charged with appraising the value of LACE Company's IP and other assets. The panel performed an appropriate economic analysis, and in 2010 informed the government that LACE Company was owed an excess of $200 million (US). Naturally, the government was not eager to hear this result. The government did not act on this report and made no effort to offer the owners of LACE Company the $200 million as called for under their own legal structure. After receiving the report calling for the government to reimburse LACE Company for more than $200 million, the government did subsequently react by offering LACE Company approximately $20,000,000, roughly one tenth of what their own expert committee had called for in compensation.

Thus, the dispute was joined and the international arbitration began. The arbitration was to be held under the auspices of ICSID, was to be binding, and without recourse. Settlement of the amount awarded would be directly out of the World Bank account of Government X. Thus, the stage was set for the hearing in front of the Work Bank in 2016.

The Valuation Process, Issues, and Experts

Because Government X had already been instructed by its own appraisal commission that the value of the assets was in excess of Two Hundred Million, they were in an awkward position. First, that valuation was already on the table and, second, they had to find an expert who could walk them back from that position. Thus, they sought a group that had worked for them before on multiple occasions and specifically they sought a "Dr. Smith" who appeared for them in multiple other expropriation hearings over the prior four or five years.

Dr. Smith can best be described as a man of flexible ethics and moveable opinions. He is able to change his own earlier conclusions while testifying if fundamental flaws are pointed out to him using the excuse of subordinate miscalculations. The key issues were the following:

- What discount rate should be used? 15% or 20%?
- What exchange rate should be used? Four to the dollar or eight to the dollar?
- What valuation date should be used? The date of expropriation or the date of the hearing?
- What growth rate should be used? 2% or a more realistic 3.4%?
- Finally, what cost of goods sold should be used? The company's actual experience of 65% or an inflated 90% as proposed by Dr. Smith?

As experts for LACE Company, our approach was to use a 16% discount rate, even allowing for a quite high country risk factor in calculating our cost of capital, as we can see from (Figure 12.1).

For the exchange rate to be used, in order to not penalize the company's owners, we used the exchange rate as it existed at the time of taking, which was four to one. Dr. Smith used an exchange rate of eight to one, which he justified by saying that over time, the local currency would degrade down to the eight to one ratio. However, he could not state a reason as to why he would devalue the currency in this manner. The third area of debate was what date to use for the valuation. As we discussed earlier in this chapter, one mustn't penalize the owner of the assets by using a valuation date earlier than the date of the tribunal. This would reward the government such that they would not have to pay the time value of money to the owner of the asset since that owner has been waiting patiently for what was then six years (and is now eight years) since the expropriation. Thus, the appropriate date of valuation, in my view, is always the date of the arbitration.

The final two issues were growth rate and cost of goods sold. Growth rate was set by Dr. Smith at an artificially low 1.9% compounded, whereas the growth rate for coffee consumption in Latin America has historically been 3.4%, which is the number we used. This makes a substantial difference when projecting revenues and profits over time. Most importantly, however, was the selection of the cost of goods sold (COGS). Dr. Smith used a 90% COGS, which is far beyond anything that anyone experiences in the coffee industry and far beyond reasonable. There was no rationale for selection of this number. Thus, a very high cost of goods sold combined with a very low growth rate and an artificial exchange rate, which effectively cut revenues in half, were layered on top of a very high discount rate, which

Figure 12.1 Discount Rate Analysis

Discount Rate Analysis	
Equity Cost of Capital	
Item	**Rate**
Risk Free Rate	*4.3%*
Expected Equity Market Return	*11.8%*
Equity Risk Premium	*7.5%*
Unlevered Beta	*0.56*
Levered Beta	*1.21*
Country Risk Premium	*15.5%*
Equity Cost of Capital	**32.2%**
Rounded	***32.0%***

Benchmark Rates	
20-year Note Yield as at November 10, 2009	***4.3%***
Morningstar, 209 Small Composite WACC	***7.8%***
Morningstar, 209 Small Composite WACC + size premium	***11.5%***
Morningstar, 209, 5yr Avg. Debt/Total Capital, Small Composite	***19.6%***
Integra, SIC 2835, Long-term Debt/Total Assets	***18.7%***

Cost of Debt Capital
Factors considered in Company Specific Risk include:
Current yield greater than 7% for Triple B rated Corporate Debt
Company is smaller than most Corporate Debt issuers
17% yield for High Yield Bond Index

Weighted Average Cost of Capital	
Equity Cost of Capital	*32.2%*
Debt Cost of Capital	*10.0%*
Capital Structure:	
% Equity	*36.2%*
% Debt	*63.8%*
WACC	***15.86%***
Rounded	***16.0%***

depressed value substantially. In effect, the combination of these factors had a multiplying effect that decreased his valuation by several orders of magnitude.

Concluded Values

Dr. Smith's layering of his assumptions, one upon the other, managed to reduce the original government appraisal committee's estimated value from the $200 million down to just above $20 million. This is easy to understand when one reviews the litany of assumptions in the paragraph above. If, however, one makes more reasoned assumptions, the discounted cash flow analysis comes to a value of between $175 million and $200 million. In an alternative calculation, using the market multiples method and based on comparable companies provided by Dr. Smith, we found a valuation conclusion of just above $200 million.

Figure 12.2 shows values plotted out. The darker line represents CONSOR's DCF valuations plotted at three points in time. We then plotted Dr. Smith's conclusions of value had he done a market multiple approach; those are plotted on the lighter grey line. You will see that had Dr. Smith used a market multiple approach, his valuations would parallel those of the CONSOR team. Finally, you will see at the bottom left a dot that is his calculation based on a discounted cash flow valuation.

The chart speaks for itself. Clearly, Dr. Smith attempted to manipulate his DCF assumptions to the maximum extent possible. However, his market multiple valuations clearly are embarrassing to him and obviously prove that his DCF analysis is not worth the paper upon which he printed it. The quote from Kantor's book explains why Dr. Smith's DCF value must be ignored.

Mark Kantor, in *Valuation for Arbitration*, notes, "If valuations reached by two methodologies are widely inconsistent with each other, that can be a strong signal something is awry.

Figure 12.2 Opposing Expert DCF Undervalues Company

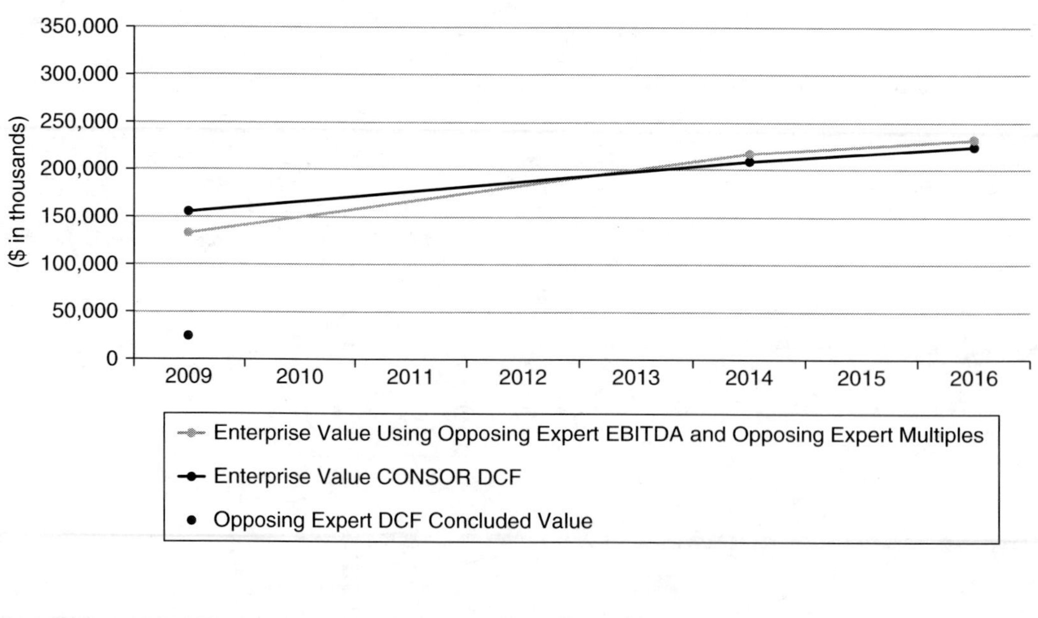

If several valuation methods produce consistent results, arbitrators may take greater comfort from the valuations."[1]

Case Study 2: British American Tobacco v. the Hong Kong Government

This is a different type of international arbitration, as the valuation work takes the form of a report only. No testimony was possible. The report that we submitted speaks for the expert and was submitted by counsel for British American Tobacco. This report was presented to the government tribunal that was hearing evidence on regulations being proposed by the Department of Health in Hong Kong. That hearing on these new proposals accepted pleadings from the affected tobacco companies in Hong Kong.

After the submittal of our report and other materials by the tobacco companies, a ruling was subsequently made. That ruling, as we understand it, was not favorable to the tobacco companies. While it was our understanding that an appeal was possible, it was not likely to be successful, as the regulations were to be implemented as originally proposed.

CONSOR was retained by counsel on behalf of British American Tobacco (BAT) to analyze the impact of tobacco control measures that were being proposed by the Department of Health in Hong Kong. Under the current regulations, there is a stipulation that health warnings should take up to 50% of retail packaging. Under the new regulations, the amount of graphic health warnings was to be increased to a size that covers at least 85% of the two largest surfaces of the cigarette packages/retail container. Very specific terms are spelled out in the new proposed health regulations as to where and how those graphic health warnings should be placed.

We were asked to analyze the impact on BAT brands of increasing the portion of the packaging on their cigarette products that would be covered with graphic health warnings, i.e., increasing the health warnings from 50% of packaging to 85%. Most importantly, we were asked to address the potential loss in value to BAT, especially the loss in value of BAT's trademarks and other brand asset IP.

The analysis specifically addressed the calculation of loss of brand equity value that includes trademarks, trade dress, packaging designs, copyright designs, and the value of other IP elements, which we collectively refer to as the brand IP. The analysis was done as of June 2015.

The Importance of Brand IP to the Tobacco Industry

In the tobacco and cigarette industry, trademarks and brand IP are extremely valuable assets to their owners who typically are also their manufacturers. These assets serve as the primary factor by which consumers are able to differentiate one brand from another. If the proposed measures were implemented, it would directly encumber a company's ability to capitalize on their brands in marketing to their consumers. This was particularly true for BAT, a global

12-1 Mark Kantor, *Valuation for Arbitration* 27 (2010).

tobacco group that sells their brands in more than 200 markets. These measures in Hong Kong would obviously directly affect BAT in that marketplace and also would have a spill-over effect in adjacent markets where the same brands are being sold. It is important to know that BAT has a holding company for its trademarks and other IP and then licenses brand IP to operating companies such as the one in Hong Kong, as well as throughout the world.

Trademarks and other brand IP are the most significant factors by which consumers distinguish between competing cigarettes. Encumbrance and reduction of the brand IP on packaging, because of increasingly restrictive health warnings, will reduce the value of that brand and its associated goodwill. This reduction of the space and the resulting factor by which consumers can distinguish between competing brands and products diminishes the competitive advantage in value of the brand owners' IP. If brands were to be completely removed from cigarette product packaging, consumers would be unable to distinguish one brand from another.

Due to the increasing globalization of commerce and major consumer brands, a reduction in value of brand IP in one local market will therefore have adverse effects on the global value of brand IP. As an example, consider Adidas, who uses the Adidas trademark and three-stripe trade dress on its packaging and product. If a licensee were not able to use the trademark, but only the trade dress, the royalty rate would be lower than that charged to a licensee who was able to use both the trademark and the trade dress. This concept is useful in understanding the impact of the proposed health warnings that, if applied to the BAT product, would reduce BAT's ability to use either their trademark or their trade dress on their product.

Finally, in preparing for the valuation process, we reviewed the Hong Kong Health Departments proposal. In doing so, we did not see any reference in their analysis of the impact of their proposals that address the loss in value of the trademarks and brand IP held by BAT and other cigarette manufacturers. There is no indication that the Department of Health realizes that the increased restrictions in packaging contained in their proposals would damage the value of the BAT brand IP. The purpose of our analysis and our report was to analyze and quantify the amount of value lost and therefore the amount of damages incurred.

Valuation Process

Previously, we referred to the licensing of trademarks to various operating companies by BAT. By definition, each piece of IP is different, and royalty rates being used will always vary. Therefore, the relief from royalty approach is most appropriate here, as each BAT brand can have appropriate royalty rates set for them. Also, we were able to do so since comparable royalty rate transaction data were available. If the health department measures were implemented, tobacco companies in Hong Kong will be encumbered by limiting the space in which they can utilize their trademarks and brand IP. As a result, the royalty rates that can be changed would be lowered.

The reduction in royalty rates that BAT and other manufacturers would be relieved of paying as a result of their diminished ability to use certain trademarks and trade dress can accurately be determined. The loss in brand IP value, therefore, is measured as the present value of diminished royalty payments. As a result, the relief from royalty approach is the most accurate approach in this case and has been relied upon in our analysis. The loss in brand value is calculated as the present value of lost royalty revenue in the form of reduced royalty rates.

In order to establish a revenue base upon which to calculate the future royalties, we simply extended out BAT's revenues in 2014 using historical sales data in the Hong Kong market. We were also able to establish average prices per cigarette and apply historical growth rates of a relatively modest 1% annual future growth rate. This growth rate would decline over time, as cigarette smoking becomes less socially acceptable for reasons including health, economics, and social pressure.

At the same time, average royalty rates for BAT-branded cigarettes were established. These rates range from 10 to 12%. We were also able to study what happens when encumbrances are placed on a trademark from other marketplaces and other environments, as would be the case if the health department measures were implemented in Hong Kong. That reduction in value reflects the extent of the encumbrance. It was our estimation that if the measures were implemented, the reduction in royalty rates would approximate 75% since the reduction in remaining useful space on the package was in the range of 75% (going from 50% of package space available for trade dress and trademark exposure to 15% is an effective reduction of approximately 70%).

As we can see in Figure 12.3, royalty rates decrease as coverage display is reduced, and they decrease relatively rapidly. The implication is clear. If the licensee doesn't have enough space to display both trademarks and trade dress, the point of paying a royalty to use the brand IP is diminished, and the royalty rates decline quite quickly. Note that the relationship between the encumbrance on the use of the brand IP is not proportional to the reduction in royalty rates. As the space applied to product IP is reduced, premium products become more generic. This results in the commoditization of a premium brand that more swiftly impairs its market value and the royalty rate it can command.

Figure 12.3 Royalty Rates vs. Package Space

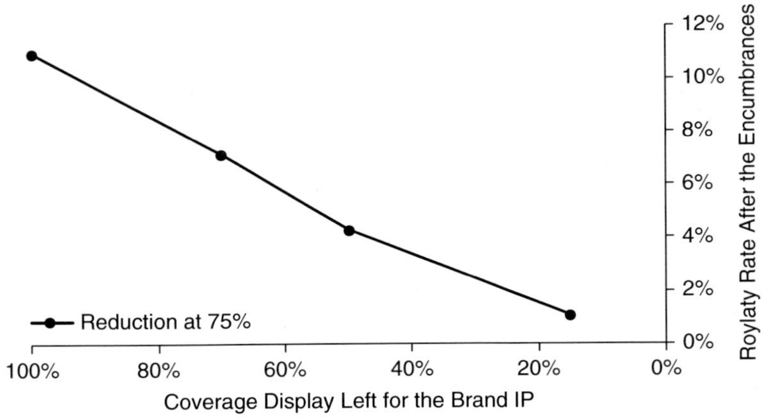

Figure 12.4 Reduced Royalty Flows

Year	BAT After Tax Hypothetical Royalty Charge at 50% Warnings Label Encumbrance	BAT After Tax Royalty Charge at 85% Warning Label Encumbrance (Lower Bound 60% Reduction)	BAT After Tax Royalty Charge at 85% Warning Label Encumbrance (Lower Bound 75% Reduction)
2015	$ 7,162,632	$ 2,865,053	$ 1,790,658
2016	7,282,346	2,912,938	1,820,586
2017	7,404,060	2,961,624	1,851,015
2018	7,527,808	3,011,123	1,881,952
2019	7,653,625	3,061,450	1,913,406
2020	7,781,545	3,112,618	1,945,386
2021	7,911,602	3,164,641	1,977,901
2022	8,043,833	3,217,533	2,010,958
Total	**$60,767,451**	**$24,306,981**	**$15,191,863**

Figure 12.5 IP Volume Reduction

BAT	Value
BAT Hong Kong Present Brand IP Value at 50% Warnings Label Encumbrance	$167,847,000
BAT After Tax Royalty Charge at 85% Warning Label Encumbrance (Lower Bound 60% Reduction)	$ 67,139,000
BAT After Tax Royalty Charge at 85% Warning Label Encumbrance (Lower Bound 75% Reduction)	$ 41,962,000

Figure 12.4 provides a striking illustration of what happens to royalties and royalty rates when packaging space and royalties are reduced by 75%. The decrease is sudden, rapid, and sustained. In the eight years from 2015 to 2022, total projected royalties under the as-is scenario go from $60.8 million to $15.2 million under the 75% reduction scenario.

Value Conclusions

Having considered the impact of the proposed health warnings on royalty rates and the brand IP, our conclusions are straightforward. The value of the BAT brands, as measured by the value of their trademark, trade dress, and other IP, will drop substantially—and quickly.

Figure 12.5 has three entries. The top entry shows the present value of the BAT brand IP as it exists today at $168 million. The middle entry shows the value of the BAT brand IP with the new regulations in place assuming at least a 60% reduction in royalty and a value of $67 million. The bottom entry with a 75% reduction shows a $42 million value.

The Importance of Arbitration

As projects and markets become more multinational and global in nature, the amount of international arbitration will grow. In virtually every arbitration, IP is an integral part of the dispute. Every arbitration is unique, particularly those that involve sovereign states. Each venue is unique in arbitration, and the rules can be challenging and ever-changing as the people at BAT found out in Hong Kong. Also, without a BIT or a similar underlining treaty, much of the power shifts to the sovereign state when one is engaged in arbitration. Thus, an arbitration can become a very one-sided environment if a party finds itself engaged in a dispute against a sovereign state.

The valuation work in international arbitration must be held to the highest possible standards. The quality of the research and due diligence, as well as the depth of the analysis, cries out for professionalism of the highest order. The other side of the arbitration will certainly bring their A game to the table, and credibility is all important, as typically there is no appeal from an arbitration. One final caveat on arbitration. The process to its final ruling can be very long and usually time consuming for a number reasons, some of which are political, some of which are economic, and some of which simply have to do with time demands the arbitrators place on themselves. Arbitration is typically not a full-time job for a top arbitrator but a voluntary or part-time avocation.

Chapter 13

Valuation of Application Based, Digital Platform Ventures, and Internet Assets

In writing the *Intellectual Property Primer* in 2007, there was no section on application based ventures (ABVs), digital-based ventures, or Internet assets. Why? Because a few years prior, the great dot-com crash had occurred. The bottom had fallen out of prices for Internet-based stocks, and little or nothing was being said about either the stocks or methods to value them. Much has changed since that time. The market and the public's appetite for social media, digital-based assets, and app-based companies has increased substantially. The understanding of the value of these companies has also changed and become more grounded in reality.

We now move from valuing discreet intellectual property (IP) to the enterprise value of a company whose sole assets are IP. In this chapter we take a brief look at the history of what used to be known as Internet-based companies and set the scene for how these same assets can be valued today. We will look at case studies from projects of actual values in transactions, litigation, and initial public offerings (IPOs). This chapter provides a better understanding of both what these assets are and how they can be valued today.

An Overview of Application Based Ventures

What does the all-encompassing term "application based ventures" include? The terms Internet companies, social media companies, website companies, digital or data platform companies as well as "new economy companies" are all used in parallel and interchangeably. For our purposes, application based ventures, or ABV, is the umbrella term that covers all of these.

An ABV is a nontangible asset-based company. It finds its value primarily in its IP and intangible assets. Value is based almost exclusively on this part of its asset base. It is heavily dependent on algorithms, software, business method patents, proprietary and technical know-how, private data, databases, and trade secrets.

Further, ABV values are often user dependent, and without a strong, growing, or stable base of users, these companies often find themselves in paralysis positions. In addition, their financial statements can be dense, namely, financially opaque to analysts. For this reason, they are often difficult to value, particularly using traditional valuation methods. Even then, for most analysts, collecting data and establishing appropriate metrics to value these companies is rarely easy.

More important, most analysts aren't particularly good at valuing this type of company or these types of assets. As a result, value is usually based on traffic/users, ad revenue/subscriber data, or other monetization potential. However, the most sophisticated analysts on Wall Street are often misled when identifying the true value of these companies.

The Snapchat Case

The measures of value change for ABVs as they change with growth. Initially, value often comes from measuring clicks or number of views, to the number of users, to a multiple of users, going on to a measure of ad revenues, profits, and growth. An example of the difficulty that continues to vex Wall Street in the valuation process for ABVs is Snapchat. Since its public offering in early 2017, its lead bank, Morgan Stanley, is still being quizzed about its original valuation and the methodologies used thereon. As many readers will recall, Snapchat went public at $28.00 a share but immediately declined by more than 20%. It then spent many months struggling to regain its original IPO price.

In several articles that were published in the 90 days after the original offering by Morgan Stanley, questions were raised about their analysis. It became clear that Morgan Stanley had to readjust their analysis supporting the IPO price for Snapchat on at least three occasions. On one occasion, they had to adjust their revenue forecasts and put out a note to that effect. On another occasion prior to the IPO, they had to correct their cash flow forecasts. On yet another occasion, they had to adjust downward the weighted average cost of capital percentage used in order to be able to hold the target $28.00 a share IPO price. Why do we mention this? Because it is a quick illustration, or mini case study, of how difficult it is for even a sophisticated investment house like Morgan Stanley to accurately value the IPO shares of an ABV without constantly having to adjust their calculations. This is simply an alert to anyone reading this chapter or investing in shares of an ABV to cautiously read all the research.

In the remainder of this chapter, we will talk about the earlier history of ABVs and what is known as the dot-com bust or the dot-com crash of 2000. We will also cover the short intervening history and then focus on methodologies for valuation, both then and now. The chapter will conclude with actual case studies using methodologies that we feel are appropriate when working in the world of IP and intangible assets that form the core backbone of value for ABVs.

A Sense of History: The Dot-Com Crash of 2000

Few of us today remember the intensity of the dot-com crash of 2000, and few of us believe or can credit the steepness of the rise in value and the abrupt fall in value of dot-com stocks at that time. In order to get a sense of the proportion of the crash at the end of 2000, think of this statistic: the Bloomberg index of 280 Internet stocks stood at about $2.95 trillion at its peak during calendar year 2000. By the end of that year, it had fallen to $1.2 trillion, a loss of $1.75 trillion! Value losses like that are hard to imagine in any circumstance.

Here are a couple of examples. Cisco Systems, which had been a pioneer in the market and went public in 1990, lost $210 billion in market value that year. Yahoo lost $102 billion. America Online lost $92 billion in a single year. Of the 280 stocks in the index, three quarters of them had lost 80% or more of their value in a single year. This followed a three-year bubble period in which investors chased prices up at such a fast rate that anyone with a broker and a fast trading style could make money. Immediately after the crash, everyone talked about the tulip craze in Holland in the 1700s as a parallel to what had just occurred on Wall Street.

Why did this happen? Because there was no solid valuation system for these stocks. In fact, there was no solid value for many of these stocks, putting aside some of the classic survivors such as Sysco, America Online, and Yahoo, which in the long term proved their value. Before the implosion in 2000 and the ultimate market crash, there was no system of valuation for what were then known as Internet stocks and what we now call application based ventures. All that mattered at the time were revenues, if any. If there were no revenues, some of the following metrics were used, strange as they may now seem today:

- Number of websites,
- Number of domain names,
- Number of subscribers, and
- Number of trademark applications.

In other words, there were no valuation standards for many of these companies. As a consequence, investors found out in late 2000 that there was no value for many of these companies. In that wide-open environment of no value and no valuation standards, more than 500 Internet- and technology-related IPOs took place in 1999 and 2000. This was part of a continuing trend of hundreds of IPOs in each of the prior years. Figure 13.1 shows just how

Figure 13.1 Dot.Com Boom

Rank	Company	Date Went Public	Offer Price	First-Day Close	Percentage Change
1	Theglobe.com	11/13/98	$ 9	$ 64	606%
2	Foundry Networks	09/28/99	$25	$156	525%
3	Cobalt Networks	11/05/99	$22	$128	482%
4	Marketwatch.com	01/15/99	$17	$ 98	474%
5	Akami Technologies	10/29/99	$26	$145	458%
6	Sycamore Networks	10/22/99	$38	$185	386%
7	Ask Jeeves	07/01/99	$14	$ 65	364%
8	Finisar Corp.	12/12/99	$19	$ 87	357%
9	Crossroads Systems	10/20/99	$18	$ 79	337%
10	Priceline.com	03/30/99	$16	$ 69	331%
					Avg. Gain: 432%

Source: Hoover.com.

big the gains were in some of these IPOs. Obviously, it was worth it for those management teams to take their companies public. Those teams saw 300, 400, even 700% jumps in value on the first day of trading for their new IPOs.

The First Decade: The Quiet Days

After the crash of 2000, there followed a period of quiet in the Internet world that hadn't been seen since the great crash of 1929 and stock market collapse of the early 1930s. Some of the companies that flew high and crashed hard include the following:

- Global Crossing was a telecommunications company that was founded in 1997. It went public in 1999 and reached a market capitalization of $47 billion in early 2000. By the beginning of 2002, they filed for bankruptcy.
- Infospace also went public in 1999, and its stock reached $1,305 per share in March of 2000. However, by 2002, its stock was trading at $2 per share.
- The Learning Company was one of the hottest, brightest, and quickest flare-ups to be seen. It was bought by Mattel in 1999 for $3.5 billion. It did not prove to be the success that Mattel management had hoped for. They turned around and sold it the next year for $27 million.
- A similar example of a quick disposal after an acquisition is Lycos, a company that was purchased by Terra networks in 2000 for $12.5 billion. It was later sold in 2004 to Korean-based Daum Communications for $95 million.
- Finally, Pets.com went public in 1998 to great fanfare and great hopes for the future. It was caught in the dot-com crash in 2000 and subsequently filed for bankruptcy at the end of that year.

At the height of the Internet- and technology-based IPO slowdown, the year 2008 brought only one ABV-based IPO to market. Thereafter, excitement in technology began to build again. More specifically, social media companies clearly had made their initial impact not only on consumers but on worldwide markets. As a result, the second decade brought changes to ABVs.

New IPOs and New Valuation Methodologies in a New Decade: Four Comparative Case Studies

In 2011, LinkedIn became the first of the major new social media companies to hit the IPO market, and it did so successfully. It went public and raised approximately $275 million, placing a market value on itself of roughly $3.0 billion. Its shares traded consistently from opening day onward.

By contrast, the following year, Facebook opened the ABV market further with its IPO in May of that year. At that time, Facebook priced its offering at $38 a share, which valued the company at $104 billion. The problem was that the market perceived the valuations as being significantly overpriced, and while the market cap for the company was later restated to be $90 billion, it nonetheless was viewed as excessive. As a result, over that first year of trading, the stock came down from its IPO price of $38 to as low as $20. It did recover over the next two years. Nonetheless, this IPO valuation cast serious doubt on valuation methods for IPOs.

Next, we look at two IPOs with similar profiles. The first is Twitter, which went public in November 2013 at an IPO price of $26 a share. This immediately surged to $45 a share, which expresses itself as a $4 billion market cap. Twitter continued to trade at a premium over its IPO price on a consistent basis.

By contrast, a few years later, Snap and its Snapchat service went public in March 2017. Often viewed as a competitive social media platform to Twitter, the Snap IPO price of $17 a share could not be maintained and dropped quickly, remaining below opening trading prices for the balance of 2017.

This brings us to the issues of valuation. If we compare the first two companies, LinkedIn and Facebook, which had much in common at the time of their IPOs, we can look at a basic valuation concept to see the difference in how their advisors priced the offerings:

- First, LinkedIn. At the time of the offering, they had approximately 100 million unique users at a total valuation of approximately $3.0 billion, for a value per unique user of $30.
- One year later, Facebook went public, with 900 million users and a total market cap of $104 billion, for a valuation metric of $115 per unique user.
- Thus, the difference between these two valuation metrics—LinkedIn at $30 per user and Facebook at $115 per user—tells us that LinkedIn should maintain its IPO price with no difficulty, while Facebook was easily predicted to drop from its original offering price.

In the second pair of companies identified above, Twitter and Snapchat, we see the same dichotomy. In the case of Twitter, it went public at an IPO of $26 with a market cap of approximately $14.5 to $15.0 billion, equivalent to approximately $58 to $60 per unique user. Snapchat, on the other hand, went public at $17 per share and a total market valuation of $24 billion, with 158 million unique users and a value per unique user of $160 dollars. Thus, the difference between the two companies, where Twitter valued itself at roughly $60 per unique user and Snapchat valued itself at $160 per unique user, is immediate and obvious. Using a metric of dollars per unique user illustrates the dichotomy in valuations between LinkedIn and Facebook and Twitter and Snapchat. While not the only method of valuation, it is certainly one that is useful for asset testing a valuation for an ABV.

Today's Valuation Conditions and Methodologies

The valuation of an ABV is different today than it was in 2008 or 2010. Today, an IPO for an ABV-based company must live up to higher standards. They must have greater stability while at the same time being larger and more complex in scope. There are several differences that drive these statements. First, of course, are higher standards for IPOs. Through the early years of this millennium, an IPO didn't need a minimum amount of revenue. Today, for a company to be listed on the NASDAQ, they are required to have aggregate pre-tax earnings in the prior three years of at least $11 million. Thinking back to 1999, many companies had no revenues at all.

Second, because there are stricter standards for public offerings today, many chief executives and their brands are more IPO adverse. In the current market, private sources of funds let early investors sell some of their shares at a profit, allowing an IPO to be postponed until later stages. This, in turn, has reduced the pressure on companies to go public or to be acquired.

In addition, as we look at valuation today, one of the most important factors in the value equation is that the amount of capital required to start a successful ABV is substantially lower than it was back at the turn of the millennium. In large part, this is due to the fact that technology services such as the Cloud make it much less expensive to start up a successful ABV operation. Instead of spending millions to buy and operate big computer systems, one can simply contract to a Cloud computing service.

As a corollary to the above, there are a number of venture funding firms, both private and larger hedge and other funds, that are willing to provide the capital to early investors and developers of ABVs. This allows companies that formerly had to look to the IPO route for capitalization to find their funds elsewhere. Snapchat is one example. In 2015, a couple of years before they went public, Snap Inc. was able to reach out to private sources in order to raise $1.2 billion in cash from a group of well-funded private investors.

Finally, and in some ways most importantly, there is far less debt in the ABV community than there was in 1998 through 2001. This reflects the fact that the cost of building up a new technology company or an ABV has been reduced as the cost of technology has been reduced. This means that a current technology company's capital structure, while remaining relatively light on the asset side of its balance sheet, also is far less burdened with debt.

The Valuation Question Answered

Now, we move to the question of how does one value these companies. The standard answer is, let's value the cash flows. When the cash flows are not available, what other measures do we use? Let's start with the standard methodologies—income, market, and cost. The income approach is, of course, the cash flow approach wherever possible. The market approach is used most frequently with ABVs, but the type of market approach is different. One looks at ratios of comparable companies, and one calculates comparable multiples, such as enterprise value to sales, or number of users to sales, or number of users to ad dollars. Or one can look at comparable buyouts of other companies. Of course, one can use a price to free cash flow analysis.

The cost approach can be enabled with an ABV, but it is a different form of cost approach than one thinks of with a more traditionally structured company. It's an asset value that is based on looking at a liquidation or distressed sale approach. The valuation expert can estimate the fair value for all of the ABV's assets while also subtracting fair value for its liabilities in order to determine a net worth under a liquidation scenario. While this cost approach is useful, it is used only as a no-less-than value analysis in our view.

Finally, we come to what I think is the most appropriate method for valuing ABV companies or online Internet companies, and that is a variation of the market approach using metrics appropriate to Internet or social media companies. These metrics typically focus on the following:

- Users, particularly unique users;
- Stickiness, repetitive uses, multiple uses, and focused users; and
- Website rankings as to content, visits, and advertising.

Trend analysis of both types of factors—users and websites rankings—is critical in valuation of an ABV.

In the end, it is market comparables combined with analysis of the company's users/stickiness and customer loyalty that often form the basis of the analysis of value. This combined with market comparables based on revenue ratios, total revenues, ad dollars, or other fiscal measurements form a critical part of the analysis.

Finally, we see some of these techniques used as we move into the case studies to conclude this chapter. These short case studies are based on actual client work, and you will see that they use five approaches to valuation:

- Website rankings,
- Market multiples,
- Unique user analysis,
- Discounted cash flow based on an income approach, and
- Traditional revenue multiples.

Case Study 1: Fan-Based Website

This first valuation is based on an actual transaction analysis. The purpose of which was a possible acquisition by a large retailer of an affiliated fan-based website that was started by an independent group of aficionados of the retailer. The site was started as a source of information for customers interested in products from the retailer and was not affiliated in any way with the retailer. Think of it as a sort of "SEARSFANS" website. The information that was contained on the websites pages was offered as a compilation of different individuals experiences with products from "Sears." The founders of the site were not professionals and assumed no responsibility for the accuracy of the information on the site. Sears is a registered trademark of Sears Brands, LLC and was not intended in any way to be used by SEARSFANS as a trademark. The site SEARSFANS did not charge a membership fee to its users. After reviewing the website, it was our understanding that advertising was the only source of revenue for the SEARSFAN website.

Figure 13.2 Alexa Rankings

*Alexa ranks are shown for the acquisition date as presented by flippa.com.

Domain Name	Global Alexa Rank
http://www.sears.com/	318
http://www.SEARSFANS.com/	79,802

Website Rankings

There are a number of publicly available sources that measure the strength and activity of a website relative to other websites. Two of the most widely utilized sources are Alexa Rank and Google PageRank. A list of rankings and website statistics for SEARSFANS is provided in Figure 13.2.

Alexa Rank

Alexa is a web information company, founded in 1996, that provides a ranking system that tracks more than 30 million websites worldwide. As described on alexa.com, Alexa is the leading provider of free, global web metrics. You can search Alexa to discover the most successful sites on the web by keyword, category, or country. You can use their analytics for competitive analysis, benchmarking, market research, and business development. Alexa's Pro tools can optimize any company's presence on the web."

Google PageRank

Google founders Larry Page and Sergey Brin developed PageRank at Stanford. At the time that Page and Brin met, search engines typically linked to pages that had the highest keyword density. Therefore, people could game the system by repeating the same phrase over and over to attract higher search page results.

In general, webpages with a higher PageRank are more likely to appear at the top of Google search results.

Market Approach: Content Similar to SEARSFANS

Due to the abundance of publicly available information on recent arm's-length website acquisitions, the market approach provides a strong indication of value. As a set of comparable transactions (Comps), 15 websites with content similar to SEARSFANS that had been sold in 2013 were identified. We then determined the purchase price multiple per daily unique visitor. By applying that multiple to SEARSFANS's number of unique daily visitors, we arrive at a market-based value.

Figure 13.3 Google Page Rankings

Domain Name	Google PageRank
http://www.sears.com/us/	7
http://www.SEARSFANS.com/	4

Figure 13.4 Visitor Multiples

†Rounded to the nearest thousand.

Domain	Price Multiple Per Daily Unique Visitor
pattjudd.com	22.23
themaisonette.net	1.50
homedesignideas.com	47.11
mzvirgo.com	9.67
dickoatts.com	35.57
castlives.com	8.36
peterjon.com	11.96
lroonle.com	5.00
hometrendesign.com	4.61
lamidge.com	8.41
roomdecorationideas.org	13.78
apcconcept.com	19.66
therightathome.com	7.49
aledman.net	11.09
tophomeideas.com	4.51
Lower quartile	6.24
Median	9.67
Mean	14.06
Uppe rquartile	16.72
	SEARSFANS Valuation
Daily unique visitors	9,694
Value at median multiple†	**$94,000**
Value at upper quartile multiple†	**$162,000**

Since SEARSFANS has a higher Alexa Rank than all 15 Comps, a higher Google PageRank than 14 of the 15 Comps, and a longer history of use than all 15 Comps, the multiple that would likely be applied to SEARSFANS would be between the median and the upper quartile. This results in a valuation range of $94,000 to $162,000. The analysis of comparable transactions and market-based valuation is provided in Figure 13.4.

Market Approach: Similar Number of Unique Daily Visitors to SEARSFANS

Market data for the acquisition of websites that host content that is similar to content on SEARSFANS was limited to websites with substantially fewer unique daily users. To test for a possible size bias in the market-based valuation multiple, a second group of Comps was analyzed for websites with a similar number of unique daily visitors as SEARSFANS.

As with the Comps for websites with similar content, SEARSFANS has a longer operating history than 13 of the 15 similar-sized Comps had at the time of their acquisition. As a result, the multiple that would likely be applied to SEARSFANS in an arm's-length transaction would be between the median and the upper quartile. This results in a valuation range of $90,000 to $160,000. The analysis of comparable transactions and market-based valuation is provided in Figure 13.5.

Figure 13.5 Price Multiples

Domain	Price Multiple Per Daily Unique Visitor
thegardenhelper.com	28.22
ewallpapers.eu	3.95
militarybases.com	30.00
twitrbackgrounds.com	9.78
tiptoptens.com	5.00
petpeopleplace.com	23.74
minecraftskins.com	2.22
tf2wiki.net	3.50
twitrobot.com	19.12
spyrestudios.com	5.90
ecofriend.com	7.74
gotop100.com	12.20
mydellmini.com	4.67
dzineblog.com	9.27
mobile-barcodes.com	13.89
Lower quartile	4.83
Median	9.27
Mean	11.95
Upper quartile	16.50
	Daily Unique Visitors
Searsfans.com	9,694
Value at median multiple	**$90,000**
Value at upper quartile multiple	**$160,000**

Income Approach

The income approach can also be used to determine the website value by calculating the present value of future income streams. To discount future earnings, we used a discount rate that was representative of the level of risk involved in an investment in SEARSFANS.

Using the median daily revenue estimate of $56 (Figure 13.) results in a value of $120,000. The income approach analysis is illustrated in Figure 13.6.

Figure 13.6 SEARSFANS Income Approach Valuation

Annual income	a			$ 20,440
Discount rate		b	20%	
Growth rate	c		3%	
SEARSFAN value		**a/(b–c)**		**$120,000**

Conclusion

Based on the information provided to us and on the research and analysis summarized above, our opinion is that the value of SEARSFANS is as follows:

- $94,000 to $162,000 using the market approach for Comps with similar content to SEARSFANS.
- $90,000 to $160,000 using the market approach for Comps with similar numbers of daily unique visitors to SEARSFANS.
- $120,000 using the income approach.

This case illustrates the approach to valuation of website assets using both the market approach and the income approach. Further, within the market approach, it illustrates how one can use comparables based on both content and number of unique visitors. Finally, we recommended to our client that a single point of value would be a conclusion of $125,000. The outcome was a successful acquisition of the website by our client.

Case Study 2: Dual Valuation: Video Assets in Litigation; *Hulk Hogan v. Gawker.com* and Gawker.com

In this highly publicized case from 2012,[1] Terry Bollea, aka Hulk Hogan, sued the website Gawker.com (Website) for violating his right of publicity. Specifically, we were asked to provide an opinion of value and, therefore, damages regarding the increase in value of the Website that resulted after Gawker posted a video there. In the video (Video), Mr. Bollea engaged in private consensual sexual relations with a Ms. Heather Clem obtained through private sources and without the permission of Mr. Bollea or Ms. Clem.

According to data published in February 2014 by the promotion agency the Marketing Arm, Inc., "Hulk Hogan has a 96% awareness among a general population in the U.S. This is one of the highest awareness levels of any athlete/celebrity in the U.S." As of December 17, 2014, Hulk Hogan had 1,110,000 followers on Twitter and more than 3.9 million likes on Facebook.

Gawker.com

Gawker Media, LLC, is an American online media company and blog network. Its website Gawker.com focuses on celebrities and the media industry. Gawker was founded in 2002 by Nick Denton, a *Financial Times* veteran, with the gadget blog Gizmodo.com. The company's flagship blog, Gawker.com, was founded later that year as a New York media and gossip blog. Gawker depends on advertisers for revenue, and revenue is driven by the number of unique users who in turn are driven to the site by unique content such as the Hulk Hogan video.

13-1 *Bollea v. Gawker Media, LLC*, No. 8:12-cv-02348-T-27TBM, 2012 U.S. Dist. LEXIS 162711 (M.D. Fla. Nov. 13, 2012).

In mid-2007, without his knowledge or consent, Mr. Bollea was videotaped while engaged in private consensual sexual relations in a private bedroom with Heather Clem. Unknown to Mr. Bollea and Ms. Clem, the private bedroom was under surveillance and the encounter was recorded. Mr. Bollea did not give anyone permission to record him.

On October 4, 2012, Gawker posted a 1 minute and 41 second "highlight reel" of the secretly filmed recording on the Website. Prior to publishing the Video, Gawker added English subtitles to it. A 1,440-word narrative describing the Video written by former Gawker.com editor A.J. Daulerio also was posted on the Website. The Video received 8,610,124 page views and 5,357,572 unique page views on the Website. Numerous other media outlets and websites also shared and republished the Gawker-edited Video on their own websites.

Shortly after the Video was initially published on the Website, Mr. Bollea's attorney promptly demanded that Gawker remove the Video from Gawker.com; however, Gawker refused. The Video eventually was removed from the Website on or about April 25, 2013, pursuant to a temporary injunction issued by Judge Pamela A.M. Campbell in this action. Yet, Gawker linked to a third-party website that was playing the Video. Despite the injunction mandating that the narrative also be removed from the Website, Gawker refused.

Valuation Analysis

Due to the availability of information regarding transactions that involve comparable websites, we relied on the market approach in this case. Specifically, we analyzed the increase in value of Gawker.com based on market multiples, a variation of the market approach. The use of market multiples allows for the valuation of comparable assets based on a ratio to some common denominator. This is based on the theory that a ratio that compares value to some firm-specific variable is the same across firms.

For the purpose of our analysis, we relied on monthly unique users as a benchmark to compare similar websites. Over the last several years, we have valued numerous websites using monthly unique user multiples in the context of litigation and private transactions. Employees have also taught this methodology extensively in valuation presentations and continuing legal education webinars.

Valuing the Business and the Hulk Hogan Video

Based on the open research context of the situation, we chose to use the market approach as the most reasonable method for determining the increase in value of Gawker.com. Our analysis included the following steps:

1. We relied on a market-based monthly unique user value multiple as a benchmark to compare the value of other websites similar to Gawker.com.
2. We then calculated the benefit to Gawker by analyzing the change in value of Gawker.com from September 30, 2012 (before the Video was posted on the Website), to April 30, 2013 (after the Video was taken down), thus establishing the value of the entire business.

3. The change in value of Gawker.com attributable to Gawker posting the Video on the Website was then allocated based on the unique user traffic that was generated by the Video, thus establishing the value of the discreet IP in the video.

Gawker's Use of Monthly Unique Users

Gawker uses monthly unique user data, reported by Quantcast, in the analysis of its operating performance. As an indication of the importance Gawker places on website traffic, monthly unique user data reported by Quantcast are currently used as the principal metric for determining employee bonuses. These bonuses are calculated based on the website's performance in relation to previously determined targets. As described by Gawker Chief Operating Officer Scott Kidder, "The bonus pool is calculated as a percentage over target. So, for example, if the site is 10 percent over target it will receive 10 percent of its payroll, its labor budget, as a bonus pool."

Comparable Websites

Historical monthly unique user data for Gawker.com was obtained from Quantcast. To determine the value of the Website at various points in time, we needed to determine a market multiple per monthly unique user. This required identification of transactions that involved comparable websites with similar monetization potential.

Six comparable websites were identified (Figure 13.7). While the experience offered by some of the comparable websites differs from that of Gawker.com, all are content-based websites and not e-commerce websites. Similarly, all generate revenue from advertising. As a result, all have similar monetization from monthly unique uses.

Website traffic fluctuates from month to month. An arm's-length buyer or investor would not rely on a single month's performance because vast fluctuations in user traffic will occur with nearly all websites. Instead, they would look at the average monthly traffic the site had over some prior period of time, typically 12 months. As such, it was prudent in our analysis

Figure 13.7 Comparable Website Values

Valuation Multiple Per Monthly Unique User			
Comparable Website	**Monthly Unique User**	**Company Value**	**Monthly Unique User Multiple**
BleacherReport.com	25,599,849	$ 170,000	6.64X
Buzzfeed.com	135,925,889	$ 850,000,000	6.25X
HuffingtonPost.com	25,000,000	$ 295,900,000	11.84X
Ozy.com	5,130,718	$ 12,000,000	23.39X
Grandparents.com	754,832	$ 31,280,800	41.44X
Yelp.com	136,283,099	$3,604,851,060	26.45X

Minimum	**$ 6.25x**
Average	**19.34x**
Maximum	41.44x

Figure 13.8 Minimum Value of Video

Value of Gawker.com Attributable to the Video (Lower Bound)				
Month Ended		**Trailing Twelve Month Average Monthly Uniques**	**Valuation Multiple**	**Value of Gawker.com**
	Source:	*Doc 11*	*Exhibit 3*	
September 30, 2012		11,989,092	6.25x	74,972,679
April 30, 2013		14,788,578	6.25x	92,479,008
Change		**2,799,486**		**$17,506,329**

Value of Gawker.com Attributable to the Video	
Total Unique Pageviews of the Video	5,357,572
Months the Video was Posted on Gawker.com	6.71
Average Monthly Unique Views of the Video	**798,821**
Change in Trailing Twelve Month Average Monthly Uniques to Gawker.com	2,799,486
Average Monthly Unique Views of the Video	798,821
Change Attributable to the Video	**28.53%**
Change in Value of Gawker.com	$17,506,329
Change Attributable to Video	28.53%
Value of Gawker.com Attributable to the Video (Lower Bound)	**$4,995,000**

to calculate the monthly unique user multiple using the average monthly unique users for the 12 months prior to the date the Website was being valued.

A summary of our monthly unique user multiple analysis is presented in Figure 13.7.

We used both the minimum and average multiples for our valuation. The minimum multiple provides a conservative no-less-than value, whereas the average multiple provides a reasonable indication of the actual value of a single unique user. These multiples, which again represent the value of one individual unique user, will be used in our analysis of the increase in value of Gawker.com that is attributable to the posting of the Video.

Value of the Video to Gawker

To calculate the value of Gawker.com before the Video was posted, we applied the market-based monthly unique user multiples, identified above, to the average monthly unique users for the 12 months prior to September 30, 2012. To calculate the value after the Video was removed, we applied the same monthly unique user multiples to the average monthly unique users for the 12 months prior to April 30, 2013. Our analysis using the minimum and average multiples are presented in Figure 13.8 and 13.9.

The Video received 5,357,572 unique views on Gawker.com during the 6.71 months that it was posted on the Website. This represents an average of 798,821 unique views per month, which represent 28.53% of the change in average monthly unique views from September 30, 2012, to April 30, 2013.

Both from an industry perspective and through Gawker's own use of monthly unique users as a measure of value, an increase in monthly unique users has a direct and positive impact on the value of a website. As the Video was responsible for 28.53% of the increase in monthly unique user traffic to Gawker.com, the Video was therefore responsible for 28.53% of the increase in value of the Website.

Figure 13.9 Upper Bound of Value

Value of Gawker.com Attributable to the Video (Upper Bound)			
Month Ended	**Trailing Twelve Month Average Monthly Uniques**	**Valuation Multiple**	**Value of Gawker.com**
Source:	*Doc 11*	*Exhibit 3*	
September 30, 2012	11,989,092	19.34x	231,810,148
April 30, 2013	14,788,578	19.34x	285,938,464
Change	**2,799,486**		**$54,128,315**
Value of Gawker.com Attributable to the Video			
Total Unique Pageviews of the Video	5,357,572		
Months the Video was Posted on Gawker.com	6.71		
Average Monthly Unique Views of the Video	**798,821**		
Change in Trailing Twelve Month Average Monthly Uniques to Gawker.com	2,799,486		
Average Monthly Unique Views of the Video	798,821		
Change Attributable to the Video	**28.53%**		
Change in Value of Gawker.com	$54,128,315		
Change Attributable to Video	28.53%		
Value of Gawker.com Attributable to the Video (Upper Bound)	**$15,445,000**		

As shown in Figure 13.8, using the minimum monthly unique user multiple of $6.25, our analysis indicates that the increase in value of Gawker.com attributable to the Video is at least $4,995,000.

Alternatively, as presented in Figure 13.9, using the average monthly unique user multiple of $19.34, the increase in value of Gawker.com attributable to the Video is more likely $15,445,000.

As shown above, the ABV value of Gawker.com was $285.9 million as of April 30, 2013. The increase in value of Gawker.com was $54.1 million.

Mini Case Study: Huffington Post

One last anecdotal case study serves to illustrate how things have changed. In the summer of 2011, the Huffington Post was acquired by AOL for an acquisition price of $315 million. In doing the analysis as to an adequate price, AOL's approach was three-fold, as we understand it:

- First, was a price based on a multiple of ad revenue. In 2010, ad revenues were approximately $31 million, so a multiple of 10 times net ad revenues was established as the level of value for acquisition.
- Second, the Huffington Post had more than 26 million viewers at the time of acquisition, and a price of $12 per unique user was established. This is a conservative figure and well in line with comparable websites.
- Finally, a price per thousand page views was established apparently based on revenue generated on approximately 4.8 billion page views over the course of 2010. This meant

that 1,000 page views were worth approximately $6.25. Again, this is well in line with comparable ABV new age information sources.

The point here is that in the last six years, valuation analysts have begun to firmly grasp how best to value these assets. In my view, the examples of the Huffington Post, Gawker.com, and SEARSFANS illustrate that new methodologies are based on traditional methods of comparability and income approaches and are being melted together to move forward as larger and larger ABV-type companies come to the forefront.

Conclusion

This chapter has been a bridge to the future of IP valuation, looking at the value and valuation of ABVs or Internet ventures as some people call them. What we have seen is that metrics for valuing and measuring a company's worth are changing. All of the traditional measures of discounted cash flow remain tried and true, but there is a greater use of different market multiple techniques coming into play, concepts such as unique users or page views based on a multiple common to comparative companies, and they are becoming more and more prevalent.

Chapter 14

The Future of Intellectual Property and Valuation

The Status Today: Where Each Class of Intellectual Property Finds Itself in 2018

The previous chapters were devoted to each of the major classes of intellectual property (IP), from right of publicity to trade secrets, and trademarks to patents and copyrights. Before we take a look ahead in this last chapter, it's useful to review where we are today. Today's status of each key IP class is summarized in the following paragraphs.

Patents

In recent years, several prominent cases have altered the patent landscape in the United States by providing guidance on what is patent eligible. Further, the new America Invents Act has changed the rules, making ours an open file, first to file system. This has changed the status of patents and has lowered the value of these assets. In early 2018, the International IP Index found that the U.S. patent system had fallen to twelfth place in the world, ranking below such countries as China, Japan, and Hungary. The U.S. Chamber of Commerce attributes this decline to a growing level of uncertainty for innovators, particularly in relation to patent protection and technology licensing. We find uncertainties in the patent system that have resulted from inconsistent interpretation of Supreme Court attempts to define patent-eligible subject matter. Further, innovators face challenges in post-grant opposition proceedings such as inter partes reviews, which involve a great deal of cost and lack of predictability for those who file patents compared with other post-grant opposition systems in other countries. In other words, the value of patents is being challenged.

Trade Secrets

Trade secrets have made up a lot of ground in recent decades in terms of protection and utilization. As the business landscape continues to evolve rapidly due to increased technology utilization and globalization, one could argue that trade secrets are now viewed as more important than patents in the IP world. Over the past decade we've seen how the value and usage of trade secrets have increased. We can state with some certainty that in the coming years, trade secrets, particularly those that involve the collection and manipulation of data, will be one of the primary forms of development of valuable IP.

Copyrights

In today's digital world, copyrights play a bigger role in the expansion of IP in our daily lives. The laws that protect copyrights in the developed world have extended the lives of creative works of all types, and protection is more rigorous today than it was a decade ago. This has resulted in higher values for copyrights as well as longer lives, and there is a greater emphasis and importance on performing accurate valuations for these assets. We don't expect these trends to change in the near future. This is particularly true due to the emergence of virtual reality and artificial intelligence technologies, which will affect copyright configurations, usage, value, and litigation over the next few decades.

Trademarks

The rate of trademark applications and registrations has been increasing for the last 25 years, and the rate of growth has increased markedly since 2009. As the number of registered trademarks continues to rise, the once static definition of a trademark is gradually adapting to the advances in technology and the creativity of the human mind. Notably, sensory trademarks such as smell, sound, texture, and color are now part of the legal landscape.

An important illustration of the increasing role of trademarks in international IP strategies is the Chinese approach. China increased its trademark applications by roughly 250% from 2008 to 2015, and this growth continues today. Clearly, the Chinese are moving from a patent-only registration strategy to a patent and trademark strategy.

Why do we see this increase in trademark registrations in the United States and in other key markets around the world? Because the useful life of most patents is significantly less than 20 years. As innovation and technology continue to accelerate, older patents often become obsolete as new technological advancements push those older patents and patent applications out of the way. Trademarks, however, have an indefinite life span (if they are continuously in use). As trademarks age, their value often increases. Thus, we see trademarks as a key area within the IP family that not only will continue to grow, but growth will outpace that of most other areas of IP.

Right of Publicity

While a specialized area of IP that is protected under a patchwork of various state protections as opposed to federal protection, right of publicity (ROP) is an area of rapid growth due to the increased use of celebrity imagery and branding rights via licensing, promotion, and endorsement. Most often, athletes, actors, celebrities, and other persons of interest exercise these rights. ROP is fueled by the three fast-growing areas of law, marketing, and valuation.

ROP is one of the fastest-changing areas in IP law, one of the fastest-changing areas of marketing and branding, and one of the fastest-growing areas of licensing and merchandising—and therefore of valuation.

ROP activities continue to grow at a relatively rapid pace. In 2017, licensing industry research estimated that retail sales for licensed products using celebrities' ROP were approximately $5.9 billion. This is up 2.2% from previous years and represents only a part of the picture; it does not include activity or revenue from endorsements, promotions, and other ROP usages.

Application-based Digital Platform Ventures

Application-based ventures (ABVs)—what does this include? The phrases "Internet companies," "social media platforms," "website companies," and "digital platform companies" are all used interchangeably along with "new age economy companies." As we discussed in chapter 11, "application-based ventures" is the umbrella term that covers all of these. An ABV finds its value primarily in its IP and intangible asset base. That value is heavily dependent on assets such as algorithm software, business method patents, technical know-how, private data, and trade secrets, to name a few.

Approximately two decades ago, the great dot.com crash occurred; the bottom fell out of prices for Internet-based stocks and many companies that resembled an ABV. At the time, little was said about either the stocks themselves or the methods to value. Much has changed. Today, valuation of an ABV has become sophisticated. Now we see that the metrics for valuing and measuring a company's worth have changed. The traditional measures of discounting cash flow remain tried and true, but a greater use of different market multiple techniques has come into play, with concepts such as unique users and page view multiples becoming more common. Most importantly, we see that values for digital platforms can be substantial, whether it's a $1.2 billion purchase of Instagram or a Snapchat public offering with an initial market valuation of $24 billion. It is obvious that a substantial market for ABV assets and investments exists as does an interest among investors to pay substantial premiums for this type of IP.

Foretelling the Future

In the case of IP, foretelling the future is a necessary evil. The very nature of IP, with its constantly changing body of assets and changing valuation requirements, means that an underlying trend—fortune telling—is a requirement of most IP valuation professionals.

What have the last 13 chapters taught us? If nothing else, two basic things. First, the nature of IP is changing. The breadth and range of trademarks is changing. The types of patents have changed, both traditional patents and business method patents. The range of copyrights has expanded. The rise in utility and value of trade secrets and an increased emphasis on rights and protection have been documented. Finally, of course, ROP and other name and likeness assets continue to increase in value.

What's the second thing that we've learned? It is that valuation techniques and methodologies are changing and adapting everywhere. As the face of IP changes to include new-and traditional IP with more apps, more chat rooms, more platforms, more social media, and more digital assets in general, new valuation methodologies and/or adaptive ones have moved to the forefront. Important among these is the so-called smallest saleable practicing patent unit (SSPPU) concept. This is a fancy phrase for simply identifying the smallest unit of value inside any larger body of IP (or any bundle of assets) and then valuing that smallest value unit (SVU). And, with increasing IP complexity and higher volumes of litigation, other valuation techniques are being refined and used:

- The Edgeworth Box
- The Nash Bargaining Solution
- Alternative Market Multiple Approaches
- Unique User Reference Multiples
- The Coarse Theorem

The Big Four Dominate: Society, Technology and IP, Value, and Valuation

According to Capital IQ and other research sources, as of early 2018, four companies—Apple, Facebook, Google, and Amazon—had a market capitalization of approximately $3.0 billion, probably the largest conglomeration of market cap value ever seen among four companies. How do we put this into perspective? Let's look at Amazon. It's market cap of roughly $670 billion is worth more than the total stock market value of its nearest retail competitors—Walmart, Costco, T.J. Maxx, Target, Kohl's, Nordstrom, Macy's, Bed Bath & Beyond, Sacks Fifth Avenue, JC Penny, and Sears/K-Mart—combined. Another financial measure is that Apple's profits, which were roughly $50 billion in 2016, are greater than the total revenue of Coca Cola. Beyond revenue, what kind of influence do the Big Four have on our society and on our IP? Here are a few examples:

- Facebook has more than 2.1 billion monthly users.
- Amazon serves 65 million households, two thirds of American households, virtually every month.
- Facebook owns four of the five top apps available on social media.
- Google controls more than 92% of the Internet search market.
- The Apple iPhone product family dominates global personal telecommunications.

These numbers tell you about the social impact and control that the Big Four have over not only the stock market and society but over the development of IP, social media, new apps, and new forms of (online and offline) technology; in turn, exerting IP domination and concentration.

We must watch these four companies over the next 10 years, along with Netflix, because their sheer size makes it virtually impossible to accurately value all of their IP as a whole. This is where the concept of the "smallest unit of value" comes into play and where, I believe, the valuation exercise for IP, particularly when it's held by an Apple or a Google/Alphabet or a Facebook, is being challenged. It's the concept of the SVU. When valuing assets held by one of the Big Four or other social media or IP giant, the assets need to be broken down into their smallest elements, so they can be both accurately valued and comparatively valued.

Valuing these assets will also require new analytic discipline over the next decade for two reasons. First, each company generates substantial revenue per employee, but none of them generate the amount of social benefits that more traditional corporations like Proctor & Gamble, Xerox, or even Microsoft does. Instead, they create huge amounts of cash flow that doesn't necessarily benefit society or the surrounding orbit of supporting suppliers and corporate partners.

Second, these four companies pay one of the lowest effective tax rates of any group of companies (prior to the new tax law passed in early 2018). The effective tax rate among the Big Four was roughly 15%, far lower than one would find with any other representative group of four American companies. The valuation of these entities, and other large platforms/ABV entities, is going to be difficult, and so SVU will grow as a valuation tool.

Domination and Concentration of IP in Media–Content and Communications–Connectivity

In the section above, we briefly talked about the Big Four dominating society, social media, and the Internet world. There is also domination and concentration going on in two other areas that have very large components of IP embedded into their businesses. In the worlds of media–content and communications–connectivity, we have witnessed a growing concentration over the past several years and we can certainly look forward to a domination of these two areas by a handful of companies in the coming decade. However, this domination of communications–connectivity and media–content by companies such as China Mobile, AT&T, and Disney is also being challenged by the Big Four.

At first, this may sound counterintuitive. However, the Big Four and the Internet arena in which they operate do directly compete or compliment the areas of media–content and communications–connectivity. First, as to communications–connectivity, we see that the world's top five telecommunication–connectivity companies are:

- China Mobile Ltd.,
- Verizon Communications Inc.,
- AT&T Inc.,
- Vodafone Group PLC, and
- Nippon Telegraph and Telephone (T&T) Corp.

The total market capitalization of these five was approximately $800 billion at the beginning of 2018. This market cap was approximately the same as the market cap of Amazon at the same point in time. In other words, Amazon is as big as the world's top five telecommunications–connectivity companies. Perhaps more importantly is that Amazon is beginning to compete with China Mobile, AT&T, and Nippon T&T by offering Cloud computing services and by offering content in much the same way that AT&T offers content through its DirecTV acquisition.

We see the same degree of concentration and domination of an IP-intense business in media–content. The five largest media companies at the beginning of 2018 were:

- Google/Alphabet, which dominates in search engine advertising, but is also a huge player in display advertising and video advertising through its YouTube platform.
- The Walt Disney Company. Through its subsidiaries such as the Disney Channel, ABC networks, and its affiliated ESPN networks, the company is able to offer multiple platforms including a stake in Hulu.
- Comcast, which owns media giant NBC Universal cable and broadcast divisions that include USA Network, Sci-fi, and CNBC, as well as a dozen international TV channels and networks.
- 21st Century Fox with its global holdings in the British broadcasting company, Sky, as well as Star India, Fox Broadcastings, and Fox Sports television companies. It also has film entertainment and direct broadcast satellite TV income.
- Finally, Facebook because of the company's all-encompassing mobile technology, which encourages its users to visit the site multiple times each day. Its mobile revenue is growing quickly at a double-digit rate.
- Looming over all of these is Netflix, which had 125 million users and a market cap of $185 billion in mid-2018.

The point is this—in media and content as well as in communications and connectivity, there is the obvious increased concentration of IP into a handful of dominant players. As a result, the size of the IP portfolios owned by these companies is at a point where valuation is becoming more difficult. Valuation professionals will need to be able to break down the assets of companies like these into the SVU and the smallest business unit (SBU) in order to be able to accurately value these large conglomerations of IP assets.

Contextual and Jurisdictional Knowledge Management: The Cloud Is Now

In 2006, Amazon Web Services opened its first Cloud computing service company. Fast forward to the beginning of 2018, and we find them operating at an annual revenue level that is approaching $25 billion. However, they're not the only big players to offer options in Cloud computing. Microsoft, Google, and IBM have also expanded their own Cloud computing centers at a rapid rate, as they bring big new clients into their own clouds. The consulting firm Forrester Research predicts that by 2025, 80% of America's companies will use Cloud computing services or will have built their own clouds. In other words, that old roomful of servers down on the third floor of the headquarters complex will soon no longer exist.

What does all this mean when we speak of the Cloud and IP? It means faster creation of IP, better protection, and more secure management and control of proprietary data and trade secrets. Going forward, it will also mean bigger and better codified families of IP inside corporations and perhaps bigger disputes, and more litigation, over the ownership of IP—and not just Internet-based IP. Hopefully, however, the Cloud will bring greater security and better definition over the parameters of what each company owns and controls.

Apps and Chats–Platforms and Forums

IP of all types, but particularly those related to digital assets, social media, and related assets, will continue to grow at a compound rate of greater than 5% per year. Growth will not only be in the number of apps but also in the type of assets and apps around which IP content and social media platforms will be built. This will include the technology used to drive social media, as well as in the breadth and range of apps being offered.

For example, at the beginning of 2018 there were approximately 3.5 million apps available at the Google Play Store. To give some indication of growth: Figure 14.1 shows that in May 2012 there were 500,000 apps available. Growth doubled in one year to 1 million apps in 2013. The number re-doubled over the next two years to 2 million apps in February of 2016 and reached 3.5 million at the end of 2017. Equal growth has been seen at the Apple Store where, to date, more than 2.5 million apps are available; some are free, of course, while many others are available for purchase and renewal.

When looking at these assets, the valuation issues are multiple, the most important being that with each additional app that enters the marketplace, the value of all the other apps declines (miniscule as it may be), and therein lies new valuation issues. First, how does one do an accurate valuation? Second, how does one account for this ever-decreasing size of the slice of the pie that's offered with each new app that enters the marketplace? A valuation approach must take into consideration the discrete market to which the asset is aimed. We believe that user multiplier valuation techniques or income approach techniques would be most useful here.

In addition, one must be aware of the obsolescence of apps and other digital assets as new competitors enter the ever-shifting IP content world. Another concern that immediately

Figure 14.1 Number of Available Apps at the Google Play Store

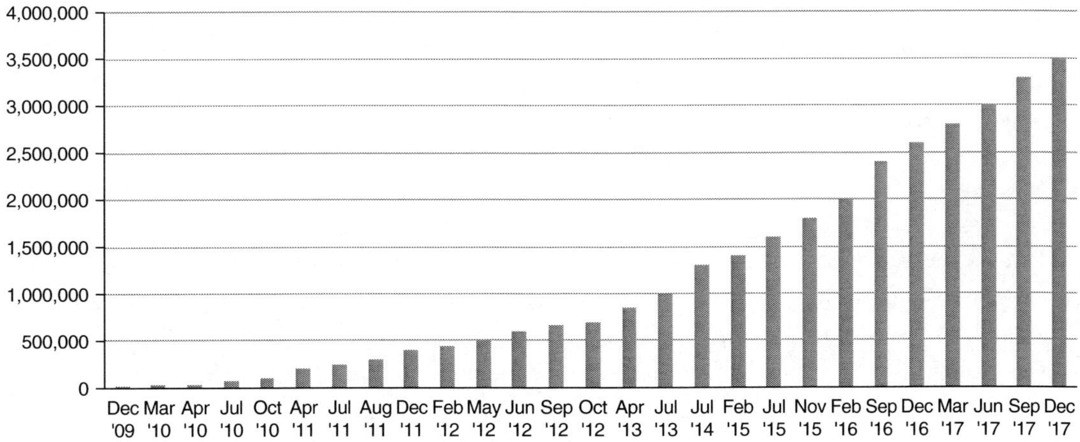

becomes an issue is the shortened effective life span for these assets. With each additional app, or each additional new social media platform, or each new messenger service, or each new technology that's showcased on the Internet, one has to assume, at least initially, that there's a shortened life for competitive apps, chats, social media, and other directly or tangentially competitive IP.

What the world of IP will face with this online development will be specialty and adaptive content in social media apps, platforms, and technology. As we see it, the ability to compete effectively against the Big Four plus Netflix in content and services is going to depend, to a great extent, on specialization, e.g., for specialty messaging services such as Snapchat (of course, on a much smaller basis) and/or special language or ethnic messaging services. Other examples might include the following:

- Specialty geographic and/or location-specific online platforms and services;
- Special needs services that are food related, health issues related, and/or private social issues related, such as sexual orientation;
- Technology related apps, such as those aimed at followers of the late Dr. Stephen Hawking;
- Content specialist or category-related specialist sites devoted to anything from the mundane, such as early American furniture, to the truly obscure, such as the collection of African beetle husks; and
- The societal specialist media platforms, apps, and technology offering insights into ethnic, religious, educational, occult, and every other interest.

The point is that this proliferation of apps, platforms, and technology-driven social media in a hundred or a thousand new areas will continue. Equally important, the methods needed to value these assets must be refined and must mature quickly as this movement toward online and Internet-based app and technology-developed IP will continue to proliferate whether we wish it to or not.

The Creation of New IP with Mechanical Means

A further unique development in this past decade has been the appearance of mechanical and non-human techniques to develop different types of intellectual property – and drawing the question "who is the owner of the IP", if in fact a machine or algorithm has created that intellectual property. Some simple examples, complex as they may seem, include the following:

- The appearance of artificial intelligence has led to the writing of music, design of art, the creation of fashion, such as tee shirts. And, this barely begins to describe all that artificial intelligence is doing and going to do. And thus, creating copyright material. But who holds the copyright? Not the artificial intelligence machinery. But what human being would be the copyright or trademark holder? That's the question that has to be answered.
- Virtual reality is another area that holds great promise, and it too creates new copyrightable material and material that can be trademarked. Again, the question becomes are

these new forms of IP attributable to a particular individual human being? That issue has to be addressed.

- In a similar vein, the advent of 3D printing, where totally new designs can either be copyrighted or registered as a trademark or even developed into a design patent, is now with us. How does this impact the ownership of intellectual property, and also how does it impact the counterfeiting of IP?
- Blockchain Technology in which we see the creation of Bitcoin and Crypto Currencies can also be used to create counterfeit currencies as well as other IP. How will this be monitored?

All these new and rapidly blooming technologies are quickly affecting the use of copyrights, trademarks and design patents; more importantly, asking questions as to ownership of the creative material. Finally, we need to think about how one values these creations. Are the valuations going to have any discounts from full market value because of issues surrounding the creation and ownership of the particular design, copyright, or trademark? These questions are not yet settled and valuation techniques and methodologies will have to be developed to answer these questions.

How Multiplying Apps, Specialty Platforms, and Expanding Social Media Will Impact IP and Its Valuation and Management

Finally, I want to share my view of what is going to happen in the next 10 years as the face of IP is impacted:

- Fourth: There will be an accelerated pace of change.
- First: There is going to be some loss of control over discrete pieces of IP as more social and digital IP is registered.
- Second: We will see infringement at a much higher rate than we are accustomed to.
- Third: New forms of IP are going to present themselves, and these new forms of IP will be a hybrid of copyrights, trademarks, and trade secrets.
- Fifth: An avalanche of new social media and Internet-based brands or IP identifiers (if not formally being identified as brands) will appear.
- Sixth: The opportunity for new distribution channels is certainly presenting itself via the Cloud and via new platforms offered by digital-based companies and the Internet.
- Seventh: We're going to be faced with more complex litigation that is going to lead to jurisdictional disputes because of the Cloud.
- Eighth: We're going to find the US Patent and Trademark Office in a bit of a shambles over the next decade as they attempt to keep up with the changes being wrought in the world of social media and IP on a global basis.

As we constantly preach in any discussion of IP and value, context is always critical. The context in which we've written the previous few pages can be summarized against the shadow of a few major thoughts:

- The impact of the Big Four, Apple, Google, Facebook, and Amazon—will continue over the next decade;

- The rise of nonsovereign wealth, best illustrated by Bitcoin and its sister currencies, as well as the issue of how one values those assets, will grow as an international issue.
- Extra-jurisdictional knowledge management will grow in importance; issues of value and valuation of assets within the Cloud including Cloud-based apps;
- There will be expanded use of new valuation techniques (e.g., SVU and SSPPU);
- Refinement and increased use of mechanical based IP via block chain, AI and other new technologies) will add a new dimension; and
- At least a cursory understanding of the climate of the "internet of everything" is a must.

These are the emerging contextual elements that we believe will have the most bearing on IP valuation over the next decade or so.

Concluding Thoughts

As my advisors at Harvard once taught me: the only constant in life is change.

In the world of IP, I learned long ago that this is absolutely true. Today, we find ourselves with an increase in value of almost all IP groups, with the possible exception of patents. We also find ourselves in a time of great social change. We find ourselves under the Cloud with the Big Four companies, plus Netflix, increasing their dominance in content, media, connectivity, and communications.

Finally, we find ourselves as valuation professionals looking at different and more appropriate ways to value these IP assets. The new focus will be on valuation techniques that make the valuation exercise more manageable by looking at one of two approaches. Either the SVU or SBU should increasingly be the focus of the valuation professional. Rather than attempting to value the entire entity, it is my opinion that much like the SSPPU concept that we discussed several times throughout this book, the SVU should be used when valuing a company with multiple pieces of IP. Alternately, with a very large entities such as Alphabet or Disney, one must look at the SBU approach in order to be able to accurately value all that these companies own in IP.

Finally, I hope that this book conveys that this is a time of great change in the world of IP and a time of even greater change in the world of IP evaluation and valuation.

As I said in the introduction of my first book, "I have attempted to strike a balance between complexity and simplicity, trying to avoid being too technical and obscure as well as too pedantic. This is a tricky balance and I hope the reader finds that I was able to maintain it."

I conclude this book as I began that first book, with that very same thought.

Index

T

About the ABA Section of Intellectual Property Law

From its strength within the American Bar Association, the ABA Section of Intellectual Property Law (ABA-IPL) advances the development and improvement of intellectual property laws and their fair and just administration. The Section furthers the goals of its members by sharing knowledge and balanced insight on the full spectrum of intellectual property law and practice, including patents, trademarks, copyright, design, and trade secrets. Providing a forum for rich perspectives and reasoned commentary, ABA-IPL serves as the ABA voice of intellectual property law within the profession, before policy makers, and with the public.

ABA Section of Intellectual Property Law (ABA-IPL)
Order today! Call 800-285-2221
Monday-Friday, 8:00 a.m. – 5:00 p.m., CT
or visit www.ambar.org/iplbooks.

Qty	Title	Regular Price	ABA-IPL Member Price	Total
_____	ADR Advocacy, Strategies, and Practices for Intellectual Property and Technology Cases, 2nd Ed. (5370231)	$149.95	$119.95	$_____
_____	ANDA Litigation, 2nd Ed. (5370223)	$369.00	$289.00	$_____
_____	Antitrust Issues in Intellectual Property Law (5370222)	$149.95	$119.95	$_____
_____	Arbitrating Patent Disputes (5370229)	$89.95	$74.95	$_____
_____	Careers in IP Law (5370204) (The ebook is complimentary with ABA-IPL Section membership)	$24.95	$16.95	$_____
_____	Chinese Expansion in the EU (5370224)	$169.95	$134.95	$_____
_____	Computer Games and Virtual Worlds (5370172)	$69.95	$55.95	$_____
_____	Copyright Litigation Strategies (5370228)	$369.00	$285.00	$_____
_____	Copyright Remedies (5370208)	$89.95	$74.95	$_____
_____	Copyright Termination Law (5370226)	$139.95	$109.95	$_____
_____	Crash Course on U.S. Patent Law (5370221)	$39.95	$34.95	$_____
_____	The DMCA Handbook, Second Edition (5370234)	$79.95	$64.95	$_____
_____	The Essential Case Law Guide to PTAB Trials (5370233)	$249.95	$199.95	$_____
_____	Fundamentals of Intellectual Property Law (5370218)	$89.95	$69.95	$_____
_____	Fundamentals of Intellectual Property Valuation (5370143)	$69.95	$49.95	$_____
_____	Intellectural Property and Technology Due Diligence (5370236)	$219.95	$179.95	$_____
_____	The Intellectual Property Law Handbook, 2nd Ed. (5620154)	$139.95	$109.95	$_____
_____	IP Attorney's Handbook for Insurance Coverage in Intellectual Property Disputes, 2nd Ed. (5370210)	$139.95	$129.95	$_____
_____	IP Protection in China (5370217)	$139.95	$109.95	$_____
_____	IP Valuation for the Future (5370237)	$89.95	$59.95	$_____
_____	A Lawyer's Guide to Section 337 Investigations before the U.S.International Trade Commission, 3rd Ed. (5370219)	$129.95	$99.95	$_____
_____	Legal Guide to Video Game Development, 2nd Ed. (5370227)	$74.95	$59.95	$_____
_____	A Legal Strategist's Guide to Trademark Trial and Appeal Board Practice, 3rd Ed. (5370220)	$169.95	$139.95	$_____
_____	Marketing Your Invention (5370165)	$20.00	$15.00	$_____
_____	Music & Copyright in America (5370201)	$97.95	$67.95	$_____
_____	New Practitioner's Guide to Intellectual Property (5370198)	$89.95	$69.95	$_____
_____	Patent Freedom to Operate Searches, Opinions, Techniques, and Studies (5370230)	$139.95	$109.95	$_____
_____	Patent Neutral (5370232)	$89.95	$69.95	$_____
_____	Patent Obviousness in the Wake of *KSR International Co. v. Teleflex Inc.* (5370189)	$129.95	$103.95	$_____